ADVANCE PRAISE

"Peter speaks with conviction about a concept he calls 'human-spirited leadership.' What a wonderful phrase! Perhaps it is the true essence of *Wonderlicious*. He leads us through a series of courses that continue to build, evoking lessons acquired in the demanding and discerning world of hospitality. The key ingredient, as you might guess, is 'wonder'. This central theme, stark in its simplicity, is explained with intellectual rigour, and just like any recent convert, I find myself becoming a fanatical follower. I applaud the appetite for life that is manifested throughout and have no doubt I will have recourse to refer to it over and over again in what is tantamount to a Handbook for Life. I feel that there has never been anything quite like *Wonderlicious* ever before."

— Graham Shapiro, Award-winning British Inventor, Designer and Digital Entrepreneur | **United Kingdom**

"My career began as a waiter at Rhodes 24 in Tower 42, where Peter was the General Manager. That's where I fell in love with the hospitality industry. There's a very real, personal connection to the later chapters, which brought back so many incredible memories. What I love most is that Peter has distilled a lifetime of wonder and hospitality into a book that provides any organization with easy ways to apply these 'delicious principles' to their own industry. *Wonderlicious* will absolutely be on my bedside table—and in my heart—for years to come."

— Sam Rhodes, General Manager, Rhodes W1 | **Dubai**

"I wonder, who wrote the Book of Love? Well, Peter Merrett did, masterfully intertwining profound insights with captivating stories. *Wonderlicious* is a vital, heartful, and delightful read in a world where we need to see, create, and appreciate the wonderful again. This is a must-read for anyone seeking renewed inspiration, hope and joy . . . for themselves, their community, and their business. Simply, yes, wonderful."

— Glenn Capelli, Sir Winston Churchill Fellow, CSP | **Australia**

"I couldn't put this book down, I was captivated from the first page. *Wonderlicious* is more than a book—it's a timely refreshment that has completely transformed my outlook on both business and life. Each 'recipe' offers fresh inspiration and a renewed sense of hope and possibility. A truly extraordinary read."

— Masahiro Kishimoto, President, Kishimoto Estate Co Ltd | **Japan**

"*Wonderlicious* is an instant classic and a modern masterpiece. It redefines customer service with humility, elevating it to a transformative art. Packed with actionable insights, it's essential reading for all business leaders."

— Dale Beaumont, Founder & CEO, Business Blueprint | **Australia**

"*Wonderlicious* is full of stories and insights developed over an inspiring career in hospitality, real estate, corporate coaching, and now, award-winning speaking. Peter reinvented customer service in commercial real estate at London's Tower 42 in a manner that is still emulated globally. His focus on the power of language, 'make it right service,' and the superpower that is thinking creatively while exceeding expectations, provides insights into striving to be extraordinary. Having fun, inspiring others, and never settling are qualities we all aspire to. I am grateful Peter shared his wisdom, enthusiasm, and magic with us in these *Wonderlicious* pages."

— Henry Chamberlain, President and COO, BOMA International | **North America**

"In a world that yearns for more joy, more lightness, and more hope, you are holding in your hands not a book but a little treasure chest that's brimming with wonder. Not flimsy fairytales or silly fantasies, but indeed a life-enriching guide, with the truth of not only what world-class cultures and service leadership with wonder actually look like but also how to bring it to life. While this might be part business book, part celebration of humility, part refreshment for the soul, this is also a book that has no time to be left on the shelf."

—Doug Lipp, former Head of Disney University Training Team
at Walt Disney Studios, Speaker, and Author of *Disney U* | **North America**

"Don't ever employ Peter Merrett to do spreadsheets. He's crap! Instead, ask him to share with you how to create the most incredibly wonderful business that delivers on the bottom line and that everyone wants to be a part of."

—Derek Williams, Founder, The WOW! Awards | **United Kingdom**

"Not only is Peter outstanding in the quality of everything he does, he is also a wonderfull human with a good heart. *Wonderlicious* is a seriously brilliant book—a hand-crafted guide for creating a wonder-filled, successful, best-in-class organization. When he coaches from the renowned 'Wonder Room' or delivers keynote presentations to thousands of corporate leaders, one thing remains the same: his audiences always walk away feeling revitalized and excited, ready to reinvent their lives, leadership practices, and businesses.

Wonderlicious is going to do that on a global scale. He has spent his luxury-hotel and corporate career showing the world how to infuse service with wonder, reinvent the way teams are inspired, and add the extraordinary to the otherwise ordinary routines of life."

— Amanda Gore, International Hall of Fame
Keynote Speaker and Author | **North America**

"Reading *Wonderlicious* is like finding an icy cold bottle of water in the middle of a dry, barren desert. It's everything the world needs now, more than ever."

— Dr. Jodi Richardson, Speaker, Author,
and Host of *Well, hello anxiety: The Podcast* | **Australia**

"I worry about wonder. I worry that somewhere along the way, we've let it slip behind the endless scroll of Insta and Facebook reels. But every now and then it sneaks back in—the fleeting, breathtaking reminders of how beautiful life truly is. Wouldn't it be wonderful to have a book that shows you how to see and celebrate these moments of wonder every single day? I reckon *Wonderlicious* might be it—properly so. Read this book, thank me later!"

— Maz Farrelly, Award-Winning TV Producer,
International Keynote Speaker | **Australia**

"In *Wonderlicious*, Peter Merrett dishes up an inspiring and absorbing account of his adventures from Professional Chef to International Keynote Speaker and his pursuit of 'wonder' in the service experience."

— Jeremy Larkins, Director of Sales & Marketing,
Customer Science Group | **Australia**

"Peter Merrett's *Wonderlicious* is a truly wonder-filled guide to breathing life, joy, and magic back into the world of leadership and customer service. His unique ability to bring a sense of wonder into everything he touches is truly inspiring. Peter invites readers on a joyful adventure—showing us all how to lead with heart and deliver service that not only meets customers expectations but brings pure joy to the lives we touch. He reminds us that with a little curiosity, kindness, and creativity, we can rediscover the wonder in even the smallest moments. This book isn't just about customer service – it's about reigniting that spark of wonder in our leadership and our lives."

— Tony Randello, CEO, Aveo | **Australia**

"Peter really tantalizes us with his insight into the service and hospitality world, tempting us in each recipe (chapter) with the next compelling story. A true smorgasbord of life lessons that I devoured. Outstanding."

— Adam Gray, Michelin-Starred Chef | **United Kingdom**

"*Wonderlicious* reignited my sense of wonder and reminded me of the inspirational experiences that can be found in everyday life. I highly recommend this book to anyone looking to spark their own passions in order to live more fully and lead from the heart."

— Connie O'Murray, Managing Director,
Jones Lang LaSalle Americas, Inc. | **North America**

"I once had the confidence to hand Peter a blank sheet of paper with an invitation to write his own script. My reward was that he helped us develop a world-leading office brand. At Tower 42, he united a diverse group of facilities-management contractors into a world-class, customer-focused team. The magic ingredient? Peter's unshakeable belief in people and his empowering leadership. *Wonderlicious* brings his recipes to life, helping people become the best that they can be and showing us all how to make a difference."

— Christopher Lacey, Former CEO, Sir Richard Sutton Limited | **United Kingdom**

"*Wonderlicious* reminds us that we are at our creative best when we approach challenges with purpose, intent, and, most importantly, fun. Peter's personal story, rooted in humility, is wholly absorbing with such freshness, intensity and power. His reflections on self-discovery are stunningly articulated and deeply relatable, offering moments that will resonate with every reader. This book isn't just about reaching a destination—it's about enjoying the adventure along the way."

— Neil Gopal, CEO, South African Property Owners Association | **South Africa**

"For CEOs, CMOs, business leaders, and owners, *Wonderlicious* is more than just a source of inspiration—it's like having your own motivational coach and practical guide to leading with heart. Each paragraph, each page, feels like a personal conversation with Peter Merrett. His vivid, real-life stories remind us that leadership isn't just about managing tasks or hitting targets. Those goals will follow naturally when you inspire teams, nurture relationships, and create an environment where both employees and customers can thrive. Peter's approach—emphasizing human connection, kindness, and attention to detail—shows that the qualities which cost little can bring the greatest return. The advice in this book is not just inspiring but deeply practical, ready to be applied in your professional life. *Wonderlicious* will leave a lasting impression, long after you've turned the last page."

— Jeannette Flynn, Director of 4D Marketing Pty Ltd | **Australia**

"Using the metaphor of preparing a banquet, Peter satisfied my hunger for a refreshingly playful approach to awe and the role it can play in bringing more happiness into our lives. It goes beyond mere intellectual engagement, offering a fun and nourishing experience for the reader's spirit. It just made my short list of favorite books."

— Jill Badonsky, Author/Illustrator of *The Awe-manac: A Daily Dose of Wonder* and *The Muse is In: An Owner's Manual to Your Creativity* | **North America**

"*Wonderlicious* is a delightful feast and a masterclass in leadership and service. Through heartfelt moments of human connection and authenticity, each chapter serves up rich stories that both inspire and ignite wonder. The wisdom within lingers like a fine after-taste, leaving you satisfied yet hungry for more. This isn't just a book—it's a banquet for the soul."

— David XiaoOu Chen, Chairman & CEO,
Fields of Gold Capital & Asset Mgt | **China**

"There are few who embody the essence of whimsy and wonder like Peter Merrett. If you are looking to reignite the spark of delight and joy in your life or business, *Wonderlicious* is the book for you."

— Michael McQueen, Multi-Award-Winning Keynote Speaker
and Bestselling Author of *Mindstuck* | **Australia**

"Peter Merrett leaves one with a unique sense of experience, a reminder about the beautiful aspects of life that we often miss—how to encourage one another, how to celebrate, and how to get back to what matters. It's so rare to meet someone as gifted as Peter who has this ability. When I first met Peter he had just won *The Office Building of the Year* award for Tower 42. His lessons in customer service were brilliant. In this book, Peter expands this on so many levels; you will truly enjoy the journey."

— Randal Froebelius, President, Equity ICI Real Estate Services Inc. | **Canada**

WONDERLICIOUS

Bringing Wonder Back to Life, Leadership and Service

Peter Merrett

Inspired by Truly WonderFULL Real Events

Illustrated by Jasmine Hromjak

E
* * *

Editing: Jennifer Goulden
Editing and Layout: Chris Arnold
Illustrations: Jasmine Hromjak
ISBN (Hardcover): 978–1–0689121–2–2
ISBN (Paperback): 978–1–0689121–3–9
ISBN (e-Book): 978–1–0689121–4–6
First Hardcover Edition Printed in Canada: April 2025
1 2 3 4 5 6 7 8 9 10
ENTOURAGE
Published by Entourage Media
www.entouragemedia.ca

For my boys, Zachary and Jake:
The best thing I have ever been called is *Daddy*.
Thank you for filling my life with endless joy and wonder!

MENU

Foreword: *"Oh, What Wonder Awaits!"* xv

"

Man does not suddenly become aware or infused with wonder,
it is something we are born with. No child need be told its secret;
he keeps it until the influence of gadgetry and the indifference of
teenage satiation extinguish its intuitive joy.

Sigurd Olsen

Wonderlicious *adjective*

| ˌwən-dər-ˈli-shəs |

An overwhelming sensation of delight, surprise, or unbridled joy caused by
an experience that is unexpected, unfamiliar, wonderful, delicious, magical.
The sense of feeling welcomed, safe, included, connected, and seen.
The new gold standard for life, leadership, and service.

Foreword:
"OH, WHAT WONDER AWAITS!"

with Doug Lipp
Former Head of Disney University Training Team
at Walt Disney Studios, Speaker, and Author of *Disney U*

I first met Peter on a sunny day in Scottsdale, Arizona. We were brought together to perform a keynote "duet" for JLL's annual Management University conference in April 2015, a gathering of one thousand of their senior managers and leaders. It was Peter's first major keynote of his soon-to-be (yet-to-be-discovered) new profession and love. We had various briefing calls with the client to paint the picture of their exciting vision—to create a ninety-minute interactive experience from the stage. I performed the opening forty-five minutes with lessons from my time with Disney, then theatrically handed it to Peter to close our special production with forty-five minutes of Wonder. It was such a fun moment for both of us.

However, I still clearly remember watching Peter's reaction of disbelief, as the audience stood and joyfully cheered with applause as he closed. He had put his full heart on the line and they thanked him for it. He called me up to the stage to share the moment together. We hugged in front of everyone, and only I could see his tears. He hid them well.

I saw something I haven't often seen through my years as an international speaker. I provided Peter with some direct feedback afterwards and told him: the energy with which he shared his passion and knowledge reminded me of Walt Disney. He has fun while educating at the same time.

What I experienced that day, the same as our audience, was his special way of guiding people away from the monotony and wearisomeness of everyday life. I have since come to realize he has fully embraced this as his purpose in life, and it always makes me smile like a proud parent as I watch his restlessness with normality and his underwhelm with all things ordinary. As you turn the following pages, you will, for your pleasure and benefit, learn from his simplistic ways of finding an easier and better way to approach everything and anything.

In a world that yearns for more joy, more lightness, and more hope, you are holding in your hands not a book but a little treasure chest that's brimming with wonder. Not flimsy fairy tales or silly fantasies, but indeed a life-enriching guide, with the truth of not only what world-class cultures and service leadership with wonder actually look like, but also how to bring it back to life.

What I love most about *Wonderlicious* is that it's real. It is a message of encouragement that we all desire—how to go easier on ourselves and each other and return color to our otherwise gray ways.

Peter has a way of pushing away the fog and clouds to renew us with the shine of fresh light and hope. He isn't apprehensive in showering us with real life wonder. Nor is he hesitant in bringing us down a few gears to cut right through the challenges of our modern world—to provide us with a refreshing reminder that life can be fun and bright, as much as it's often serious and distracted, and recharge our inner fulfillment through moments forgotten.

His mind works in a fascinating way, and I applaud his selfless enjoyment of making people not just feel good and happy, but appreciated, recognized and valued. I am in awe of his constant state of wonderment. When we are together, if I see something that looks black and white, he sees exactly the same with an array of color, as if his eyes have the lens of a kaleidoscope.

Young children—all of our little people the whole world over—see boundless possibility and awe with everything and anything all around them. They overflow with curiosity and exasperation over the smallest of moments. Their wide-eyed astonishment the first time they realize the reflection in the mirror is theirs; their first taste of ice cream that causes the realization that life just became even more exciting. Even something so small as noticing a leaf fall from a tree—to them they see a piece of magic. It's the most marvelous thing they've ever seen, and in that moment, it becomes the most fascinating object ever known to man. To them this isn't just a leaf, and they want everyone to see it, touch it, and hear all about its wide array of amazing superpowers.

This used to be us, all of us. Then we grew up and left our sense of wonder behind. We covered it up, believing it is only reserved for the little people and stopped noticing the awe in our everyday lives. Through our adult work lives we let it pass us by unnoticed as we conform within our disinfected ways of process and procedure. There is no time for this "fluff" some may believe, yet deep inside us, the little people are still there, ready and waiting to bring a torrent of curiosity and imagination.

Peter's approach to life, his determination to constantly cultivate a sense of wonder—in some of the smallest things—rings familiar with another creative leader: Walt Disney. My career at Disney helped me learn from so many brilliant leaders who in turn learned directly from the maestro of whimsy. Walt implored his staff to never overlook even the smallest details. In looking for opportunities to improve the quality of Disneyland, or a movie, Walt demonstrated, and expected, a childlike level of enthusiasm and risk-taking.

For many years, I've lived by the wisdom tucked away in the following philosophy from Walt Disney, shared through the ages as it was passed from mentor to student: *The trouble with people is they grow up, they forget what it's like to be twelve years old.*

Peter proudly embraces his inner child when dreaming up and producing thought-provoking solutions to seemingly insurmountable challenges.

Ahead of another time we performed together, I fondly remember sitting in the afternoon sunshine with Peter in 2017 at my home in Sacramento, California. He described to me his ambitions of writing this book, which would be inspired by his culinary and hospitality past, with "delicious recipes." He mentioned the title *Wonderlicious*, which at the time seemed to be fantasy, but I knew he was dreaming up something special. However, I acutely know just how daunted he was by the prospect, and therefore I feel incredibly proud that he not only persevered and the world can now benefit from this message. More so, I admire how he took the time to attain a deeper sense of who he is and of why sharing this message is so important to him.

I shared with Peter a personal lesson my father passed on to me during my own book writing escapades. Many years ago, my father said, *"B-I-C,"* to me. While I was trying to write my first book, he would insist to me, "You've got to sit down! Put your butt in the chair." I have written seven books since this, so I enjoyed passing on my father's three magic letters B-I-C to Peter. "Butt In Chair" served me well and I am so pleased he actually listened to my advice!

I stake my claim though that this is more than a book; it's a lighthouse for guiding us back to life and business with heart. I know this has taken him several years to bring to life, but you can tell. It's a labor of love and I salute him for never giving up on it.

If there is anything I should warn you about, it is this: please don't be fooled by his whimsical ways. Peter's work is wizardry. This is a creation of wonder for you, by someone who's actually done and experienced everything they are writing about. There are no untested theories in the pages ahead, which is a rare treasure.

While this might be part business book, part celebration of humility, part refreshment for the soul, this is a book that has no time to be left on the shelf.

So, in this moment with you here, please let me proudly raise the curtain and eagerly exclaim: "Oh, what wonder awaits!"

APERITIFS

—

A TOAST
TO WONDER

"

All around you, in every moment,
The world is offering you a feast for the senses.
Songs are playing,
Tasty food is on the table,
Fragrances are in the air,
Colors fill the eyes with light.

You who long for union,
Attend the banquet with loving focus.
The outer and inner world
Open to each other.
Oneness of vision, oneness of heart.

Right here, in the midst of it all,
Mount that elation, ascend with it,
Become identical
With the ecstatic essence
Embracing both worlds.

Lorin Roche

Introduction:
HOW IT'S MADE

"

My mouth watered so much my taste buds put on shower caps
Carole Fowkes

The creation of *Wonderlicious* is the inspired result of—and tribute to—the wonderful leaders I have had the fortunate pleasure of working with over the past three decades. They showed me the great power of humility, instilling in me their timeless lessons of creating prestigious, profitable, and multi-award-winning cultures that value, appreciate, and recognize people. This is also a tribute to the teams I myself have had the honor of leading, the big-hearted people who dared to be different and bring wonder to life with me.

During my time in hospitality, I took notes on the things that truly mattered. A *lot* of notes. I had a vision, even then, of writing a book others could enjoy and cherish, celebrating humility and connection. Back then, I dreamt it would turn into what it has indeed now become—something that is a little bit different. A book of humble truth and reality, uncovering role-model leadership, best-in-class customer service, and never-ending imagination.

The following pages are filled with my favorite recipes of wonder—taste-tested lessons learned throughout my hotel and hospitality roles. You will discover how I went on to apply these recipes to corporate business, and then scale with international acclaim. My dream is to inspire and encourage you to bring recipes of wonder into your life, both personally and professionally.

Twists and Turns

I was trained professionally as a chef then climbed the ranks of various luxury hotel leadership roles. From there, I went on to introduce and apply the hospitality lessons I learned to my role as general manager of Tower 42, the landmark commercial office high-rise in London, which as a result, went on to become named the best office building in the world. Having seen the best and worst of team and customer service cultures in business (and in life), I'm here to not only reflect on both, but also provide practical insights to bring refreshing magic and wonder to your everyday life.

This book will twist and turn and weave you in and out of my childhood, my working life, from the kitchen to hotels, through to the final section of this book and the three closing recipes. To provide a culmination and example of what is possible when you combine all the recipes.

I am grateful to have spent recent years as a trusted advisor and professional speaker, working with some of the world's leading corporations, organizations, and hotel chains, inspiring them to look beyond what is necessary and embrace the pure joy that comes from adding wonder to every act of service. It is my mission to show every person, from the concierge to the c-suite, that it is possible to bring wonder back into their work again.

No Chapters

Staying true to my culinary and hospitality upbringing and background, this is a book without *Chapters*.

I have carried the metaphor of *Recipes* through my whole working life inside and outside of the kitchen. I have always been fascinated and inspired by how chefs create and express themselves within their recipes to create a truthful reflection of their mastery. They test, play, taste, practice and relentlessly experiment with their ingredients—to create honesty and emotional connection through their food—the reason behind their adored hospitality.

I have applied this level of imagination to all that follows, and proudly serve you a *banquet* of wonder, to tantalize all your senses.

Every palette is different; yours is personal to you and the following recipes illustrate various possibilities and inspirations. Use and adapt these to your preference, remembering a recipe is only a framework to guide your own adventure as you choose.

Each Recipe Builds on the One Before

You may have traditional cookery and recipe books at home that you pick up and flip between your favorites from time to time. Maybe the pages are bent, folded, or bookmarked, have coffee stains on them, and show all the signs of good use. This is true of this book as well; you'll read sections that you will undoubtedly highlight and mark the pages, and I want this for you.

Whilst you wouldn't typically sit down to read a cookbook from front to back, this book is different. Here, each page leads to the next, and the best way to read this book—in the first sitting at least—is from front to back. I sincerely hope *Wonderlicious* will live on your coffee table and become a treasured resource in your life and work.

Taste-Tested

All of the stories, ideas, and ingredients featured here are a celebration of the three greatest things I have been fortunate to learn over the past three decades—fun, care, and common sense.

Everything that follows has either happened for me, to me, or by me—taste-tested.

Every page you turn, I hope to not only inspire and refresh your thoughts but reach through to your heart with what lies ahead.

To a bright and pleasurable place—a fascinating place.

A wonderlicious place.

Please make yourself at home and let us begin.

It's time . . . to open up the Wonder.

Bon Appetit!

Prologue:
LET'S SET THE TABLE

"

I would rather have a mind opened by wonder, than one closed by belief

Gerry Spence

T he air was impossibly heavy and wet. It was like trying to inhale the inside of a hot steam oven, yet the full weight of the heat was still to come. It was only 6 a.m. in India as the early morning sun was rising slowly over the splendor of the Taj Mahal, as if conducting the greatest light show ever seen. In overwhelmed silence, my two traveling companions and I sat watching in awe as the Taj Mahal's grandeur transitioned through every shade of pink to the brightest brilliance of pristine white.

We'd made it. Long had I dreamt of seeing it, and here we were. We had been told to come early, before the crowds arrived. An eye-watering eight million visitors come through every year, some days up to seventy thousand people, so it was especially exciting to have it almost to ourselves, just us, along with a handful of other early risers. The three of us didn't say much to each other, nor did we need to. We didn't run around taking selfies. We got just a couple of photos and then put our cameras away. We were too deep in our curiosity. We ran our fingertips across its walls and lay on the grass to silently stare at its grace.

It felt as if I had stepped back in time to my five-year-old self, unashamed and overwhelmed with joy. It wasn't only seeing the four-hundred-year-old Taj Mahal that was filling me with awe, nor was it being present with one of the Seven Wonders of the World. This wasn't *it*. The sheer magnitude of the moment was coming from all my senses with everything that was happening all around me, every single piece and part that was contributing equally to the feeling of *it*.

It was the combination of the sights and sounds, the scent and taste, the touch—and the people. And it was all combined together like an expertly mixed cocktail. Without question, the Taj Mahal is a magnificent sight with its unique architecture and radiant glow, but upon closer inspection, I was equally fascinated watching the people silently and proudly tending to the grounds as if they were their own. How the gardeners were attentively sweeping the vista for the day ahead—it was the way they were doing it, with love.

The earthy, aromatic scent and taste that hung in the air played its part. The distant engine sound of the occasional boat passing on the Yamuna River behind us echoed through the stillness of the moment, and a hundred birds in the trees sang a hearty good morning chorus to us. It was all of this, especially our laughter, that came from us trying to quench our thirst with our now-hot bottles of water.

It was the way we had been excitedly welcomed on arrival with warm hospitality, as if it was the first time they had done it. "Come, come, come, please," said the lady from one of the ticket booths, urgently gesturing us to follow her to the entrance. "There she is," the lady said, beaming eagerly, with her arm outstretched, giving us the Taj Mahal—as if it was hers.

Our wondrous moment abruptly disappeared at the speed of a balloon popping as we headed to the exit and stepped into the chaos outside on the street—the endless line of buses honking their horns impatiently at one another as they dropped off the massive crowds, which were now frantically pushing past us, clamoring, shouting, and racing to see the Taj. It was as if they had just been given the order from the trenches to "charge," with a sea of selfie sticks in the air like bayonets and cameras clicking in a wild frenzy as if the world was about to end in the next three minutes.

We noticed that our welcome hosts were now cowering inside their ticket booths to avoid the stampede. I gave our lady a fleeting wave in the distance and shot her a look to say *Good luck!* The smile she shot back at me and the glint in her eye said, *Thank you! I'm going to need it!*

We disappeared like a puff of smoke into the crowds and headed to the train station to make our great escape.

The Beauty before Us

There are ever flowing moments of awe all around us every minute of every day, flying in every direction. Yet we fall guilty of not noticing or realizing and believe that our sense of wonder is something just reserved for coming out in short bursts for one-off special occasions—like decorating the tree on Christmas Eve, blowing out birthday cake candles, or visiting the Taj Mahal at sunrise.

The moment we are born, we arrive into the world brimming with a unique and invisible sense of fascination. As human beings we are all innately created and hardwired to need everyday wonder.

As young children, it didn't take much for us to step inside the color, joy, and fascination of our everyday pleasure. From our early baby and toddler years, this continued to blossom and electrify our very being. As our teenage years rolled into our adult years—what many people consider "becoming a grown-up"—our serious and complicated world then took over to cleverly distract us from the wonder. Using everything in its power to stop us from seeing it—making us believe it doesn't exist anymore, or worse, making us believe it's not necessary anymore, that wonder belongs only to young children. Like the flowers of blossom falling from the tree until the branches became bare, wonder didn't disappear or leave us, we just let it go.

We stopped seeing it.

We forgot how it felt.

We switched the wonder engine off and prematurely put it away. However, like a bird in the sky or a fish in the water, you already live amidst the wonderful. Yet you don't need a trek to India, or to ride a camel around the Great Pyramids of Giza, or to visit the Hanging Gardens of Babylon to see and feel the wonder that's all around us. It's always here and on constant supply to be shared—at home with our families and at work with our colleagues and customers.

Okay so yes, I realize exploring the Taj Mahal at sunrise is undoubtedly a once in a lifetime opportunity of unparalleled wonder. However, twenty or so years later, I still return *there* every day in my mind; it is my everyday wonder. Whenever I check into a hotel, visit an airport or shopping mall, explore a new restaurant, walk into a coffee shop, enter an office building, or go to the bank, it is exactly the same. The Taj Mahal is in my subconscious. It is who I am, it's what I do, it's what I look for in my day to day.

This is what we learned in hotels. Sensing and noticing everything around us in its totality was ingrained in us in our work and training. Being aware of, and in tune with, the emotional depth of everything inside any given moment—this the work of true connection within the present moment—with wonder.

Missing the Magic

"We are all doomed!" Just switch on the TV for the latest news and you will get an up-to-the-beat confirmation of this, with a fresh fix of gloom. Turn on the radio, pick up a newspaper, or go into social media and you'll find more of the same.

Our adult lives are certainly challenged by the exhausting weight of uncertainty coming from many directions. At the same time, we are told we have to work harder and somehow figure out how to cope with fatigue and digital distraction. We live in a time that is fixated with constant reinvention, under the strain and relentless bombardment of everything that's coming next—the next thing we need to think about, the next life-changing gadget, the next upgraded piece of software, the next must-know tips for this or the next life-changing tricks for that.

We live in a constant pursuit of being *there*, of rushing toward tomorrow, instead of recognizing what we're missing *here—right now.*

The warming exchange of a hearty "Good morning," the expression of a sincere "Well done," a thoughtful "Thank you," and the fascination of meaningful eye contact . . . All moments of wonder that many have lost sight of.

I struggle to see the purity and joy of the human spirit, which is often missing in life, work, and business today. It makes my head speak a language that my heart doesn't understand. I hate watching children being tranquilized into silence with devices and gadgets. As adults, we too have forgotten to look up and so we miss the innocence and joy of taking in our surroundings—seeking out shapes in the clouds, marveling at the colors of a sunrise, and connecting personally with others. Through us, our children are learning the same. It is terrifying that this is our idea of normal.

I agonize observing the same in business today. Where organizations are so frantically engrossed in everything coming tomorrow, they forget to appreciate what is happening today. They miss the magic and the goodness and all the little things unfolding before them in the present moment.

Imagine Wonder

Amongst the often-confronting noise of life, there is hope, rich opportunity, possibility, and pleasure. Way beyond the pressure of process, systems, and automation lies the most powerful and influential resource of all—your sense of wonder.

Imagine if we could see the wonder once again and turn our gray, digitally distracted existence back into the full multi-color wonderlicious one we left behind in our childhoods.

What if we could dial down the noise of today and turn up the joy and laughter in our offices and workplaces? Imagine if we could create wildly attractive business cultures that excite employees and delight customers.

More than anything, imagine if we started each day letting the people we live with, lead, and serve know they are valued, appreciated, and recognized.

Now that would be wonderlicious . . .

HORS D'OEUVRES

—

PRESENCE

"

*We delight in the beauty
of the butterfly, but rarely
admit the changes it has
gone through to achieve
that beauty*

Maya Angelou

BUTTERFLIES IN A JAR

I must never forget the significance of Wednesday, 28 June 2016. I spent the day with my dear friend Neil Gopal, CEO of the South African Property Owners Association. Together, we had just attended the Building Owners and Managers Association annual conference in Washington DC, and before our flights home, we had a day off to explore the picturesque and historical little streets of Old Town Alexandria.

Neil is one of the most senior leaders that I know, representing the commercial real estate industry of South Africa. He is, however, also one of the most warm-hearted and gentle-mannered people I have ever met. Whenever we speak together, there is nothing else on his mind—he is always fully present in the moment. As we slowly walked around the beautiful little winding streets, I poured my heart out with my dreams. They had become so strong. My love of speaking had grown and my ideas for starting my own business were bubbling away, but I still had my wonderful senior corporate role in Australia, which I also loved.

Over lunch in a small, local restaurant, Neil paused and said something across the table that changed the course of my direction in life. It was profound, and it was exactly what I needed to hear.

"Do you know what you are?" he asked quietly with a smile, sipping on his iced tea.

I shook my head and sat forward intently.

Just above a whisper he said, "You're like a butterfly in a jar. You're flying around with all your dreams and ideas, but you've got the lid screwed on tight."

I couldn't speak.

"Are you able to undo the lid?" he asked, then paused to hold my gaze for a moment. "Because it's time to let yourself fly."

I still couldn't speak.

"Like setting free butterflies from a jar, once the lid comes off, it will be like releasing yourself into the wind."

It wasn't only the depth of his encouragement but the combination of his belief in me that lifted me up. More than anything, I felt the impact of his care and permission to take the lid off the jar. This exact moment is what started to change the course of my life. On the flight home I urgently sat and wrote notes to capture all of his words. I didn't want to forget any single part of what he had said.

So, eight years on, it feels particularly surreal to share these words with you here. I remember thinking that if I ever wrote a book, those words would become an important part of it.

Ever since that moment, the imagery of *butterflies in a jar* has become a favorite visual that plays over in my subconscious mind. It has guided me to relate to life at a much deeper and broader level. I have since realized the darker side of the analogy, and at the same time I have grown an acute appreciation of what it actually looks and feels like to be inside the jar. It has given me clarity and a deeper understanding of company cultures and service environments that are suffering and suffocating.

When I visit organizations and businesses, or experience restaurants, hotels, and other service-based establishments, I often find myself visualizing the glass jar with the lid screwed on tight—where the atmosphere is stuffy, wonderLESS, and the people are notedly constrained. They are bogged down by complex processes and sometimes discouraged from expressing their imagination and creativity. The environment is disorganized and unproductive—which makes sense because the air supply is cut off.

Then there are the business and workplace environments with the lid *off* the jar.

Like butterflies in the wind, these are the people who are surrounded by encouraging leadership and are lit up with joy.

They have an air of adventure and delight. In comparison to people working inside suffocating workplaces, these people are weightless in their pursuit of wonder.

This is our time to get the lid off the jar—let's get started . . .

Recipe 1:
A RETURN TO WONDER

"

You've always had the power my dear . . .
you just had to learn it for yourself.
Glinda the Good

"All aboard!" the jolly station master shouted at the top of his voice in between blowing his ear-piercing whistle.

I love India. It's one of the most vibrant and alive places on earth.

Along with my two traveling companions, we left the Taj Mahal to dodge the crowds and made it to the train for our great escape. Our hearts dropped when we found even bigger crowds at the train station and imagined we might be stranded there for days before we would be able to actually get onto a train. There were so many people and no way we were all going on this train, maybe they had ten back-up trains close behind this one to handle the numbers.

"All aboard!" he continued to bellow. There was nothing at all orderly about it, but miraculously we made it inside and got a seat on one of the wooden benches. All the carriages were filled to surely double capacity and yet more people continued to squeeze in and around us. It was impossibly hot and almost terrifying, but bizarrely it also felt ridiculously exciting!

We were wedged in so tight I could literally only move my hands, every other part of me was pinned and powerless. To this day I have no idea how they got so many people on that train. Behind me there was a man with his goat. Nearby, someone else balanced a basket of chickens. People sat on each other's laps, some were up on the roof, and others hung off the outside of the doors. Yet no one was complaining or agitated, it seemed just like a normal day to them, and we loved it—every single part of it. The thing that hit us so hard was how everyone was entirely present in the moment, no one was distracted. Under the immense weight, the train creaked and groaned as it pulled away, providing some relief with a brief breeze.

Here we were inside what felt like the biggest party we had ever been to. Everyone appeared to know each other, and the sound of conversation was deafening and exhilarating—and beautiful. Somehow, like an impossible magic act came the *chaiwala*—a man selling his tea, working his way through the carriage, climbing over everyone with his huge stainless-steel container filled with warm chai.

There were hundreds of faces in front of the three of us; some started nudging each other as if to say, "You ask him."

A lady with a bright, happy face piped up and asked: "Please, excuse me, what is your good name?" Her neighbors giggled in anticipation.

"Peter," I replied, wishing I could wipe away the beads of sweat running down my forehead and face.

"Pizza?" she exclaimed with surprise. She and her neighbors debated the pronunciation until they eventually wound up at Peter. "Please, excuse me, what is your profession?"

"I am a hotel manager in England and am on a break traveling for a year." My answer caused more fascinating debate. There was clearly something they all wanted to know so they eagerly nudged her some more to ask me.

"Please, excuse me Mr. Peter, is it true there is a train that goes under the sea from your country to France?"

Everyone stared at me, impatiently waiting for my response. My trip in India was in 2001 and the Channel Tunnel had famously opened several years earlier in 1994.

"Yes, that's right!" I exclaimed. They looked back at me in utter disbelief. I had confirmed that it wasn't a myth they had heard. It was real. I quickly realized I had to share the story of this groundbreaking engineering, by simplifying it to make up for our language barriers.

"Well, in England we started digging a big tunnel under the sea toward France, and the people in France did the same thing, they started digging a tunnel toward England!" I resisted the urge to make a digging motion with my hands to illustrate my point because it would require more space to move. "The digging took us six years until the day we met in the middle! Now there are trains that go back and forth between both countries."

This caused even more giggling and astonished debate between everyone. The innocence of the moment was completely glorious. Everyone was part of the moment, present and all together in unison, like one very big family gathered around the fire to tell stories.

The nine hours spent on this train felt like an eternity, but still wasn't long enough! I so miss the exhilarating moments of humble wonder like this—where everyone is undistracted and fascinated with each other, deeply connected and present together.

Diverse, included and equal—as one.

Part of me is jealous that the wonderful people of India live like this every day. Many have nothing, but at the same time, they have everything.

Stop and See

When was that last time you woke and, before you reached for your cell phone, you reached for the curtains instead to breathe in the beauty of the new day? You notice the clouds and the sky, the stillness and space of the moment, the sounds of the morning, the movement of the leaves in the trees. You go downstairs and notice your family and how much they make you laugh, how charming your kids are, how beautiful your partner is, the wondrous taste of that first sip of fresh coffee.

You eagerly head into work because you love the sense of arrival and warm greeting of welcome each day. More than anything you enjoy the calmness and reassurance this brings to the start of your day. You realize how brilliant it is to work at your company and how much you like the people around you. For all the companies you could have worked at, you chose this one. And they chose you. And here you are.

Or, perhaps the same as yesterday, your day started with a sense of overwhelm by everything in front of you? Your phone brought you into your waking moments, pinging alerts into your morning opening and you continued scrolling as you brushed your teeth. Your journey to work was hectic as usual, you flew through the coffee shop but didn't notice who served you. No one would ever know what you've been through in the lead up to getting to work. You went through chaos getting the kids to school, your train was delayed, or you got stuck in heavy traffic. You found your desk and considered the tasks in front of you, sorting through your emails and messages. The boss didn't see you arrive, and you ran to the first meeting of the day. You were at the table, but no one seemed to notice. You felt unseen and you knew the next day was destined to be exactly the same.

We live in a time where we are consumed and busy. Being busy is glorified, leaving many of us to balance both our ambition and the constant search—no, the *chase*—for what's coming next. We don't stop to breathe, to acknowledge, to celebrate the present. With it we lose sight of the beauty all around us in the now.

Yet just under the surface and deep inside us lies a sense of wonder that remains dormant, yet hopeful for its release.

ONCE UPON A TIME

Once upon a time—in a previously familiar land—being amongst and in tune with our sense of wonder used to be easy. As young children, we didn't even know it was happening; it was unconscious and effortless.

It was our natural default state of pleasure—a boundless place of presence and possibility. It was forever bubbling away inside, fueled by our innocent interest in everything ordinary. Our curiosity made anything and everything extraordinary and acted as our compass, our superpower that made it all possible.

I close my eyes to see my five-year-old self—the sunlight fills my eyes, and my mind is full of color. A magnifying glass gives me invincible powers, and I can turn a cardboard box and a flashlight into a magical wonderland. I scream with excited delight to catch a little burst of bubbles in the air with every ounce of my being.

My heart is radiating—I can see the wonder and I am invincible. My imagination runs wild with joy, and I feel as if I can conquer absolutely anything.

When I open my eyes again, the world is back to gray and serious. I shudder. The wonder is gone.

Cereal Boxes and Mud Pies

One of my favorite memories from childhood was how present and kind my parents were, and I am incredibly thankful for this. Growing up, my father's career moved us to live in various locations around the UK, from the friendly little village of Coedpoeth on the outskirts of Wrexham in North Wales to the bustling city of Wolverhampton in the West Midlands and then to the vibrant city of Sunderland in the northeast. They were modest little bungalows, townhouses, and terraces, and they were happy homes.

More than anything, I remember being surrounded by their limitless encouragement to curiously explore and imagine. In the early years my mum used to give me the cereal box to read at breakfast. I climbed trees and made mud pies at the bottom of the garden. The times we used a camera were mainly when we went on family holidays—Dad would buy some rolls of film to capture our memories. But I don't remember them ever forcing me and my sister to stop what we were doing every five seconds for a picture. We just existed together, exploring freely with everyday moments.

Both sets of my grandparents were wonderful role models for me. Being from small rural communities, they embodied humility and grace. While we didn't see them "enough," we did visit them often. I loved their presence and enjoyed copying their respectful table manners at the dinner table. Both of my grandmothers had a unique way of setting their table each day for breakfast, as if it was the most important ritual of the day. They always took the utmost care in everything—setting the place settings neatly, arranging the pots of homemade jam, carving thick slices of fresh bread, and making perfect boiled eggs. They just wanted to make everything nice. Whether it was breakfast, lunch, or dinner, everyone was welcome at the table—as long as they washed their hands, and sat down with a smile, along with a story ready to share.

Feeling encouraged throughout my childhood inspired an enduring sense of wonder that continues to grow within me to this day. My parents and grandparents were from a generation in which kindness was currency. My grandparents taught this to my parents who taught it to me, and now I'm teaching the same to my sons. My hope is to share the same with you here.

We didn't go on extravagant expensive family holidays, France was just a three-hour drive and one ferry ride from our home, so we would go on little adventures there.

I remember one year clearer than others. I was seven and my parents took me and my little two-year-old sister Hilary to stay in a little farmhouse near Annecy—a quaint, picturesque old town in the southern Auvergne-Rhône-Alpes region. To me and my sister, it was like the set of a magical fairy tale.

We visited the local *boulangerie* (a French bakery) each morning to buy fresh bread and pastries straight from the oven. The scent that greeted us before we opened the bakery door made us excited in anticipation. Our presence would be announced by the little bell fastened to the top of the door.

Mum knelt in front of me, looked me in the eye, whispered what to say and reassured me how I should express it. We smiled and nodded together. I can still feel her comforting hand on my back, as she gently urged me to take the few steps toward the lady at the counter.

I took a deep breath and said: "Bonjour madame, s'il vous plaît, puis-je avoir une baguette et quatre pains au chocolat?" It meant, "Good morning, madam, please may I have one baguette and four chocolate pastries?"

The lady beamed a big smile at my effort to speak proper French. I turned around and ran as fast as I could into my mum's arms.

"See! I knew you could do it!" she said.

I thankfully realize that moments of wonder like those of my childhood have never left me. They have inspired me my whole working life.

I am just thankful that Mum didn't step forward to speak for me, shielding me from potential failure. Instead, she remained present, unhurried, and engaged in my learning, always encouraging me to take a risk, and showering me with recognition afterwards. Here lie some of the most potent ingredients of the joy lost in our work today—all of which I will eagerly uncover, especially for you in the following recipes.

Lost in Time

Some may say, with a bit of a huff, there is no time for wonder anymore because, "We aren't children anymore!" So, we brush the wonder off, believing there is no place or time for the "fluff." We just stay busy and continuously chase our disconnected existence and suppress sharing the wonder that lives deep inside us.

If I had magical superpowers, I would use them to gift every child in the world the ability to make wonder an unbreakable sense—one that would continue to blossom throughout all the years of their life—an antidote to the disillusionment of adulthood. Wonder would act as a never-ending spark of joy that lights our way through daily life, now and forever.

The reality is, there isn't anyone the world over who couldn't do with some more wonder and joy in their lives, to rejuvenate their humility and fulfillment and provide a deeper sense of positive connection in the moment of now.

But where did our sense of wonder go?

Seeing Only Possibilities

I am not completely sure how it happened, but I am thankful that my five-year-old sense of wonderment has never left me. In fact, it has grown stronger with time, through many serendipitous moments.

In high school, my strongest subject was pottery! I excelled in every part of it. I was fascinated with clay, this raw and interesting organic earthy material. All I could see in front of me was the potential, the challenge, and the adventure of turning it into something unexpected and magical. Whilst many of my friends were upstairs in the "clever" classrooms accumulating their impressive grades, I didn't know at the time that I was uncovering and learning the method of my life's purpose—creating unexpected possibilities.

On my last day of school, my mum waited at the school gates along with all the other mums. I watched from the windows of the front door as all my friends excitedly waved their certificates in the air, laden with their amazing grades, looking for praise as they ran into their mother's arms. I hesitated and waited for a moment, feeling anxious. Then walked forward to sheepishly hand Mum my certificate. In bold at the top was my highest grade—an A in pottery. She leaned forward and gave me the biggest hug.

To this day, I remember her words vividly as she looked me in the eye and whispered, "Don't worry darling, the world will always need plates!"

No disappointment, no judgment, and no embarrassment—just encouragement.

After a few adjacent skips and gleeful twirls in work and life, pottery ultimately inspired me to then train professionally as a chef. For me it was the same. Learning how to connect emotion with fresh ingredients in the kitchen provided the same sensation as when I would shape something unexpected from clay. This eye for *what could be*—instead of *what was*—grew, as did my career, influencing my approach to work in hotels and in the corporate leadership roles I held. I saw the wonder and possibility of making simple things joyfully magnificent. I was filled with wonder, and that meant soaking up the many lessons I learned from working with many of the most wonderful human-spirited leaders in the world—the leaders who encouraged wonder. I am beyond thankful for their heart-led guidance.

These were the leaders throughout my career who were laser focused on profitability, business growth and customer loyalty. However, in equal measure they also gave me clear permission to go out and search for the uncommon. To stay restless (never settle) and focus on uncovering the possibility in everyday moments. This became a mission statement for me.

So Much Waste

Being amongst wonder and awe isn't just about joy and delight or going on amazing adventures. It isn't balloons and chocolate cake, or rainbows and lollipops, or fairy tales and sparkles. Wonder goes way deeper. We are creatures of wonder, and it represents our ability to fully see and be. It doesn't only help us to create feelings of amazement, but also the feelings of calm and contentment—a sense of peace. It provides reassurance and fulfillment—a place of growth. Wonder, especially within our adult lives, in business and through the core of organization culture, isn't "fluffy things" or "silly things," but the *very things* that cause a nourishing depth of authentic connection.

I see businesses, organizations, and corporations all around the world creating huge amounts of unnecessary waste—not traditional rubbish, but opportunity waste—unseen loss, the missed opportunities, opportunity cost, quantifiable waste . . .

I am talking about the waste of losing people who are burning out and then opting out. Waste from disconnected recruitment and onboarding methods. Waste with low team productivity, high employee turnover, and vacancies. Waste with missed customer loyalty opportunities, missed sales, disengaged teams from unappealing leadership, and the list goes on.

It makes huge volumes of waste—of time, energy, and humility—not forgetting profitability.

A lack of wonder comes at great cost. It isn't only about taking picnics at sunset or causing surprise delight for someone, but also about waste reduction and a positive return to the bottom line. Whether you are a business leader of a large corporation, exclusive restaurant, international airline, or solo entrepreneur, the scenario is exactly the same.

Through the pages ahead, I'm going to show you the ways to not only bring wonder back into your life, but also how to reduce the waste.

Finding Wonder Again

Wonderlicious will simplify the complicated. It will share the refreshing lessons and methods of humility that I learned from the leaders through my life and career—their fascination of seeing the best in people and giving them room to flourish. The leaders who went out of their way to make their people feel seen, heard and noticed—to continuously tell us how we mattered and inspired us to make a difference.

This is my dream: to shower you with encouragement to rekindle your sense of awe and wonder in your everyday life—at home, at work and in business. To breathe fresh air into possibility and connection.

At the same time for us to join together to spread and encourage everyone's wonder further.

To roll a ball of snow together until it becomes so colossal and wondrous in size, it takes us all to be together to keep it growing and moving.

Recipe 1 Recap:
A RETURN TO WONDER

In a world consumed by hyper-connected busyness, reclaiming your sense of wonder is not just a nostalgic fantasy but a vital way back to fulfillment. As you break free from distraction, you'll find that wonder still lives inside you, patiently waiting to be rediscovered, celebrated, and shared.

Ingredients:

* ★ The ability to explore the possibilities, embrace the unexpected, and be captivated by everything around you.
* ★ A focus on creating genuine human connections.
* ★ Sincerity, kindness, and compassion.
* ★ A willingness and determination to be the source of positivity and inspiration for joyful awe in your team.
* ★ A purposeful focus on the present.
* ★ The cultivation of gratitude for the here and now, sharing it freely.

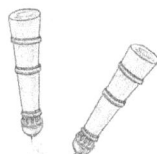

Substitutions to Make this Recipe Your Own:

If you can't board a busy train in India, try walking through a crowded city square. Absorb the excitement in the chatter, the light in people's eyes, and the vibrancy in the variety of people. Find the magic and embrace it.

Handy Hints:

To switch wonder on as your compass to a life filled with purpose, connection, and boundless joy, notice the wonder around you. Before diving into your daily routine—whether it's the sunrise, the laughter of loved ones, a moment of silent thought, or the aroma of fresh coffee—wholeheartedly savor every single one of these simple pleasures and be the role model to those around you.

Recipe 2:
LEADING HAND IN HAND

"

As human beings, our job in life is to help people realize how rare and valuable each one of us really is, that each of us has something that no one else has—or ever will have—something inside that is unique to all time. It's our job to encourage each other to discover that uniqueness and to provide ways of developing its expression.

Fred Rogers

For as long as I can remember, I have loved the warm, wise, and reassuring humility of Fred Rogers (better known to the world as Mr. Rogers). He was a generous, gentle soul who selflessly encouraged the world to see *and be* the wonder.

To help inspire wonderful business cultures around the world, imagine if these words lived on from Mr. Rogers and in fact became the heart of modern-day leadership? Imagine if the essence of this quote was up on the wall of organizations everywhere, inside the front cover of every employee welcome pack, and followed by leaders the world over as their compass? Not just words on a sign to sound nice but lived and breathed by everyone as second nature. Whilst this is a quote by Mr. Rogers, these words paint the picture of exactly what I was lucky enough to experience at the start of my working life.

Working inside a vibrant, human-spirited workplace culture radiating with positive leadership is like going on a treasure hunt. Except in this hunt, you are given easy clues to where all the prizes are hidden! It is similar to trying to navigate blindfolded through an impossible maze, except in this maze, someone takes your hand and guides you to the exit.

Wonderful, enchanting leaders have the map, compass, and a complete navigation system (their heart) that guides and directs their people along the right path. They are expert at giving directions so that no one gets lost or disorientated. As a result, they create a spirited workplace people love, a service culture guests adore, and an environment where everyone can thrive in their work.

A decade prior to my trip to India, I started my first hotel management role. I went on this treasure hunt and wore the blindfold through that maze. For those three years, I wasn't "at work." Instead, I was the recipient of the greatest heart-led leadership master class anyone could only dream to receive. From the moment I arrived for my first day, I felt at home.

Unfolding the Map

During our little family adventures to France, my little sister and I were captivated when Dad drove the car onto a big ferry that then took us across the English Channel. We were further mesmerized when we exited the ferry into France, and he started driving on the wrong side of the road! We were fascinated by how none of the road signs seemed to make any sense and that Mum had a map so big, it nearly blocked the entire windscreen. How we never crashed I will never know.

Mum was excellent at map reading, giving dad precise in-the-moment directions, and helping to show him the way. She was always calm and encouraging. Dad would concentrate on the road and drive precisely within the speed limit and prided himself on getting us to our destination safely. Sometimes though, Mum would have to admit a mistake (and we knew it pained her to say it, because of Dad's reaction).

"I think we are going in the wrong direction," she would say bravely, casually, and undramatically. "That left turn back there, we should have gone right, sorry."

To dad it was as if the world was ending. He would grow cross and clench his teeth.

"It's alright darling," Mum would say warmly, trying to lighten the moment and reassure my dad that it wasn't actually the disaster he thought it was. But just in case, me and my sister would dive for cover under all the bags in the back seat until the car was back on track and calm was restored.

We didn't have internet or easy online maps back then to get effortless directions and navigation to where we were heading. We could have easily ended up anywhere (including going in completely the wrong direction!), but we had the safety of knowing Mum would always help us find our way.

If Dad had tried to read the map while also navigating the foreign signposts amongst the busy traffic, we would have surely ended up in Timbuktu or in a ditch. Or he would have had to keep continuously stopping to check the map.

There was a lesson for me there. I realized it when I arrived for my first hotel management role. Amazingly it was as if my mum had passed the map to the hotel's general manager, Malcolm Powell. He was sharing the directions, just like she used to do.

Making Work the Most Enchanting Spell

Even though it was over three decades ago in England's North East, I vividly remember the day like it was yesterday. Leaving the busy main road and turning into the long, winding tree-lined driveway to Redworth Hall, it led me to an enchanting seventeenth-century Jacobean manor house, hidden away in a magical woodland. It was like stepping inside a breathtaking fairy tale. I was a young and naïve twenty-year-old when I arrived for my first day as assistant manager of Food & Beverage. I never imagined the adventure that lay in front of me, to be part of the team opening the hotel was a dream come true.

From my first glimpse of the majestic manor house, it was love at first sight. This was certainly the case too for Malcolm Powell and our chairman, John Sanderson upon their initial visit in late 1989 and subsequent purchase of the three-hundred-year-old property.

Following my earlier time with Tomorrow's Leisure as a weekend banqueting waiter and trainee manager, I was excited to now be reporting to Mr. Powell (as we called him then) for the first time.

Walking into Redworth Hall moved you; it instantly took you back in time. You could sense the voices of the lords and ladies who had inhabited the property for centuries before us. In the heart of the house was the original Great Hall, with a magnificent vaulted ceiling, two huge stone fireplaces, and a minstrel's gallery. There were seventeen individual and home-like presented bedrooms and suites, two beautiful lounges adjacent to the front door with ornate ceilings and oak paneled walls, and a lovely cozy dining room. The property was oozing charm and soul from its illustrious past.

The plans were ambitious, and some believed we were ridiculously audacious. We would open with the manor house and be fully operational with its seventeen bedrooms. At the same time over the following short twelve months, along with a vast array of builders and specialist tradesmen, we would add a large courtyard extension with eighty-three individually designed bedrooms and suites, an opulent Roman themed spa and pool, an additional restaurant, and extensive conference and banqueting facilities.

The designs were clever; to seamlessly blend the new extension with the seventeenth-century hall, thus making the luxurious addition completely invisible to the eye from the front of the manor house. More than anything, we would take every step to preserve the character of this historical gem. We soon realized that the dream went so much deeper and way beyond the fabric and fixtures of the property. It was all about the wonder and connection the whole team would be creating.

There was no book of process-laden rules that bound us. We were given the opportunity to think, act, and experience things for ourselves, which provided us with the opportunity to see the limitless potential. My teammates and I were lucky to have a workplace that encouraged us to put wonder on a pedestal. We were judged more on our ability to embrace that wonder than by anything else.

Malcolm had an unwavering, unnerving, on-your-toes kind of presence. You might not see him walk in the front door of the hotel in the morning, but you knew he was in the building, you could sense his presence. It was both inspiring and terrifying. Knowing he had just arrived made the hairs on your head tingle with fear—not a horrible or uncomfortable fear, but an invigorating, exciting, and positive type of fear. His eye contact alone could make you want to dissolve into the carpet.

Whilst we all might have suffered an air of apprehension in his presence, we weren't running around the hotel scared—in fact it was the opposite. We drew great strength from our abundance of respect and trust in him. He was authentic and led with his heart, which fueled our confidence. Malcolm was clear on his expectations, giving precise instructions and setting the highest of standards. However, the bright light that shone above all of this, was his warm encouragement of open boundaries—for everyone to be 100% their best self, to fully embrace our initiative and intuition.

As the senior leader, you might imagine that he would be sitting in his office all day surrounded by plans and paperwork. (We didn't have computers and email when we opened Redworth, just a wall of pigeonholes in the general office to share our paper messages and memos.) But Malcolm never hid away. He was involved, interested, and participated in everything. He explained how we put on a show each and every day for our guests, and as our leader, he drove our collective passion.

He was direct but open, clear but fair.

He was busy but he was present, strong-willed but uncomplicated.

He was fast to pick up something that wasn't right and just as quick to acknowledge something that was.

The pressure and demands of his senior role were huge—to deliver this massive expansion development on time and to budget, and at the same time create a profitable business. But Malcolm wasn't the "boss in charge," hidden behind his own agenda, barking out the orders. Never did he preach or dictate, only guided.

He directed like an orchestra conductor, encouraged like a ringmaster, and led the way like the pied piper. He had our best interests at heart, and we all responded willingly.

He traded suffocating rules, processes, and procedures for clear guidelines and fresh, clean oxygen—for us all to just get on with it.

Creating Belonging through Wonderlicious Leadership

We learned firsthand that the vitality of mental health throughout a workplace culture comes not from weekly team happy hours, cupcakes, and yoga sessions, but from good managers and leaders.

None of us across the whole team turned up to just perform our own role, nor were we only working *with* each other. We were working *for* each other. This was the base of our newly forming culture. It was effortless, it was inclusive, it was invigorating—and Malcolm's human-spirited leadership was the spark. He gave us permission to look after each other. Our culture thrived without any big ceremonious fanfare. It was organic, fresh, and wonderlicious.

There was no classism, no elitism. Housekeeping worked *for* the front office team. The front office team worked *for* the housekeeping team. It was the same with our brigade of chefs and the restaurant team and vice versa. Everyone was joined together in spirit, like we had concocted an adhesive and wonderful super glue.

We were not only creating an exquisite hotel experience, but also a profitable business. Malcolm showed us the way; he worked *for* us, and we also worked *for* him—with pleasure. He humanized our workplace and the rewards rippled through the team and the business like a mighty wave that swept all the way to the bottom line of profitability.

From Black & White to Color

Our weekly heads of department meetings were purposeful, incredibly engaging by design, and were never just a meeting. We used each moment that we gathered together to reflect, plan, rehearse, and share our ideas of innovation. As chair of each meeting, Malcolm created an open and spacious environment that was inclusive. Everyone was equal, all of our voices mattered, and we all felt safe to speak up. He showed us what freely sharing our ideas actually looked like—he demonstrated it, and we copied him.

Malcolm would often say, "How we do anything, is how we must do everything." He laid the clear foundation of permission for us to be our best selves, looking after each other, our guests, and guided every fiber of our presence. It was down to us to do something brave, do something unexpected, do things that made a difference to ourselves and our guests' experiences.

I clearly remember the feeling I had when I heard the word *must* as Malcolm said it—how we do anything is how we *must* do everything. Removing the word *must* would have made this just another statement. If he had used *should* instead of *must*, it would have sounded optional. The word *must* clearly define the consistency of our intention.

"To some," he said, "greeting a guest, answering the phone, presenting a dinner menu, serving tea, delivering room service, checking in a guest, or saying farewell is all considered service . . ." he paused, letting us soak in the words, then added, "like a transaction, and anyone can do that."

He taught us what service should be: "Service is the black and white. It's down to us to look beyond the transaction and focus on the feeling we create with every single moment of our service."

Malcolm taught us, "This is hospitality—how we add color to the black and white. The feeling from our authentic connection, service, and present connection combined hand in hand. The feeling we provide through and from our service." He reminded us, "There's no point in us having telephones in every department if we don't answer them warmly!"

Malcolm's focus on hospitality became the north star and the top of the compass for everyone at the hotel.

Many businesses and organizations may say they *do* or *have* customer service, but how many can actually explain what that truly means? I frequently see business leaders investing huge amounts of time and focus on the deliberation and introduction of complicated systems and expensive big-budget solutions to provide "innovative, ground-breaking customer service." They are distracted in the relentless pursuit for what they believe they should be doing next, an ongoing search for the hottest piece of tech magic, or the latest software gadgets that promise a new way of customer amazement.

So, they miss it—the moment, the feeling, the sense and innocence of enchantment, the pleasured connection within the moment—*beyond the transaction.*

Whilst many hotel teams and leaders are masterful at planning ahead using sales forecasts, occupancy targets, and the latest trends and innovations, they are equally focused, if not more so, with the present. Driving and delivering their brand promise while living in the moment of now.

Check, Check, and Then Check It Again

While the huge expansion program was underway, we were more than just a team; we were together as one and our guests saw that. They started going out of their way to tell us how they loved the feeling we were creating with our hospitality—except for one morning in late 1990 . . .

I was the early-shift duty manager. We were fairly quiet as the building works were all underway, but this day we were hosting an event in the Great Hall. I can't recall what I was doing at the time, but just know that around 9 a.m. I was sitting alone attending to something in the hotel general office. However, I remember what happened next as if it happened this morning.

Malcolm flew through the office door.

"Mr. Merrett," he said, followed by a long and highly awkward pause. Something was very wrong. "Can you please tell me why the conference organizer is down in reception asking me why we haven't served their morning tea?"

I had a lump in my throat. I froze. I couldn't swallow.

"Why are you here sitting at your desk?"

His piercing eye contact pinned me, motionless, to the floor. "Mr. Merrett, what kind of example are you setting to the team out there by sitting in here? Every detail, every day, you have to check, check, and then check it again."

I was dying inside and felt my eyes glazing over. I instantly felt devastated, I must have looked at the morning's plans incorrectly.

"You are not in the moment. This is your hotel, open your eyes and get it sorted. Please."

I edged past him and scurried off down the hallway, feeling sick to my stomach.

It was a tough lesson and no, it never happened again. However, looking back now I am pleased this moment actually happened. I obviously had no idea at the time the effect that Malcolm would have on my life at the beginning of my career.

Yes, sometimes he had to point out mistakes, but he never held a grudge or suffocated us with blame. Never were we left to stew in our anxiety. Later that day he invited me to sit with him in the lounge. He calmly asked, "So what did you learn from this morning?" We unpacked it together and made it right.

Here lies the purest form of what healthy, human-spirited leadership looks like and actually is, a behind-the-scenes look at the secret door to an amazing workplace and culture. The moments like this with Malcolm are what I often think of, and frequently refer to, as the greatest life-learning moments of my life. He wasn't only the general manager in charge, but our role model. We copied him and provided the same humility with our own teams across the hotel as he did with us. Another reason why we had a low employee turnover.

More than anything, Malcolm showed us all how to remain in the moment, busy *being* not busy *doing*. I dread the thought of what would have happened had I not been offered the job at Redworth Hall. If I hadn't had such an influential leader at the start of my career, all the serendipitous moments that have happened since may never have come to pass.

"Check, check, and then check it again." To this day, his words are hard-wired in my brain, clear as day. In fact, they have been my daily mantra for the past thirty years.

DOING IT RIGHT STAYS WITH YOU FOREVER

We deliberately chose one single word to define our service culture—*pleasure*. Not only the united and collective pleasure in our hospitality and service delivery, but the pleasure we were creating—as a place of work for our team, and for the joy of our guests.

It quickly became our natural default way—leading with movement and rhythm. By walking and being, rather than sitting and doing, we were all out on and around the hotel floors, visible and engaged in the moment with everything going on around us. It was as simple as it was profound. Day in, day out, it's just what we did.

As Malcolm taught us, if everyone only ever sits and reacts, they will only ever be in a state of doing. The moment we look up and look around, take a breath and have a really good look, the view is pretty amazing. Yet these special powers aren't reserved for hotel leadership and can be applied to transform any workplace environment or business sector.

We began growing our team in preparation for the transition from seventeen to one hundred bedrooms, along with all the other facilities. We were a management team of twelve in the beginning, and we all got involved with the many interviews. Top of our recruitment strategy was personality and heart. More than anything, we wanted to create a fun place to work because that is what fosters true hospitality. We met some amazing characters and started building our dream team.

Considerable thought was put into our interview questions, like:

- What do you enjoy doing outside of work?
- What's your favorite movie?
- Why would you like to work here?
- How did you last help someone?

We were fascinated to uncover the character, nature, and personality of our candidates. The responses to these types of questions revealed the sparkle in their eyes. We much preferred that over the traditional technical questions that don't incite authenticity.

We employed various local people from the surrounding villages plus several others from as far as London and the far north of Scotland. We found various amazing chefs, friendly restaurant team members, and eager housekeepers. We could feel the buzz of excitement within our growing team of personalities.

We decided we would establish a culture of hospitality based on the same feeling of welcome we traditionally create at home when opening the door to friends and family. It was simple. This would be our way.

We also put the same amount of pleasure into planning how we would welcome our new team members on their first day. We knew it would be impossible to describe our real purpose to them with a mission statement on a piece of paper. So instead, we enthusiastically explained our vision in person. We vowed to never just give everyone the employee handbook and force them to figure out everything themselves. More so—and to avoid the common term of "onboarding"—we proudly referred to this as our "Team Welcome."

We went all out to provide a warm welcome to our guests, so why wouldn't we do the same for our team? It made perfect sense to us to be at the front door to welcome each and every new person upon arrival no matter what role or rank. Our goals were to share the spirit of our hearts, to explain our exacting standards, and to create a space of warmth and permission for the team to be themselves.

As a team, we were highly connected—not through force or instruction, through caring about each other. Working together as one was our way of life. When I look back on it all now, I realize we were more like a family in its truest sense—we had each other's backs without judgment or blame.

When Seeing Isn't Enough

As a little boy, my mum took me with her to the local optician shop. I would sit there silently in fascination as they masterfully played with a million lenses and gadgets. The optician team was filled with jolly characters, and I would stare in awe as they miraculously sharpened Mum's sight. Secretly, I was convinced our optician was a magician and waited patiently for him to pull a rabbit out of the hat.

I thought about those optician visits often throughout my career, especially with Malcolm, who showed and encouraged us, a team of young leaders, how to really see. We regularly walked the floors of the hotel together, and he would point out various details and then ask, "What do you notice?"

He would explain that seeing and noticing were two different things: "It's all well and good thinking we can see something, but that isn't enough. When we consciously see something—we then notice it . . . We become connected with it. That is when our eyes and hearts have joined together. It shows how much we care."

When we walked past hotel guests in the lounge deep in their conversation over morning tea, he would ask, just above a whisper, "What do you notice?"

"Guests having tea?" we would answer hesitantly.

"You've missed it!"

"Their cups are empty. Let me show you what I mean."

We stood back to watch as he stepped toward the guests and with warmth, asked them, "Could we organize a nice fresh pot of tea for you?"

The guests looked up with shocked delight and gratefully accepted.

The lesson here was clear. He told us, "When people know that we have noticed, they feel valued and as a result, great things will always happen." He reminded us that noticing wasn't only something special or specific to our guests. "We must notice the good in each other too."

Malcolm would tell us it was up to all of us not to catch our people doing things wrong, but actively notice and acknowledge them doing things well. And celebrate it!

Probably one of the things we all loved most about Malcolm was that he "walked the talk." He showed us, by demonstration, what being present actually looked like. He wasn't only our general manager and our leader; I think he was also part optician. He encouraged us to focus our lens, which became a defining lesson we all gratefully received. On reflection, it was as if he kept pulling rabbits out of the hat. It resonated deeply with me and with all of us.

Over thirty-plus years later, his words have never left me: "Don't just see something but notice it." What seemed pretty simple at the time, became one of the most profound leadership lessons I thankfully received at the perfect time—the start of my career.

Getting It Wrong to Get It Right

Our business operated seven days a week, and although we found wonder in most days, I think Sunday was possibly our fondest. The one thing we became quite famous for was Sunday Lunch and were almost always fully booked.

Sunday is traditionally a wonderful family day, with relaxed laughter and the celebration of togetherness. At the hotel, we went all out to create home-like magic, a feeling of home away from home. We would stand at the front door to warmly welcome our guests as they arrived, before bringing them inside. We would eagerly watch their reaction as they stepped inside to the Sunday scent of crispy roast potatoes, rosemary roasted lamb and pinot noir that filled the air. We encouraged a no-rush, leisurely family style of treat.

We didn't always get it right in the early days, especially with the way we were taking restaurant bookings for tables. We were using a paper and pencil diary and realized we weren't spacing the table reservations sufficiently apart. We kept joyfully saying yes to just about every request and inadvertently took too many bookings at the wrong times. It was a sharp and fast learning curve—a lesson on how not to do it. We tried to accommodate everyone whenever they liked which, of course, caused huge logistical problems, complaints about the backlog, and unnecessary calamity in the kitchens. We had an awesome team of chefs, but with everything backing up at the hotplate, we realized they were the victims of our eagerness to please.

The delays and guests grumbling about our poor, slow service were painful, but we reacted swiftly, and we put it right. With some very simple tweaks and refinement to our diary management and spacing table times appropriately, we resumed sharing an uncomplicated air of hospitality that created free-flowing guest compliments. At the same time, and of particular importance (for everyone's sanity), this also achieved a happy normality backstage in the kitchen—a massive accomplishment in itself.

As with all of our preparations, we worked closely together to refine our approach to service. We practiced, planned, talked, and then practiced some more. More than anything, we had fun taking service seriously. To us, it wasn't just about technical delivery of customer service. It was about how we wanted our guests to feel as a result of our hospitality.

Never Give Up—No Matter What Happens

With the official opening celebrations looming, we were down to the wire, twenty-four hours before the Minister of Tourism would be arriving to perform the ceremonial cutting of the ribbon and a celebratory lunch with 150 local dignitaries. There was still a monumental amount of things to do. No longer were we walking, only running now. We still had a gigantic mountain to climb, and it was all hands on deck.

Even though it felt (and undoubtedly looked) like chaos, it was a magnificent and uplifting kind of perfectly organized chaos. It was as if we were in the adrenaline-fueled grand finale of a TV reality home makeover show, with the clock frantically (and annoyingly) counting down to the big reveal. We were jumping around carpet being laid, ceilings being painted, furniture still arriving, flowering plants being planted, and a mass of vacuum cleaners going flat out everywhere.

But we did it.

Mid-morning the following day, we all lined up along both sides of the freshly vacuumed red carpet that led to the front door of our lovingly restored manor house and now 100-bedroom hotel. The minister's car arrived, he walked along the red carpet greeting us all and smiling as he stepped into our tranquil haven. Never in a million years could he have comprehended what had just happened in the final hours, minutes, and even seconds before he arrived!

We were all totally exhausted and felt like we hadn't slept for a week (perhaps because we hadn't), but we all knew this was our moment. We summoned the strength to put on our greatest show. As all of our VIP guests arrived, all they saw in front of them was a team that looked bright-eyed, polished, and bursting with pride.

We were all involved in the service of the opening lunch party. The whole management team, housekeeping, reception, sales, accounts—everyone joined the banqueting team, to assist with lunch service. Malcolm gave Pam Henderson, our Personnel and Training manager, the daunting but exciting responsibility of serving the long top table, with the minister positioned in the honored center seat. As with banqueting etiquette, we followed Pam's lead with everything she did from the top table. As she poured the first glass of wine, this was our cue to follow. As she placed the first entrée, we did the same.

It was going brilliantly. At the beginning.

We all stepped forward and stood next to our tables, ready for the cue to follow Pam in clearing the entrée plates. She was standing behind the minister, about to lean forward to lift his plate, and in slow-motion horror, we saw the expression on her face suddenly change. In an instant, she fell sideways and disappeared from view—having fainted—and was lying on the floor behind the top table. Before we could draw our shocked breath, she bounced back up to her feet, clearly dazed, but gracefully doing everything she could to hide her confused state, as if absolutely nothing had happened. From that moment on, it added another layer to the foundation of our culture. We realized we were practically invincible.

Soon after, a special celebration party was held for the entire team, including the hundreds of builders and craftsmen who were involved in bringing the venue to life. John Sanderson, our chairman, personally thanked everyone individually and proudly placed shiny thank you medals on bright ribbons—each with personalized engravings around our necks.

The Hotel Inspector & "The Digestifs"

We were always on our toes watching carefully for hotel inspectors. In hotels, this is one guest that always has royalty status. They can make you, and they can break you. They validate and award (or remove) star ratings and culinary accolades. Frustratingly, they are masterful at hiding their identity, giving very few clues as to their imminent arrival.

They book in as a regular guest, starting their inspection at the point of making an inquiry and reservation. They proceed to evaluate every minuscule interaction with you leading up to and throughout their stay. The only possible clue to their identity is that the reservation is traditionally single occupancy, with a table for one in the dining room. Our midweek guests were predominantly business travelers so single occupancy was common. Yet one time, soon after opening, one of our reception team spotted our first inspector! She happened to answer the switchboard and her antenna went up due to the unusual amount of questions they asked.

With some further research, she uncovered that, yes, he was a senior inspector with the AA, and a successful visit would provide the confirmation for our intended four-star status. We watched him like a hawk, and everything was going brilliantly. Late afternoon there was commotion in the kitchen: "The inspector is asking for some Digestives," said a junior member of the lounge team. It was an odd request to ask for a specific brand of biscuit, we thought. We decided he must have been testing us. So, one of the chefs ran to his car and raced to our little village shop who luckily had some. We proudly delivered four neatly arranged McVities Digestive Biscuits on a little plate, with a fancy paper doily. It was met with the biggest smile.

Upon departure, he revealed who he was at reception and asked to see the general manager. We hid in the corridor to try and hear his feedback. "You are all such fun and I admire how you are all leading from the floor," he aired. "The innocence of your team is divine, as is their amazing effort with everything," he said to Malcolm.

"Now, about your digestifs . . ." and he explained he was asking for a "digestif" (an alcoholic beverage served after a meal, usually meant to aid with digestion, including brandies, whiskeys, fortified wines, and herbal liqueurs), not for "Digestive Biscuits."

"For this little blunder," he said with a smile, "I gave you top marks for going the extra mile. It was one of my favorite moments!" We received our four stars and soon after opening, were crowned North East England Hotel of the Year.

Not only for our plush fixtures and fittings—for our heart.

We were on our way.

Just like throwing a boomerang into the wind, Malcolm showed and taught us that the more kindness, grace, and humility we shared with others, the more it would keep coming back.

I obviously had no idea at the time that the lessons he shared would not only go on to shape and influence my career, but they would also contribute to the foundations of my life.

Special Recipe Side Notes:

In 2022 I had a challenging trip back to the UK with the passing of my father. I hadn't seen Malcolm since I left Redworth Hall back in 1993, although we had remained in touch with occasional exchanges of messages. I took the opportunity to arrange a wonderful reunion and met at his home in Exeter.

Back then as a twenty-year-old working for Malcolm at Redworth Hall, we shook hands from time to time. In this moment of our greeting, as he opened his front door, we hugged a proper big hug. All I wanted was to have this chance to look him in the eye and say thank you. I just needed him to know the profound effect he had on me and my career. He showed me the way with his special map, and I was able to personally express my thanks.

Yet he still selflessly turned it back to me and said, "I didn't do any of it. It was your drive and enthusiasm that made you; I only tried to stimulate it."

Please know that the presence of your own authentic humility—the way you respectfully connect with others and how you show them the way, can not only last the time they are working with you—but their lifetime.

Recipe 2 Recap:
LEADING HAND IN HAND

Navigating a complex maze blindfolded, only to find a reassuring hand that guides you effortlessly to the exit, is the heart of human-spirited leadership. What could you do to be like Malcolm—the conductor, optician, ringmaster, or pied piper—of your business or workplace?

Ingredients:

* ★ Your presence, no matter how busy you think you are.
* ★ A willingness to lead from the floor, not from behind your desk.
* ★ An environment where fun, creativity, and wonder are encouraged.
* ★ A welcoming atmosphere which values everyone and demonstrates trust, authenticity, and fairness.
* ★ Clarity in direction and directions.
* ★ Empathy: recognition that mistakes are opportunities for growth and improvement.

Substitutions to Make this Recipe Your Own:

You don't have to have a seventeenth-century country house hotel to create wonder. You need only the ingredients above and the willingness to lead by the hand, share the map, and watch as the magic is created. Show your team that pleasure, excellence, and joy are the daily norms.

Recipe 3:
MISE EN PLACE

"

If you have a dream, you have a responsibility to yourself to make it come true.
Because if you don't you're just a dreamer

Marco Pierre White

Professional chefs are *magicians.*

Their work is wizardry—it's that simple and that profound. Their inspiring culinary skills create emotion and connection through fresh ingredients and their *pace, preparation,* and *organization* is mastery. Not by fluke or chance, they consciously optimize themselves for wonder. They are hard-wired with wonder; they *thrive* around wonder.

Chefs are amongst the most hard-working and busiest people on the planet—also the most prepared and organized. Despite performing the intricacy of their craft inside a relentless and unforgiving environment of intense, time-restrained pressure, they still give themselves space to search for possibility. They constantly challenge themselves to turn taste into excitement and flavors into fascination. They are curious dreamers, and they do whatever it takes to bring those dreams to life. Like any fine artist, the menu is their oil painting, turning endless blocks of blank canvas into adored pieces of art.

Their greatest superpower lies beyond the stove, in their daily presence. Being present isn't something they only switch on for one-off special occasions—it's their default setting. All excellent chefs are highly in tune with their time and organization. There is so much that we can all learn from them to enhance our own success and optimize our work for wonder.

Some of the most influential life lessons I learned at the start of my career happened at Hotel School in England. While training professionally as a chef we were taught how to excel within our chosen profession through our preparedness.

Whilst I didn't go on to work as a chef and instead followed a path in hotel management, the lessons of *pace, preparation,* and *organization* I learned from my training in the kitchen thirty-five years ago have followed me ever since. It is my default setting to the present day.

Putting Time to Good Use

With the complex and hectic demands on our daily time, it is easy to lose track of our well-intended plans, hopes, and dreams. As each day starts, and often before we know it, unpredicted interruptions, unplanned meetings, phone calls, and online distractions have a clever way of robbing us of our focus—and our wonder. Our well-intended to-do list and intentions for the day have flown out the window.

There is nothing more rewarding than the feeling of achievement at the end of a day, the satisfaction that you did something good for someone or successfully tackled any number of the tasks that you set out to complete. If the start of your day begins with a heavy sigh, it could simply be because your mind and heart are out of sync with wonder.

Your day might begin by attending a business seminar that starts late with a presenter who is distracted and fumbling. They clearly haven't prepared or thought about what they are trying to say and seem to be making it up as they go. As the day goes on, meetings run over, the office is a mess, and there is an IT failure. Time-wasting moments like this happen continuously and often deliver us to the end of the day exhausted and wondering what we actually accomplished.

As tomorrow morning begins, the clock continues to tick down once again. Before we know it and without even noticing, the following day starts over and we scratch our heads contemplating where the time went, while the well-intended list of things to do remains. And the cycle continues to roll.

This recipe shines a warm, bright light of refreshment into your daily routine to synchronize your sense of wonder with your work. Here I share my most potent personal organization system, a daily philosophy that positively fuels esteemed kitchens the world over. It's an enhanced methodology that can be effortlessly applied by anyone from any profession.

Conducting the Kitchen

A chef stepping into their kitchen at the start of their shift is the same as a conductor taking to the stage in their theater. Imagine the conductor warmly acknowledging the eager audience before turning to embrace their orchestra with a smile of reassurance. Arms outstretched and the baton pointing perfectly upwards, the entire auditorium holds their breath together in anticipation of the moment—and then the conductor's mobile phone rings; they forgot to leave it in the dressing room. To the horrified gasp of everyone in the theater, they stop to answer the call. Right there on stage. The flow of the moment is over. The experience crashes to a halt. All the tireless planning and preparation is shattered into a million pieces.

Of course, *this* would never actually happen.

Yet we all allow things *like* this to happen without even realizing it, a simple auto-pilot reaction that allows distractions that destroy our flow.

But chefs don't.

A chef arriving at their kitchen, like the conductor walking onto the stage, is the same as you stepping into your workplace, except they are masterful and disciplined at controlling distractions. Are you? Chefs have no choice but to be fully present in the moment. They have a head full of dreams yet are laser-focused, and the outside world is closed.

There are a number of the world's best chefs that I admire deeply and have followed intently throughout my career: Raymond Blanc, Albert Roux, Gary Rhodes, Nigella Lawson, Marco Pierre White, Heston Blumenthal, and Anthony Bourdain.

While they have each inspired me for different reasons, I'm in constant admiration not only of their unwavering passion but also their incredible presence—more so how they relentlessly dream and work hard to account for every single minute of their time to inspire others from their reputation.

One of my chef idols, Marco Pierre White, is fondly considered the godfather of chefs. His unique passion, grit, and dreams changed the world of gastronomy. In 1995 at thirty-three years of age, he was the first (and youngest) British chef to be awarded three Michelin stars. I met Marco for the first time in 2023, some thirty-five years on since his name was mentioned to me and my fellow chefs in the kitchen during our training. He shared his life from the stage at Sydney's State theater, and I felt unashamedly starstruck when he signed my treasured *White Heat* book as he came off stage. The whole audience was mesmerized by his presence, and especially by the stories he shared.

He said to us that evening, "I don't just cook, I dream!" Out came his large plain paper notebook and coloring pens with a camera above him to show us what he was doing.

"I make pictures in my mind of a new dish. It always starts with a thought that I visualize by dreaming, then I start to bring it to life."

He looked down at his paper and explained, "I draw a picture of it. I feel it. I design it. I list the ingredients and play with the colors, but it always starts by dreaming about it first."

You could hear a pin drop between his words and long pauses as the sound of his pens working around the paper echoed around the theater as he drew his example. Finally, he looked up and held a long pause. "But it's only when we take action that we make our dreams come true. Because if you don't, you're just a dreamer."

Mastering Time Like a Chef

1. PACE: Slow Down to Speed Up

The most influential lessons that I learned at Hotel School came with various short words of wonder phrases. In the classroom, our head chef lecturer would say, "To be successful in a professional kitchen, you will have to be effective with your time—you will fail if you are hasty or reactive." And in big chalk letters on the blackboard, he wrote the words: "Slow down to speed up."

In other words, it would become critical for our success to consciously take the time to think—to experiment, and consciously pause to play with our creativity. To save significant time in the long run and achieve a superior outcome, it would also be critical to first be prepared and organized.

My little boy Jake loves making pancakes. Every Sunday morning, it's become our fun family ritual. During this moment each week, he himself assumes the role of head chef, measuring all the ingredients of his favorite recipe. He makes the perfectly runny pancake batter mix and gives it to me as his nominated commis chef, to cook the pancakes on the stove.

On one occasion, he had a friend over and was distracted. He frantically rushed everything and skipped all the steps in the recipe. Instead of blending the sifted flour and eggs together first, then gradually adding the milk and melted butter, he raced to throw the eggs, milk, fridge-hard butter, and unsifted flour all together at the same time into the mixer and turned it on high speed. It produced a lumpy, unusable, sloppy mess, and he had to start all over again. All the ingredients were wasted, as was his time. Even though as a ten-year-old and the fact that he was head chef at that moment and I was his commis chef, I warmly shared the words with him on how he should *slow down to speed up*. He smiled and it actually seemed to connect with him quite positively—he took it on! His next batch of pancakes was his best yet. Each week he now further utilizes his state of wonder and slows down with his pace of preparation—I've noticed how he has applied the same with his homework and how he gets his school uniform ready the night before school.

In reverse—speeding up without slowing down, would be the same as rushing to the supermarket to do the weekly shopping, without first preparing a shopping list—and the time that would be wasted trying to remember what you might need. It would be like leading a team meeting before planning what you are going to say and how you are going to say it, or arriving to begin your day in the office without any pre-thought of what you are attempting to achieve from your arrival onwards.

It's exactly the same with professional hotel and restaurant kitchens around the world, except that chefs are experts at practicing the method of *slowing down to speed up*. Before they begin cooking for the service in front of them, massive thought and preparation occurs as second nature before they even step into the kitchen.

Imagine for a moment that you are a chef working in the kitchen of a one-hundred-cover restaurant. It's fully booked for dinner, meaning you will have one hundred hungry, eager diners waiting for you, the chef, to produce a culinary masterpiece to satiate the one hundred palettes in flawless execution. The numbers are easy to calculate—during a fleetingly short service time, several hundred plates and dishes will go into the dining room as patrons are served their hors d'oeuvres, appetizers, salads, entrees, sauces, sides, vegetables, and desserts. The pressure is on—but none of it will end well if you (and all the other chefs in your team) haven't properly prepared or thought about the service ahead of time. To make it a flawless service, along with the required speed, first you have to slow down to gather your thoughts, plan the service, and mentally walk through every detail of the evening ahead. This is how chefs consistently find their A-Game.

2. PREPARATION: Three Magic Words to Prepare Your Wonder

Three of my favorite words to describe the principle and state of mind that intuitively guide every chef's success are *mise en place*. It is the French culinary phrase that means putting in place or everything in its place. This small, handsome phrase packs an enormous amount of sense and influence. It describes the way chefs organize their day and prepare themselves for a demanding service, to produce a memorable dining experience efficiently and whilst under tremendous pressure.

As you say this exquisite little phrase, *mise en place*, it effortlessly glides off the tongue like a teaspoon of the finest Italian ice cream. Give it a try! Have a go in your fanciest French pronunciation: *Mee zon plass*.

Mise en place is also a state of heart and mind. It signifies an entire lifestyle of readiness and engagement applied to every single working day. Chefs have this concept running through their veins and are masters at keeping many tasks in mind simultaneously, with equal importance.

Of course, there are chefs who don't precisely plan or prepare their day in advance, and as a guest in their restaurant, you can always tell; *mise en place* is what separates amateur chefs from distinguished ones.

What chefs also call "*The Meez*" is what allows them to glide through each dish, without wasting a split second to frantically search for the things they need in the moment. Everything is at their fingertips—ready and within reach because of all the moments that happen long before firing up the ovens to begin cooking. There are precise steps that go into arranging the array of ingredients, utensils, and other components required for the forthcoming service: the pre-thought ahead of assembling the fresh ingredients; prepping the sauces and seasoning the meats; setting up each workstation; positioning the pots and pans; meeting with front of house and back of house to run through service; making sure the tables and establishment are sparkling clean, set and ready, and triple checking menus.

Every element of service is regarded as part of the *mise en place*.

American chef Anthony Bourdain wrote in his best-selling memoir *Kitchen Confidential*: "Mise en place is the religion of all good line cooks . . . As a cook, your station, and its condition, its state of readiness, is an extension of your nervous system. The universe is in order when your station is set."

He cautioned: "Without a well-tended meez, you'll soon find yourself spinning in place and calling for backup."

Bourdain was a brilliant chef who consistently demonstrated how planning is the most fundamental ingredient to any dish. He and his chefs would unfailingly plan every aspect of their menu recipes, not during the service, but before the actual service began. Exactly the same will happen when you apply the same thinking and attention to your own workday, with your "service."

3. ORGANIZATION: Clean as You Go

To optimize wonder through your day, maintaining the order of your office or work environment is of equal importance. Chefs subconsciously do this as second nature, cleaning as they go.

Working with my fellow chefs in our Hotel School kitchen was one of the most invigorating and exciting thrills of my professional life. We had a pretend—but real— restaurant that we would fill with our friends and families for us to practice on each week. There was silver cutlery that we learned how to properly polish, crisp white tablecloths on every table, and bone-china crockery to serve our culinary creations. Our obliging guinea pigs would sit and eagerly anticipate our offerings of hospitality.

Through the restaurant service doors was our professional training kitchen set out with traditional sections and a central bank of commercial ovens and stovetops covered by a large extraction canopy. Our complete focus was on the front hotplate—the heart of the kitchen—where each plate received any last adjustments in the final seconds before being sent into the dining room. I loved being in the middle of a busy dinner service because I always forgot that I was actually training. It was adrenaline-fueled precision.

All of our senses were collectively beaming on full alert. We were always anxious at the hotplate, anticipating the response and critique from our guests.

Each service was never noisy from shouting at each other. It was intense, but our *mise en place* provided calm. Chef Newby, our lead teacher, guided us through each service. He reminded us that the best kitchens around the world are never deafening with mindless yelling at each other. And that this would preserve the space for us to cook by being in tune with the sense of sound. Not just looking but listening to and judging the noises that our ingredients made as we were cooking. If chopped onions went into a tepid pan, they would be silent—not good. If they went into a pan that was too hot, the onions would screech and burn—also not the outcome we wanted.

We would put in four to five hours of preparation through the day for a two-hour dinner service, from intricate planning and preparation of our ingredients and service to our continuously cleaning down as we went. It was repeatedly drummed into us, to "clean as you go."

We had an end-of-term practical exam in the kitchen and even though this moment happened thirty-five years ago, it is seared into my memory, and I am so incredibly thankful that the moment actually happened.

We were given three hours to prepare our *mise en place*, ahead of creating a single serving of classic minestrone soup, an individual serving of beef Wellington with Madeira jus, and vanilla crème brûlée. The pressure was on and just like the TV show *MasterChef*, we were working to the clock. Our culinary teacher, Chef Newby, paced around our sections and monitored our deep concentration. The clock dramatically stopped amongst our franticness to finish. Chef Newby then went around the kitchen, giving his marks to us one by one, with a score out of ten for presentation, taste, and technical skill.

He got to my section. "This soup is delicious; the vegetables are very nicely cooked." My heart stopped as he sliced through the beef Wellington; to my relief, it was perfectly pink in the middle. "This is excellent, the mushroom duxelles is seasoned just right." He then smiled as his teaspoon cracked the caramelized-sugar top of the brûlée. "Superb," he said.

"I give you four out of ten." I am sure he saw the devastation on my face.

"Chef," he said to me. "Please look at your section!" I glance behind me. He continued, "It's a disgrace." The class started sniggering and nudging each other as he frowned at my huge pile of pots, pans, vegetable trimmings, egg shells, flour, and all the mess I'd created. "You seem to have forgotten that every good chef cleans as they go. It's a matter of pride and this disarray reflects you and your state of mind. You lost five points today for your bomb site."

His quiet, calm tone sent chills down my spine, cutting sharper than a razor blade.

"This mess represents the loose ends in your approach and reflects your attention to the job at hand." He and I both knew this was a pivotal lesson. Ever the teacher, he warned that "In the outside world in the peak of a normal service—you will sink."

He frowned some more and then walked on to mark the next section.

That moment had such an effect and influence over my life. The words of Chef Newby have never been far from my mind! I do realize that today many people, including my family, think I'm pedantic, especially when I'm in the kitchen with the way that I clean as I go. Whenever it's my turn to serve family dinner at home, there is hardly any washing up or cleaning to do afterward, it's all done.

But the same principle applies to my office workspace. It's a habit with the way that I approach my work and presence, working in a clean, organized, productive state of mind. At the end of each day in my office, I clean down my work space and leave everything ready for tomorrow.

"Cleaning as you go" will significantly benefit the completion and achievement of your daily tasks. It will provide some soothing organization with all the moving parts of any task that faces you.

Applying a Chef's Magic to Your Daily Routine

Consider the start of your workday—what's the first thing you tend to do when you arrive at your office or work environment? Examining your inbox or listening to phone messages is a common default. In many ways, this is one of the worst habits to start a day. Both activities steal and trick our focus and throw us in a reactive spin, with other people's priorities quickly distracting our own preparation for the day ahead. This is the equivalent of a chef entering their kitchen and starting their shift by doing the crossword of the morning newspaper.

When preparing for the day ahead, your thoughts might sometimes appear muddled or daunted with what you have in front of you. Your work environment might be as you left it, with the remnants of yesterday and your inbox screaming for your attention, social media notifications pinging, and your phone ringing. The well-intended to-do-list starts to fall away into the abyss through the relentless distractions.

Applying a chef's *pace, preparation,* and *organization* to your own work is a limitless and enriching method that can be applied to any task, such as leading a team meeting, creating a business report, designing a new customer experience, studying for an exam, or delivering a presentation. By not leaving any of these to a hasty last-minute chore and instead applying the simplicity of *slow down to speed up, mise en place,* and *clean as you go* to any of these examples, your colleagues, audience, and customers will now notice and enjoy your evident level of preparation.

Your Meez

In this instance, let's imagine you are delivering an internal business update presentation at work. You might add to your to-do-list (*mise en place*) the task "Business Update Presentation" and that's it. You then arrive at the moment of the presentation and deliver it on the go. The AV isn't set as you hoped; the clicker isn't working; you can't find the stats you need; you wish the room was set differently; and you finish with some random Q&A. It's uneventful and underwhelming for your attendees.

Adding your *Meez* to the task will allow you to mindfully gather all of the ingredients in advance and fully prepare your mind ahead of the experience. You will include all the components that you will need for the business update: the clear purpose of your message; the sales figures and statistics; room layout; AV requirements; and timings. You might ask yourself:

- What feeling do I want to create?
- Will I include participation and interaction?
- Should I use PowerPoint slides or a whiteboard?
- What handouts could I produce?
- How much practice time should I allow?
- What time should I arrive to set up the room?

The answers to these questions will set you up for great success before you start the presentation. Your care will shine through to your attendees, and they will love that it wasn't painful, but an engaging and impactful experience.

Think of your business update presentation like a chef preparing to serve a vegetable stir-fry. Any successful stir-fry recipe only works with attentive *mise en place*—gathering and preparing all of the ingredients in advance—because once the ingredients start to hit the hot wok, there's no time or opportunity to backtrack, no second chance, no forgiveness. The principles of your *mise en place*, your state of heart and mind, are exactly the same. For you, it is what will indeed make your business update presentation a meaningful and memorable experience—quite delicious, even.

Thirty-Five Years Later

You must do whatever works best for you—by example, my own daily *Meez* of many years is a single page Word document. I don't label this as my "To-do list" and instead at the top of the page is the title "Mise en Place." I have three very simple section headings, each colored as traffic lights: *A: Today* (Green); *B: This Week* (Amber) and *C: This Month* (Red).

At the end of each day, I simply list the things I must accomplish the following day and list these into A and add other things that come to mind into B and C. In addition to the motivation of my daily Meez, this serves me as my easy-to-view ongoing monthly plan.

I always update my Meez at the end of each day by listing my fresh points under *A: Today*. This helps me to not only familiarize myself in advance with the forthcoming day but assists me to switch off as I close each day too. Before anything else, I start each morning with a ten to fifteen-minute mini-planning session to review my Meez. In this moment I simply check the sequence of my priorities under A and front load important priorities with a fresh mind. For certain specific tasks on my list, I add them to my calendar—helping me fine-tune my day ahead. The key part of my daily ritual is to visualize that the day has finished, and I consider the accomplishment from the tasks that I have achieved.

I stay connected to *B* and watch over *C*. But each day I focus on *A* and play within the green lights. This is my personal and visual signal for movement and momentum.

Finally, at the end of my day comes the satisfying part. That's when I spend about fifteen minutes reviewing my Meez. I simply remove everything I've completed within *A*, but instead of just deleting the things I have achieved and accomplished, I move them down to the top of an ongoing "Done" page, with each of the items starting with a ticked symbol bullet point.

This is both my personal "pat on the back" and also provides me with a record for simple reference. Whenever I ask myself what I actually got done this week, month, quarter, or year, it's all there at a glance.

The Habit of Harmony

I always warmly invite anyone who is interested in learning the secret of undistracted daily productivity to step behind the scenes of any famous kitchen and work alongside a chef to witness the organization, rhythm, and rituals of their work. Whilst I realize stepping into the kitchen of Marco Pierre White or Michel Roux Jr. may not be possible for most, let this story be your guide to the wisdom gleaned from the polished silver, the frantic yet controlled service, and the mastery of professional chefs.

When this is applied as a way of life across your daily routine, even as the method across a whole business or organization, you'll be well on your way, even floating, from your blissful productivity. Just as you brush your teeth every morning, treating your *mise en place* as the same personal habit will ensure you bring the same freshness to the productivity of your day, also your readiness for wonder.

More than anything, allowing your Meez to guide you as your sixth sense, with everything in its place, is a freeing feeling—I assure you!

Recipe 3 Recap:
MISE EN PLACE

We should all take lessons from professional chefs. They are conductors, magicians, and dreamers who master countless complications and logistics as if bending time and possibilities to their will. There are many transferable benefits from the meticulous rituals of chefs that will optimize you for a wonderlicious daily routine you look forward to each morning.

Ingredients:

★ **Pace:** Slow down to speed up. Take the time to think, experiment, and play with creativity. Avoid rushing and wasted effort by setting a deliberate pace with your tasks, just as a chef carefully prepares everything for a flawless service.

★ **Preparation:** Embrace mise en place by putting everything in its place. Prepare for your day by planning how to anticipate every situation with a chef's precise consideration, organization, and arrangement of ingredients for optimal efficiency.

★ **Organization:** Clean as you go. Maintain order in your workspace to enhance productivity and clarity of mind. Just as chefs tidy while they cook to avoid chaos, incorporate this habit into your daily routine for a smooth and calm workflow.

Substitutions to Make this Recipe Your Own:

If you aren't running a kitchen, but perhaps a family home, a business, or a career instead, apply a chef's mastery to your daily routine. Start your day with the above ingredients. Intentionally avoid reactive habits (such as immediately checking emails upon waking). Adopt a chef's mindset of presence to set yourself up for success.

APPETIZER

—

HEART

"

*Seems to me it ain't the world that's so bad
but what we're doing to it, and all I'm saying is:
see what a wonderful world it would be
if only we'd give it a chance.
Love, baby—love. That's the secret.*

Louis Armstrong

A FOUNDATION OF KINDNESS

Musicians have a special way of recording timely pieces of music for the world—right at the moment it's needed most. Louis Armstrong, American trumpeter, vocalist, and one of the most influential figures in jazz history did exactly this in 1967 with "What a Wonderful World." To help ease the challenging unrest at the time in America, this was his gift, a song of heart to share some optimism and celebration of life. Over five decades later this honored Hall of Fame piece of music still holds a special place the world over. The lyrics feel as fresh, relevant, and important for us today as they did to those who first heard it back when it was released.

From the humblest beginnings in New Orleans, Louis Armstrong was a lifelong hard worker, helping his family to make ends meet by selling coal on the street at the young age of six. He was known for putting the satisfaction of others before his own; on the stage and at home with his family, he did whatever it took to make others happy. Not only famous for his gravelly voice and beaming smile, but he was also known for his big heart that he tirelessly shared with everyone.

"What a Wonderful World" was written by Bob Thiele and George David Weiss. Using just 120 words, this musical treasure resonates in perpetuity with the masses. It is timeless for its celebration of beauty in the human spirit and the world around us that we all take for granted—shaking hands with friends, looking up at the sky, saying I love you . . .

The wonder that makes life worth living is getting lost in the tempo of busyness. It has become far too easy to pass people on the streets and in the hallways of our lives without so much as a "Hello," our eyes down or focused on our phones. Even now, fifty years or so after Louis Armstrong topped the charts with this song, we are still at risk of missing the magic he sang about.

I passionately bring Louis Armstrong into this moment and onto these pages because he knew how important it was (and still is) to embrace the wonder of humanity for a better, more fulfilling way of living, working, and being. To learn how to go easier on ourselves and each other; to find the true foundation of our human motivation again, with decent and proper leadership practices of heart and care; to help navigate our modern world.

This next part of the Wonderlicious Menu weaves some honest consideration and purposeful reflection—to demystify five big bold words. Five transforming words that I have had the extraordinary fortune of learning throughout my career: *Softness is not a weakness.*

The most basic truth is that from softness comes our kindness—a formidable human strength and a sublime leadership power that can move mountains. Yet kindness is commonly underrated and frequently lost under the heavy wheels of time.

For some in the world of business and at the center of organizational culture, we are conditioned to believe that we must resolutely "march" our ambitions on, with robust vigor and grit, in the pursuit of greatness. Leaders believe it's about being hard and tough. Like us, their subconscious minds have grown to consider kindness as a weakness.

Kindness is a real foundation of soft skills that is not only crucial in life and business; it is the "soft things" that are increasingly vacant in our modern existence and also appear far more confronting to practice. It becomes easy to brush it aside as unimportant and instead of being kind, we stick with being hard and tough.

I often think that trying to function without a happy and grateful heart for the world and people around us would be like trying to launch a rocket to the moon without an engine.

There is great power in embracing the wonderful world we live in. Bring your heart with you for this part—the rocket is about to leave for the moon . . .

Recipe 4:
GIVING YOUR HEART A VOICE

"

Piglet noticed that even though he had a very small heart,
it could hold a rather large amount of gratitude.

AA Milne

The floorboards creak inside the little old house you just stumbled across by pure chance. Everything is covered with dusty white sheets, and it feels as if you've stepped inside Aladdin's cave that's been hidden away and deserted for years. Clouds of dust fill the air as you pull away the sheets to reveal the beautiful and ornate antique furniture that has been left behind. It was lost until now, waiting to be discovered—by you.

In my own mind, I imagine this old treasure chest house and parallel it with a company workplace culture. Instead of the furniture lost in time waiting to be found, it is the invincible power of our human connection that I see hidden away beneath dusty covers.

Our minds carry the daily burden of our hyper-connected existence, ongoing global unrest, and change. Everything can feel so heavy in our head that it drags down our body. Where once the mind-body connection was in sync, it's now more often disconnected. We live in our heads and, often without realizing, put our hearts on the proverbial back burner.

However, what if our heart and head connected with a depth of rhythm? Back in sync—to be more intuitive and creative—to become better leaders with freedom to create deeper relationships and connections. To belong.

I offer you some space here to let go of your head for a moment, to loosen any tangled wires and step inside your heart to find a sense of possibility through wonder. To discover what happens when you wear your heart on your sleeve and share it everywhere you go. To connect your human motivation and lift your imagination—not leaving your heart behind at home, or in the car, on the train or bus to work. Instead, taking it everywhere you go.

Okay, so please excuse the dust clouds as we pull away the covers . . .

The Other Reason Why People Love Going to Work

Whatever our craft or industry, we have the honor and responsibility to lead ourselves and others with compassion each day. Encouraging those around us with heart and noticing people doing things well is the subtle difference between the organizations that thrive and those that continue to struggle. "Treat your people well, and they will take care of your customers" is an age-old expression that is as real today as it ever was.

Relaxation spaces, fun pop-up events, and interesting outdoor areas top the reinvention list of flashy amenities designed to lure workers to their workplace and encourage job satisfaction. That said, in my experience, what truly provides joy, motivation, commitment, and excitement to go into work each day comes from genuine, heart-led leadership. People crave a working environment where they feel inspired and loyal because they know they are seen, valued, and understood. They want to know they are not alone and that their efforts matter.

All of the outdoor picnic areas, office fitness challenges, and meditation rooms in the world cannot overcome an environment where everyone feels unnoticed and discouraged.

If you want to radically transform a company culture, you need to create connections and share encouragement. That's where the wonder is—important simple practices that are commonly missed.

Lifting the Hearts of Others

There is nothing more exciting and fulfilling than being part of a business environment or workplace culture that is alive with the heart of caring leadership. As a result, the positive sparks that fly from employees can radiate a million miles. Everyone enjoys being part of it—customers, guests, and clients included.

Organizations that believe they are heart-led—and those who truly are—can be worlds apart. Heart and wonder are more than a mission statement on a piece of paper tacked to a wall. They must be a cultural component to your business's way of life. The ones who understand this are the businesses who are thriving, not wasting time in lengthy recruitment meetings debating team morale or turnover rates. People in heart-led organizations tend not to think about leaving because they find joy at work. These are the workplaces where the employees are the cheerleaders and ambassadors for others to join because they feel encouraged, noticed, and valued.

While many organizations have nice, impressive-sounding words on their website about the fabulous values of their caring culture—the reality is often completely opposite.

Joy will always be created by the simple moments in life, such as meaningfully sharing two wonderful words: "well done." This matters more than an office morning tea with cupcakes. These small, powerful words of encouragement can positively impact you and your business beyond measure. They help leaders become the positive energizer that lifts the hearts of others. Whilst remuneration is obviously important to workers, feeling seen and encouraged is equally, if not more, important.

Openly encouraging and recognizing people inside a working environment will always radiate a positive energy as warm as the sun. It has the power to single-handedly turn the tide and create an abundant, joyful workplace. On the other hand, when you keep your employees at arm's length and unnoticed, they feel invisible and isolated, grow restless, and begin looking for an employer who sees them. It all boils down to one single and commonly missing ingredient that inspires progressive work—encouragement.

The Epidemic of "Busyness"

As second nature, authentically heart-inspired leaders recognize the efforts of people with regular warm and open-hearted sincerity. I have visited and encountered many organizations across the globe where you can sense that the employees, frankly, seem miserable. You can spot it a mile off. People sitting at desks looking at screens clicking their keyboards in silence, the heart is clearly missing. Managers and leaders are either hesitant or believe they're too busy to share compliments and encouragement with their employees and teams. They miss the importance of these simple, rewarding measures.

When I visit organizations, I often notice the speed at which leaders and managers run around their offices. As if it's part of an exercise routine, they run between meetings, exchanging fleeting half glances with their colleagues.

> "How's things?"
> "Busy, you?"
> "Yes, busy, lots on."
> "Back-to-back meetings today. Busy."

It's an epidemic of *busy*. And it is infectious!

Leaders might say that their people have their KPIs, job descriptions, and targets, and that they're paid to be here, to work. I will never forget touring the offices of a company headquarters in Sydney and saw exactly this—overhearing a senior director saying across their desk to a colleague "I haven't time for this—I'm not here to babysit them too." The environment was tense and dehydrated, but this "influential director" couldn't see it.

I thought to myself at the time just how different it would be if she hadn't left her heart at home and brought it with her to work. I knew that if encouragement were her natural state, this business environment would have been so much healthier and happier. I'm not embarrassed to say that the *babysitting* comment made me want to discreetly head to their bathrooms; my eyes could have easily sprung a leak into tears, but I somehow held them back. I felt devastated for all the people sitting at their desks.

As adults, we are experts at encouraging and praising our children. However, we stop doing this freely with other adults. Even though a gold star sticker or a "nice job" comment with an actual pat on the back for a "grown-up" adult carries much the same impact and influence, we stop believing it's necessary.

Badge of Honor

I will never forget the day that I collected my eldest son Zachary from school; he was eight at the time. I parked the car and stood at the gates like I always did so that I would be there when he came out rather than sitting waiting for him up the road in the car.

The school bell rang, and the usual explosion of noise came with all the children bursting out of their classrooms and racing to escape. This day was different. In the middle of the crowd of children coming toward the gates, I saw Zac's head going up and down, jumping up as he's running to me, screaming at the top of his voice, "Daddy! Daddy!" waving a piece of paper wildly in the air.

I could sense something big had happened. I instantly went down onto my knees to meet him with level eye contact as he crashed into my arms, so hard I nearly went flying back into the road.

"You'll never guess what happened today!"

He was so full of joy and excitement it was a wonderful sight. I felt myself immediately caught up in it as well. "Slow down, slow down, take a breath! What happened? Tell me, tell me!"

"Look what I got Daddy!" He handed me a small piece of paper.

"We were in the school assembly this morning. I was sitting right at the back and the principal called me up to the front and he gave me that, Daddy!"

The paper read, "Zachary Merrett, Student of the Week." There were handwritten words underneath from his teacher "For trying so hard in the classroom, keep up the good work."

I looked into his excited eyes "Wow, Zac! This is amazing, I'm so proud of you."

He was beaming. "Daddy, all these little bumps went up my arms and down my legs, it tickled!"

"Brilliant!" I said. "They're called goose bumps!" He looked puzzled so I explained, "They come out when surprising, wonderful things happen!"

Paper Wonder

"The Principal leaned forward to me, Daddy, and whispered, "Well done," as he gave me this. Zac pointed to his "Honor Badge."

It was a bright yellow piece of paper that had gone through the school laminating machine, was cut with a pair of scissors into a little oval shape, stuck with a safety pin through it, and pinned to his shirt.

Zac's smile was huge. With his Honor Badge for the whole of the next week he was allowed to stand in the front of the line. All his friends thought he was the coolest boy in school. The thing I love most about it all is that, in reality, the badge was simply a piece of paper.

More than this, though, there is nothing academic attached to this recognition or anything related to measurement—like in business for example, measuring someone against the company's KPIs. The paper is nothing, but the acknowledgment is everything and it wasn't the little piece of paper that changed my little boy's life.

What changed his life and attitude at school was knowing his teacher had taken the time to talk to the principal and them together choosing to give him this acknowledgment, in front of the whole school and with their hearts wide open.

I admire Zac's school for doing this. The Honor Awards happen every week, so every child over the course of the year gets one.

It's not just a piece of paper. How often do you give someone in your team or business an acknowledgment with something tangible, so they feel proud and recognized enough to excitedly share the experience with their friends, partner, or parents and excitedly proclaim, "Look at what I got today!" More likely, they'll go home and (almost dismissively) say, "I got this at work today."

You see, as grown-ups, we don't think we are allowed to (excitedly) say, "Look what I got!" because we are adults now. Yet inside each of us is a little person wanting to scream, "Look what I got! Look at what the boss said to me today!"

We don't celebrate our acknowledgments like this because we have stopped playing. Even though we spend our time praising and encouraging our children, we forget to do so in adulthood and have lost sight of the importance and power of acknowledging the good in each other.

Sharing the Honor Story

Shortly after this great day, I was speaking at a conference. I don't ever do this, but I asked the event organizers if my wife and two boys could come in and sit at the back.

They eagerly agreed and Zac heard me share his Honor Award story to the large corporate audience.

As I finished, I turned on the stage and announced across the ballroom, "Zac would you mind standing up?" He stood and I said, "I would proudly like to introduce you to my son Zachary."

The entire room stood up and burst into applause.

When we arrived home Zac whispered to me, "Daddy, can you come into my bedroom please?" He closed the door behind us, and we sat cross-legged on the floor. He looked straight into my eyes, leaned forward, and whispered, "Thank you Daddy. Thank you for what you did in front of all those people, I'll never forget it."

"I want you to have this." He handed me his little Honor Badge and pinned it to my shirt, just like the principal did that day, and said, "Thank you, Daddy."

How Does It Feel?

Adults have the same innate desire for encouragement and validation as children. I'm thankful that the leaders throughout my career praised and encouraged me with their own variations of gold stars and pinned papers.

Even though your employees, colleagues, or teammates aren't walking around begging for encouragement—nor would they readily admit they need it—deep inside, it's what they crave most—your positive attention.

Encouragement has no impact without trust and presence. If anyone knows, thinks, feels, or even just suspects that it is contrived, disingenuous, or simply part of a process or procedural tick-box exercise, it loses all of its purpose. You can't (and must not) encourage someone if you don't mean it. A fly-by "well done" without sincerity is best not said at all. It has to be real. When you are connected with your sense of wonder, it just comes out of you with natural purity. Not from your head, but from your heart. Authentically said, people will always know and feel that you genuinely care.

360-Degree Moments

This isn't only a story about my son Zachary, it's a story about you—about all of us. These are the 360-degree moments of heart and encouragement that we easily lose sight of through our busyness. We tell ourselves we have no time or need for this despite the profound effect that comes from humble, authentic gestures of acknowledgment.

The culture of Zac's school is vibrant and refreshing. There is no reason that company culture should not be the same. With the impact of positive dynamics and simple, open-hearted exchanges, instant change in corporate culture and people's lives is indeed possible, if not assured.

Tiny gestures of wonder like this will always stand you apart as a present and heart-spirited human being. It is the same as texting someone your gratitude or sharing a "you are amazing" note to a service provider, calling your parents to thank them, or giving a handwritten card to your partner. When you provide your heart with a voice and blend acknowledgment with care, thought, compassion, and genuine kindness, you will be an outstanding leader; an outstanding teammate, and a wonderFULL person. You will have pride in yourself and purpose in what you do. It won't just be a job or a business; you'll have a meaningful and fulfilling life, at home and through all of your work. And the best part about this—it comes with no cost. Although it will always increase employee retention, create a culture that everyone loves to be part of, and flow through to customer satisfaction.

And you can put it into practice immediately.

Everything that happens in life and in business is based on feelings, and neither amounts to much without belonging. Recognition is a crucial ingredient: not bonuses, gifts, or rewards. Recognition is the fullest connection of the human spirit. Sharing genuine encouragement with others will always stand out as one of your most precious characteristics.

So, in this moment, please let me ask you to imagine pinning an imaginary Honor Badge on someone at home or at work, with an understanding that the way you do it will make all the difference! Say "well done" like you mean it, with every cell in your body. It is here that you will reach the heart of the wonder inside you and sincerely connect with the person standing in front of you. You will notice how their face radiates with uncomplicated joy.

Please let me share a dose of my own medicine—my own encouragement in this moment with you here, and through my heart say "well done" to you. Thank you for being here with me inside this book, on this page. Before you skip along to the next recipe, take a moment to ponder how you can make a difference to someone today with a wonderlicious moment of saying "well done" through your heart, not your head. Consider what it feels like to be the recipient of your encouragement.

The dust has now settled, the sheets have come off . . .

I hope that your heart is shining, ready, and willing to encourage yourself and others today.

GIVING YOUR HEART A VOICE

Encouragement of others in a world where chaos often dominates our thoughts is never a sign of weakness. It fosters intuition, creativity, and deeper connections. Regular sharing of encouragement has the power to transform workplaces and relationships, creating a space filled with joy, loyalty, and a sense of belonging.

Ingredients:

- ★ Sharing of genuine appreciation and praise, which fosters a vibrant, fulfilling, safe (and therefore, brave) environment.
- ★ Regular, heartfelt acknowledgment of those around you.
- ★ Authenticity and kindness in leadership at home and in your workplace.
- ★ Enjoyment of even the smallest wonderlicious moments around you each day.

Substitutions to Make this Recipe Your Own:

When state-of-the-art gym facilities or pop-up garden parties aren't possible—and aren't helping—use creativity and heart to provide a safe, exciting, motivating space people want to be in. Use your voice, use your heart, and even use a hand-crafted, paper-and-glue badge of honor if the moment calls for it. Less flash, more vulnerability. Less one-offs, more commitment to creating ripples of positivity that radiate through every interaction. Mix these ingredients together to transform both your personal and professional life. This recipe will become your superpower!

Recipe 5:
FLUENCY IN GRATITUDE

"

Feeling gratitude and not expressing it is like wrapping a present and not giving it
William Arthur Ward

"How does that sound?" Jake will ask as he practices his Slovakian dialect around the kitchen table at home. *Ďakujem* he will say out loud with the *j* silent—Slovak for "thank you." He's only in his first year at high school currently but has taken an interest in learning the second language of Suzy, his mum's side of the family who originate from the capital, Bratislava. He often hears her speaking with his grandparents and is intrigued to know what they are saying!

Then Zac will pipe up with *danke*, German for "thank you," so for good measure, I throw a French "thank you" into the exchange with *merci*. I'm always fascinated seeing all the amazing things that Zac and Jake learn at school, especially new languages. I enjoy watching them practice their fluency in pronouncing and expressing words like thank you.

It's identical to practicing and pronouncing fluency in gratitude—the language of sharing appreciation with others. Like a boomerang of goodness, the more you practice it, the more it keeps coming back to you.

This is a special little recipe to bring fluency to your thank yous and refreshment to your gratitude through wonder. If you ever feel like you are dragging a heavy iron ball and chain around with you each day, trying to lift the spirits of everyone around you—here I provide the ingredients to transform this dead weight ball and chain into a helium-filled balloon and ribbon.

The Deepest Human Desire

Ahead of remuneration, bonuses, gifts, incentives, perks, and rewards lies the ember of the deepest human desire—appreciation, the core and most basic need of our human motivation. Feeling unappreciated is one of the worst senses in life, at work, and in business culture.

It's really hard to smile when you feel unhappy.

It's challenging to become motivated if you feel your efforts go unnoticed.

It's difficult to concentrate when you feel unappreciated.

Have you ever tried to play a guitar without strings, tasted champagne without bubbles, or tried to start a car without fuel? It would be a lot like attempting to build a new house on soft soil without a foundation—destined to fail.

A business culture that doesn't share genuine appreciation for and with their people is similarly destined to fail. Without a culture of heart and wonder, there is no foundation.

The Fuel for Magic

Gratitude is the simplest and most cost-effective way of driving performance and excellence. The greatest challenge and opportunity for managers and leaders today is to shake off their hesitation or distraction from sharing meaningful compliments and praise.

When you make open-hearted appreciation the core essence of your work, business, culture, and life, it becomes fuel for incredible magic. Huge positive energy will radiate throughout a business when people know that their efforts and contributions are wholeheartedly noticed and appreciated.

It's easy to express authentic gratitude and make it a common habit and heartbeat of an organization—and just as easy to miss.

People who regularly receive sincere appreciation are more productive and more engaged. They will feel less stressed or anxious, need less time off sick, and can better handle the toughest of challenges. They will be more likely to stay in their employment for longer. On top of this, it also creates positive financial reward for a business, through reduced recruitment costs and higher customer satisfaction.

In today's challenging world, there are two words that can indeed change everything. Two of the words we crave most, yet rarely hear. They are often brushed aside as unimportant even though they always encourage, inspire, and delight, especially in times of challenge or disconnection.

They are the two words—*thank you.*

Gliding on Ice

We easily miss opportunities to express gratitude, being too busy to notice the positive things going on around us, offering a distracted "thanks" to the person standing in front of us while not looking up from our computer screen, or sending half-hearted thanks via email.

We spend much of our lives working hard to fulfill our goals and keep up with hectic daily demands. The worst thing for anyone to feel afterward is unnoticed, undervalued, or unappreciated by the leaders, or company they work with each day.

There are, however, leaders who glide through life as if they are professional ice skaters.

They thrive at work because of their ability and love of taking care of people. They go out of their way to make sure everyone feels comfortable, at home, and appreciated. They are eager to be seen by their people and encourage the best out of them. In return, they receive the strength of loyalty that is powerful enough for them to walk through walls. They spin a triple flip on the ice and the crowd throws roses into the ice rink in pure admiration. Sometimes they might slip over, but as fast as they fall, they bounce back up, buoyed by the loyal support of everyone around them.

Ted the Butcher

We live in the small friendly town of Como, a short drive south of Sydney. We feel blessed to be surrounded by such a warm-hearted community. Our resident idol is Ted Cary, our local butcher. He isn't just our butcher, but an adored and much-loved character—a soft spoken, uncomplicated man with a big, wonderFULL soul. To our community, he is a local legend.

Ted is a third-generation butcher, born in his house at the top of the garden behind the butcher shop where he has lived his whole life with his wife Pam. At the time of writing this, Ted turned eighty-six and this is the seventy-second year he's been working in his tiny butcher shop, where he started as an apprentice for his father in 1946.

The shop has barely changed since his dad, Dawson Cary, first had the shop before him starting in 1926. The pale blue ornate ceiling remains, as do the original tiles up the walls. It's like stepping back in time with good old fashioned, proud, and pleasurable shopkeeping as it used to be. There is nothing pre-prepared in the window—he doesn't do any pre-cuts or fancy marinades. Just the counter with his scales, a pile of neatly stacked white paper to wrap up your steak, and his big pencil to scribble and calculate the prices before wrapping your fresh purchase. In the middle of the shop sits the centerpiece and stage of his little theater—his butcher's block. It is here he proudly prepares everything to order right in front of you. For seven decades he has worked a six-day week by himself. Ted is there every morning before 8 a.m. getting everything ready and he's still there past 7 p.m. cleaning up, alone.

Each time I step into his little shop, the hecticness of the world outside disappears. For a number of years now, I pop in to see Ted as often as I can, at least weekly. The second the fly screen door shuts behind me, I leave everything behind for a peaceful moment. I feel happy, safe, and nostalgic.

You never hear anyone around our town saying, "I'm off to the butchers." They only say, "I'm just popping down to Ted's." At home if one of us says, "Shall we have pork chops for dinner?" I quickly say, "Yes! I'll pop to see Ted!" Then Jake will pipe in: "No

Daddy! I'll go." But the truth is, we all want to go. There's an almighty race as the four of us try to scramble to the front door first! So, we all end up going, willingly and eagerly.

Ted doesn't only serve amazing fresh meat, using the passionate skills of his craft—he gives everyone his undivided attention and his whole heart. People don't just go to Ted's to buy sausages; they go to enjoy his beautiful and full-of-wonder soul. Every time anyone steps into his little shop, it is always his humble pleasure to welcome and delight everyone. To all of his treasured customers—everyone who walks through the door—he welcomes them as if they are family. No one is more important to him than you in that moment. Ted is one of the finest storytellers I have ever heard, he knows everyone's name and tells great little jokes—the kind you still laugh at even after hearing them for the hundredth time.

Everything takes him ages, but that's part of the experience. Time stops mattering and I know that everyone would hate it if there was any rush. I have to admit I love to order a rack of lamb from Ted, just so I can stand and marvel at his wizardry knife skills. I am sure he could do it perfectly wearing a blindfold. I do feel guilty though and almost panic as he staggers out of his little cool room trying to carry the whole lamb. I almost want to jump across the counter to take over.

Some locals call him the Como Samurai! He slices your rump steak in front of you to your preferred thickness, pauses, and says to himself, "Now! Isn't that a nice-looking piece of meat?" It scares me that this much-loved art of proud hospitality and gracious service in retail is fading into the abyss. He still makes his own sausages that everyone loves and has a long list of names for them—his favorite ones: snags, bangers, and sizzlers.

I distinctly remember a number of years back, around Ted's eightieth birthday, he was presented with an OBE—we were all so happy for him! He proudly shows everyone his special gold medal on a ribbon—a surprise gift from a group of his customers, engraved with those three special words: "Over Bloody Eighty!"

For over seventy years and around twenty-thousand working days, Ted has maintained a relentlessly happy momentum. Spending every day living in the moment, in a state of complete open-hearted fulfillment. As I've proudly gotten to know Ted, he's shared with me lots of tales about what his dad taught him about running his business and showing continuous appreciation to his customers. He's told me countless stories of how every single day for seventy years he has just gone about his work in his own way and done exactly what makes him happy in serving others.

One day, when I was alone with Ted in the shop, I asked him what I had been wondering for a long time: "What's the one thing Ted?" He knew what I meant by the question.

And his gentle reply was as profound as it was so blissfully obvious. The utter simplicity of his response left me peacefully breathless, as he reflected and shared what his Dad had taught him all those years ago. He smiled, "You see, it's easy, really."

"I do what my customers want—not what I want."

Making Time

I'd been telling myself for a while that I had to do something. I just wanted to somehow say *thank you*. More than anything I simply wanted Ted to know how much love and appreciation we all had for him. I thought and thought, searching for the answer. I knew I wanted to find the right way to say and show it, and the exciting answer presented itself.

I could have just said "thank you" to Ted and verbally tried to express my appreciation, but that didn't feel meaningful enough. *That's it!* I told myself and in secret, I entered Ted in the Australian Service Excellence Awards, with the Customer Service Institute of Australia—considered by many as the Australian Oscars of customer service.

The thing was, I didn't have time, but I made the time. I did it all in surprise, pouring my heart into the written submission, and excitedly sent it off.

Ted went straight through, becoming a national finalist for Customer Service Advocate of the Year, amongst all sectors and industries across Australia. I arranged to take the awards judges to the shop to meet and surprise Ted. For them it was pure love at first sight, and Ted? Well, he was (almost) at a loss for words, and proudly glowing from the attention.

They eagerly asked Ted if they could fly him to Melbourne for their black-tie Gala Awards Dinner as their special guest. And he replied softly "I don't think I can. It wouldn't be right, you see. I can't close the shop. I can't let my customers down."

But he then turned to me and asked if I would go and represent him in his place. And what he said next completely floored us. "No one has ever done anything like this for me before. But please don't take me any further in the competition. I can't thank you enough, but it wouldn't be fair, you see. I'm at the end of what I'm doing. Give it to someone who is starting out."

So, there I am in Melbourne in my tuxedo at the huge glittering awards dinner, sitting in the middle of the one thousand excited guests for the celebrations. Halfway through the ceremony, we got to Ted's category, and they stopped everything. My heart was bursting through my chest as they put Ted's picture up on the giant screens around the massive ballroom. But I wasn't prepared for what happened next and was overcome with emotion as they invited me up to the stage, to tell everyone about Ted!

This is all I could have dreamed of; I didn't do it to get Ted a trophy. I just wanted him to know how much his customers cherished him so dearly. My only wish was for him to simply know the impact he had made on so many people, over so many years.

So, Who Says Softness Is a Weakness?

I flew home as early as I could the next morning from Melbourne and went straight to the shop to see Ted. In front of a handful of customers, I presented him with his big gold-framed certificate: "National Finalist, Customer Service Advocate of the Year." Mounted next to it was a letter to Ted that the Customer Service Institute of Australia had arranged from the Prime Minister of Australia.

He stood quietly staring at it and in his wonderful Australian twang, said: "Good on ya!"

The customers left and it was just the two of us. He admitted, "No one has ever done anything like this for me before. Why did you do it?"

I looked him straight in the eye and in an emotionally charged moment, I chose vulnerability. I somehow managed to compose myself, and said, "Ted, all I wanted to do was say thank you—for all that you do and for all you have done."

Who says that softness is a weakness? And who says it's wrong to make an old man cry? He's a proud, gentle, lovely man. He was completely beaming and discreetly tried to cover up and hide his teary eyes.

I panicked. "Oh, my goodness, Ted! I'm so sorry! I didn't mean to make you cry."

"It's okay. I'm happy that you did! Just don't tell the wife!"

Right there, in that moment—inside the teardrop rolling down Ted's cheek—was the purest essence of wonder. I desperately wanted to say how much we loved him. I didn't need to, he knew.

I proudly share this little story with you, for one important and proud reason. Ted is seventy-six years older than Zac, and the reaction was exactly the same as Zac receiving his little paper Honor Award. Whether you are six, twenty-six, forty-six, or eighty-six, this is what changes people's lives—little touches of big heart, through the fluency of our gratitude.

In that moment Ted went from being an adored and much-loved local butcher in a tiny town in the Sutherland Shire to someone of national Australian fame. But more importantly, he simply knew we cared.

He knew he was appreciated.

Don't Let the Moment Pass You By

Sometimes we confuse recognition and believe we need to reward people with gifts to make them feel appreciated. Imagine if I had given Ted cinema tickets or a shopping voucher. It would have had an entirely different outcome.

In business today and across our workplaces, these are common moments that we easily miss. Often, kind-hearted leaders get overlooked because of their perceived softness. They are seen as being weak (by the hard and tough leaders) because of it, which couldn't be further from the actual truth. The so-called weak leaders possess the greatest superpower of all—heart. Those receiving it will never see it as a weakness, only a respected strength.

Being kind and telling someone with an open heart that they are appreciated, however you do it, will always be one of the most incredible things you ever do. In German, Slovak, French, and every other language the world over, it works exactly the same. Even when you believe you don't have time, you will always find the time—at work with the people around you, your team, colleagues, and workmates, and at home with your partner, your children, and your family.

When people feel cared for and recognized, they will loyally serve their organization well. This is how positive emotions work, just like it does in any relationship. When people feel uniquely seen, understood, valued, and appreciated, their commitment to that team, leader, and organization will always be immense.

In practice, consistently shown appreciation will always fuel highly engaged and positive business workplaces that are not only profitable and stand out in their sector, but they will also create work environments that are pleasurable, loyal, and counter to fear.

We hear a lot about workplace reward programs, with many believing the more lavish they are with gifts and perks, the better they will be at stimulating workplace fulfillment. *Nothing* will ever influence engagement as much as appreciation. It is the feeling of connected human spirit that causes people to realize why they love getting up each day and going to work.

We all possess the potential to display and share the same unwavering humility of Ted. We also hold the same ability to celebrate it in ourselves and others.

When you appreciate someone, don't let the moment pass you by—you've just got to let them know.

Is there an opportunity you have already missed today?

Behind the Scenes of This Recipe:

Ted continuously promised us he would never close his shop. It was a day that our whole community dreaded. He joked that he would keep going until his big old pencil ran out. So, we kept buying him pencils!

But the day came on 25 February 2019, aged eighty-six and without any word of warning, fanfare, or any community gathering—Ted simply tore off a small corner of his butcher's paper and wrote, "Sorry, closed till further notice, Ted," and stuck it in the corner of his window. He hung up his apron on the hook and locked the door.

Ted is often spotted tending to the roses in his garden behind the shop, which he never had the time to do before now. We all miss racing to his shop each week.

Recipe 5 Recap:
FLUENCY IN GRATITUDE

The simplest of gestures have the most momentous impact. The sharing of gratitude is no exception. Those who rarely look for gratitude often deserve it most. Who are the Teds in your team, your department, business, or organization, or your home? *Hint*: they are everywhere!

Ingredients:

★ A willingness to make time for the expression of appreciation, especially to those who expect it the least.

★ Fluency in the language of gratitude, remembering how you say it is what makes the difference—tone, eye contact, and authenticity.

★ That same authenticity and tone of expression with written, texted, or emailed appreciation. Or better yet, pick up the phone to say it.

Substitutions to Make this Recipe Your Own:

Whether you are leading a team or dining out with your best friend, take gratitude to heart. Notice the server in a restaurant delivering your meal with pleasure, the helpful shopkeeper who flashed a friendly smile, and the barista who makes your coffee with care, and thank them. Sharing appreciation is one of life's finest, highest honors. It should never be thought of as a chore. It is wonderful. Then go the extra step by telling them *why* you're thankful. *That* is wonderlicious.

Recipe 6:
BECOMING THE KING OF HEARTS

"

Three things in human life are important.
The first is to be kind
The second is to be kind
And the third is to be kind

Henry James

Pick a card—any card . . .
Choosing just one from the deck of fifty-two cards, which one comes to your mind?

What if there was one single card that could magically symbolize and inspire the characteristics of modern leadership today—a card that could guide vibrant workplaces and enliven the positivity of company cultures? Additionally, what if there was a symbol that could provide a refreshing antidote for everything we have experienced across the globe through the challenging times of fires, floods, war, pandemics, and the global unrest of recent times?

Now which card might you choose?

Clubs, spades, and diamonds have little use for us with this example, although any card from the suit of hearts would work well in this moment—the Queen of Hearts, Jack of Hearts (even The Joker of Hearts would be welcome to lift the spirit of fun).

Diamonds might represent bottom-line leadership and what's lacking in the world is heart inspired leaders. So here before your eyes, the card that I bring to life is the King of Hearts (it could be the Queen but in this instance, it's the King), a special character that reflects the extraordinary heart of a vibrant and visionary leader, the powerful qualities of honesty—a heart-spirited, kind man—a fine and trusted friend.

All We Need Is Love

Organizations and businesses around the world share a challenging common goal—to not only attract and find great people to fill their vacancies but create an enjoyable, meaningful, and fulfilling workplace for their employees. Then on top of this, motivate them to stay.

Beyond the paycheck and reward incentives, the one thing we all search and crave for most, and often do not find, is positive human connection—the pure sense of belonging. Reassuring acknowledgment that shows us we are seen, heard, and wanted. Little touches of sincere heart in our work, at home, in business, across our organizations, with our employees, customers, and with each other—the type of connection that simply shows someone that their partner, colleague, manager, or leader actually cares about them. Connection with compassion and with gratitude.

Throughout my early career working in hotels, I enjoyed going to work each day. It was more than a job. It felt meaningful and fulfilling. I know that my former colleagues would agree the same. Whilst we tirelessly worked hard, it didn't ever feel like a job; it was an enriching way of life. Every day, regardless of the weight of the challenge in front of us, we knew *why* we wanted to go to work and were enthusiastic to do so. We knew we were part of something special, we felt welcome, and we felt valued because we were guided by heart-spirited leadership.

I frequently find myself searching for the beauty and emotional connection of simple, joyful daily moments of wonder. We look to complicated, automatic processes to create the magic we're looking for instead of recognizing the simplicity and wonder created by true connection and heart-centered interactions.

Many companies, start-ups, and organizations are so consumed with what's coming next, they continue to miss what's happening now. Whilst it will always be a crucial leadership skill to plan for the future and keep abreast with new innovations, the real success lies beyond the automation *mindset*. There are those who are trailblazing with brilliant, wonderFULL teams, creating magical customer cultures because of their *heart-set*. They have a hunger for showing up, being present, and reclaiming the commonly missed touches of providing pleasure by practicing open-hearted presence as their habit.

My strongest memory from my hotel days is how we were guided to craft pleasurable hospitality, for each other and our guests, by aligning our hearts as a powerful force of good. For our hearts to help inform our thoughts, decisions, and interactions.

Breaking the Monotony of Groundhog Day

Imagine experiencing wonder every day, making a habit of it so much that you unwittingly transform someone's entire day with an overflow of reassuring positivity. Even better, imagine enhancing their enjoyment of coming to work each day. It's a wonderful thought, isn't it? Let me share with you an example of the King of Hearts—somebody who stole my heart, a leader with true heart, the principal of our local primary school, Mr. Fagerstrom.

My day often starts by doing the school run for our two boys, Zac and Jake. It always turns into a frantic, nerve-testing moment trying to get them to brush their teeth, find their shoes, and get ready to actually leave the house. I often feel the urge to celebrate wildly the second we finally step out of the front door and get in the car. It happens every day. I've tried every technique to make it work more smoothly but failed. I think they do it intentionally, to see if they can break me.

In 2021, following our 107-day home-schooling lockdown in Sydney, we were all relieved to be heading back to school. As parents, we were frazzled and as for the boys, they were like caged tigers frantic to be released.

We drove to school that morning with the car windows down, music turned up, singing together and the boys bursting with excitement. Despite this, never did we anticipate the welcome that awaited our arrival. Personally, I never could have imagined that I was about to receive a brilliant masterclass in positive heart-led leadership.

As we arrived at school, all of the parents' cars slowly lined up along the side road through to the drop-off at the school gates. "Look, Daddy!" Jake squealed. There were a dozen colorful balloons tied to the school gates and a refreshing buzz filled the morning air.

But it wasn't the balloons that were causing the buzz. It was Mr. Fagerstrom, the school principal.

He was standing *outside* of the school gates, on the opposite side of the little side road, waving to each and every car as they approached. He greeted all the children by name with a bright smile and a merry "Good morning!" as they bounced out of their cars. He then excitedly ushered them for a few seconds over the crossing up to the school gates. When he was finished, he headed back to the next car to do it again. He repeated this over and over again as the parents dropped their children off, one by one. All the children were beaming—and so were the parents. The ripple of his positive leadership radiated through the whole school.

It's easy to presume that the school principal would be the one person you would rarely, if ever, see first thing in the morning. You imagine such a senior leader would be hidden away in their office at the start of the day, sorting their busy schedule, attending to their emails and messages, and preparing for their meetings. That wasn't the case here.

Mr. Fagerstrom followed his heart, which led him to personally welcome each of his students so they could start off their return to school in the best possible way. He could have easily done nothing at all that morning and let the children find their own way to their classrooms as they were used to doing. He could have delegated the task to any of the teachers and just stayed in his office.

Mr. Fagerstrom anticipated that his school children would be excited to return, but undoubtedly also be feeling dehydrated of joy after the shutdown—parched like wilted flowers in a dried up garden. It was as if he was using an imaginary watering can, filled with wonder, rejuvenating everyone with his positivity.

Making Wonder a Permanent Feature

As I drove to school the following day, I secretly hoped he would be there once again and that it hadn't only been a one-off special occasion gesture—something wonderful he had done once and then stopped. The cynical side of me said he wouldn't be there, and my optimistic side hoped that he would. To our delight, there he was, doing it all over again.

Mr. Fagerstrom is a generous, warm, humble, and uncomplicated man. We all loved him for the way he cared for the well-being of the school children. It is obviously rooted deeply in his heart.

The positive leadership shown by our beloved principal oxygenated the culture of his school. I can still imagine him getting ready for work, brushing his teeth, and making the selfless choice to personally greet everyone that day—because he could and because it would bring joy to the school.

Mr. Fagerstrom set the tone for the culture of the school, and I watched his positivity spread. The teachers started to copy him, and each mirrored the same feeling of welcome. On the very rare occasions when he's not at school, it doesn't stop. The faculty of teachers each take his lead, step into his shoes, and provide exactly the same positive sentiment and it is obvious they are proud to do so.

All the children seem to actually enjoy arriving at the school gates each morning (an amazing achievement in itself!). Yet he didn't stop there and started to do exactly the same at the end of the day—back outside of the school gates directing all the parents' cars through the drive-through to pick up the children, with another wave and a warm "see you tomorrow!" to each and every child.

No matter how busy he is each day, he is never too busy to perform his welcome and farewell routine. The sun will still rise, then set each day, and there he is, rain or shine, as his habit—every day. To all the parents, students, and also his teachers, he is a person of great wonder, someone you can't help but be inspired by.

I noticed how he radiates the same feeling online, with some of the group parent meetings that I have attended. He is never late or distracted. In each meeting, it is just as clear as the moon is round that he had given thought to what he wanted to say, how he was going to say it, and the warmth of welcome he wanted to express.

Making Seemingly Insignificant Gestures Actually Matter

The wholesome, shining leadership of Mr. Fagerstrom vividly reminds me of the incredible leaders I've had the fortune to work with throughout my career—those who embodied two defining characteristics—*heart and presence*. These special qualities create a powerful, transformative energy that fuels and distinguishes a thriving, wonderlicious workplace.

What I admired most about Mr. Fagerstrom's methods was their alignment with the principles we practiced in hotels. This included being at the front door to welcome our team and guests each day, reflecting the essence of our leadership and culture.

But does it actually matter? Take his special touch of wonder away—his present and hearty welcome—and the children would have still found their way to their classrooms before the morning bell rang. Each day would still have *functioned*, but the feeling would be very different. Here lies the simplicity of heart-spirited leadership that creates vibrant and loved cultures. Imagine the same scenario for the employees of a company—they will find their desk, office, workstation, or section. However, without any sense of welcome, without feeling noticed and without present leadership, everything falls into the monotony of wonderLESS Groundhog Day. Some will feel it would be easier to stay at home.

Relating this to your company or workplace environment, imagine if the leader or a member of the senior team was out front, in the lobby, or at the door authentically greeting everyone—every day, the same impactful feeling and welcome would be created. It would be another reason that people love to make the effort to come to work.

The beauty of this example of Mr. Fagerstrom's leadership is that it is fully transferable and will work in any business or work environment, organization, or internal department. Yet this is something that is incredibly easy to lose sight of, or be too busy to notice, or believe it's unimportant and unnecessary time wasting—so wonder remains dormant, locked away in a box. The magnificent opportunity stays lost and a culture stays flat—like a paper-thin pancake.

Noticing the Good and Celebrating It

Mr. Fagerstrom isn't just the principal of our local primary school; to us he is the *King of Hearts*. He spends his time and energy acknowledging and encouraging everyone around him—all of his department heads, teachers, and all the children. This said, I know how lonely it can be in senior leadership roles at the top of an organization. I could have seen what he was doing and thought how nice it was and just gone on with my day. But this was something that I didn't just see—I noticed. It caused me an overwhelming need to let him know, and I felt compelled to return the same gesture to him personally. I wanted him to feel the wonder that he had shared with everyone else and know the depth of his impact.

I wrote and published a short article on LinkedIn about Mr. Fagerstrom and his heart. I wanted to tell as many people as I could about what he had done to enhance the culture of our school community through his wholesome leadership. I was moved by the rapid and enthusiastic response from people around the world and from different industries contacting me to thank me for reminding them of moments of kindness like this that we have lost sight of in our daily work. From here I could have done nothing else and just been happy with the interest and comments that I had received and left it at that. But that would have been a badly missed opportunity because none of this was about me.

I wanted him to not only know what I had written, but also why I wrote it. I could have emailed the article to him, saying, "I thought you might be interested in this—see the attached," but it wouldn't have provided any understanding or connection. It would have missed the point. I could have asked the teachers if I could surprise him with it publicly during the school assembly in front of everyone, but that definitely didn't feel appropriate either. This was a private moment, not a public one. So, I printed off my article, including all the comments sent in from everyone, put it into a little folder and took it to school. I waited until all the children had gone at the end of the day, until it was just the two of us left at the gates.

I was feeling pretty nervous and managed to contain my emotion. All I wanted was to touch his heart, for him to realize and feel exactly the same emotion that he creates for so many others. I explained the background of the article and why I had done it. He was taken aback and seemed puzzled. I sensed he was about to say that he was just doing his job, and I mustered the courage to say, "Mr. Fagerstrom, we've all noticed what you've been doing and it's really special."

I continued, "On behalf of our whole community, I just wanted you to know how sincerely grateful we are for all that you do in creating such a happy school environment for everyone."

He was quite overwhelmed and at a loss for words, but sincerely grateful and I could see that I had reached through to his heart, which is all I wanted to do, as he had done for all of us.

Human Connection vs. Automation

Mr. Fagerstrom could have sent a welcome email or made a PowerPoint presentation to play on the classroom televisions, but he opted for human connection instead. The result was profound.

Just because we can "phone it in" and let technology handle things like this, doesn't mean we should. That won't create instances of true connection. It actually has the opposite effect.

Is a computer human? The answer is no. It's trained by humans, but it misses the emotional element. I don't think you could ever automate Mr. Fagerstrom, or the heart-lead and human connection of his leadership—nor would you want to.

Computers and automation are not the same as human connection, no matter how hard we try. A lot of businesses mistake having an email nurture sequence in lieu of true human connection. It's not the same thing. This also applies to automated birthday notes. There are a million examples of how we've automated things, versus how we've stopped showing up.

Automation works well when we sign up for an online course and get an immediate welcome email. Or when we book a hotel room, we get an automated confirmation, telling us what we need to know about checking in and where to find parking and those kinds of things. That's automated customer service that *helps* us, but I can guarantee you that you've never seen a hotel website that asks for a review of how beautiful their welcome email was. Whereas we will remember the person who checked us into our room, the bellman who assisted us on arrival, or the concierge who helped us get tickets to the show that we wanted.

We remember the people of the hotel that shaped the feeling of the experience. Yes, it could be that the bed was super comfortable, and the coffee was delicious. But nine times out of ten, if you look at reviews of any hospitality service, what people comment on is the feeling and the experience provided by the people, not the service received from the automated booking system. Rarely do you see technology responses in a review. Nobody goes, "My TV had fifty-two channels," or, "It was really nice that they had a clap-on clap-off light switch." Nobody cares. What we do care about is whether the establishment went out of its way to make us feel that we were welcome and valued.

If we return to a hotel, it's because we loved the feeling it gave us the last time we were there. That's how you start to build that kind of relationship with people and establish proper loyalty. When you remember my name or you remember where I'm from—that makes you know you're important and, because you feel seen, you want to be there again. A computer can't do that. You will have undoubtedly seen the restaurants where you order on a tablet, and then someone brings your food to your table. And it is fun for about a half second, until you actually need service and then it's not funny. We've taken the human spirit out for automated efficiency. Automation can be useful in certain instances, but it's not soul-led or fulfilling our connectivity.

Computers were originally used to store, manipulate, and retrieve information. And then somebody believed that computers and the automation they provide could connect us and bring us closer together, but the research shows that people have never felt further apart. So, is automation actually connecting us, or is it actually moving us further apart? How much more do we value human connection now versus twenty years ago, when we didn't have mobile phones as readily available, or forty years ago, when the average home did not have a laptop or computer?

Heart to Heart

Whilst I come with no magic wand, I come sharing the realization that our tiny actions and habits of heart will always make the biggest difference to those around us. To help us stay positively connected and do great things through the belief and humble essence of kindness, care, and thought.

My little serving of encouragement to you is this: Keep your heart open and allow it to be your compass. Also remember that whilst we might look and think we see—it's only when we consciously *notice* something that the difference will be made.

It is the moments like this that will not only guide our own heart but touch the hearts of others and, in parallel, cause massive cultural and business transformation. It takes focus and strength to purposely prioritize people over our trivial distractions. To show present leadership and humility with an open heart is to create a wonderful environment. It is something that will always cause people to talk about it—just as I am here with you now.

Play the Ace

Amongst all the noise and our ever-flowing continuous daily distractions, we will always provide our employees, teammates, and colleagues with the very reason they love coming to work each day by being there and expressing our heart. Because they feel noticed and celebrated.

Leaders who share their hearts will always have the hearts of those they lead. Whether you are the *King, Queen, Jack,* or even the *Joker* of Hearts—just don't leave your card in the deck. Whichever one represents you best, play to its strength. Wear it everywhere you go as your personal symbol and the feeling you create will always serve a perfect *Ace*!

Special Recipe Side Notes:

Another time during primary school, one of Zac's friends sadly lost his father to cancer. Our whole local community came together to warmly support the family and share their moment of grief. Several hundred people gathered at our local church for the funeral.

As the family welcomed everyone at the door, Zac's friend was sitting in the front row quietly by himself in front of his father's coffin.

I noticed Mr. Fagerstrom arrive.

Instead of just sitting down at the back, he very discreetly walked to the front amongst the many people who were finding their seats. He knelt down on both knees in front of Zac's friend and embraced him fully with a gentle hug.

His heart once again took him there—he radiated it, stood up, and found his seat at the back.

It was a simple moment of encouragement, connection, and reassurance; that he was there—and that he cared.

Recipe 6 Recap:
BECOMING THE KING OF HEARTS

In the whirlwind of modern leadership, *the King of Hearts* emerges as a beacon of positivity and hope. Amidst all the common-day challenges, his example teaches us the timeless lesson of leading with heart, kindness, and genuine connection. The world would be a better place if we all strived to be the King of Hearts.

Ingredients:

- ★ Celebration of (and preference for) the value of personalized human interaction over automation.
- ★ The fostering of meaningful relationships and loyalty through sharing your personal touch.
- ★ Leadership that begins with sincerity and compassion.
- ★ Refusal to get stuck in the monotony of routine and, instead, find opportunities to uplift and energize the present.
- ★ The creation of an environment where everyone feels seen, valued, and connected.

Substitutions to Make this Recipe Your Own:

You might be the principal of a school, the CEO of a corporation, or a parent trying to help their children get through the day. One thing remains the same—you will have opportunities to demonstrate how much you care. Whether you are the *King, Queen* (or *Joker!*) of Hearts, let your genuine spirit shine through. Wear your *Heart* symbol proudly and lead with kindness to create an environment filled with warmth and joy.

SHARING PLATES

—

CURIOSITY

"

*The whole world is a series of miracles,
but we're so used to them we call
them ordinary things*

Hans Christian Andersen

HIGHER POWER

One of my all-time favorite wonderlicious sensations is goose bumps—especially in reaction to receiving wonderful service. Often tiny, unexpected, and uncomplicated moments in life that cause you to say out loud, "Phwoarr, I've got goose bumps! Look at my arms!"

Sometimes they go up my neck and down my legs. They occur frequently by pure chance, usually through moments of surprise and thoughtful kindness, like when something wonderful happens to you and causes simple amazement. Or during conversations that are exciting, thrilling and inspiring. It happened when I surprised Ted the butcher with his framed award certificate and saw his reaction. That gave me full body goose bumps.

These millions of intermittent bumps are the body's involuntary reaction to the truth of the moment—the physical reaction to a freezing cold temperature, fear, fright, and shock. They are also the emotional reaction to a wondrous and positive connection, often inspired by pleasurable, interesting, and delightful things.

Additionally, I have always been fascinated by how creating goose-bump moments can be one of the strongest signs of excellent business growth and profitability.

Throughout my career, my teams and I were always more than just leaders creating service processes and systems, we were curious "service stylists." We purposefully went out of our way to create positive connections through the hospitality of our team and guest experiences. Everything we did, every transaction and interaction we had, was guided by a meaningful purpose—to create goose-bump moments for our guests.

Goose bumps were the north tip of our compass, our subconscious vision, our dream outcome, and our measure of true customer satisfaction. We knew that every time we created goose-bump moments for our guests, it would encourage them to keep returning, and at the same time they would tell their friends to do the same.

We applied the same focus and logic to our recruitment strategy, onboarding, and development of our employees. For every member of our team to provide service with goose-bump-inducing wonder for our guests, they first had to receive and feel it too.

Having set the bar for wonder, we studied and strove for the wondrous glint in our guests' eyes, the goose bumps on their arms, and the delight in their voices and smiles.

We consistently aimed to take delight to new heights. With anything and everything the guests touched and experienced inside our castle walls, we considered our ongoing view from a higher place.

I will never forget the first time I went to the top of the Empire State Building in New York City. At ground level, the streets were bustling with the life of everyone going about their day. I was eager to appreciate this from a completely different dimension and headed up to the top floor. As the elevator doors opened, the sheer expanse of the view from the open-air observation deck around the building's spire was breathtaking.

I went to the edge and looked down and saw the yellow taxis were toy-car tiny, and the crowds of people down below were the size of ants. The sight before me opened up a whole new dimension. I had found a place and moment to see and consider the full breadth of everything, without being in the thick of it all.

It was here in this moment that I once again realized the importance of having a clear perspective of the entire and actual view of the service you are providing.

It's time to head up, up and away—deep inside your curiosity . . .

Recipe 7:
SERVICE MAGIC

"

I will reveal you who I am.
I am your reflection

Santosh Kalwar

Every time I go on a flight, I have a familiar sensation. As the plane picks up pace down the runway and lifts off into the sky, it reminds me of the exact same feeling from my hotel days, when we designed service magic with movement and curiosity with spaciousness of height. Rarely were we stationary on the ground floor debating or only talking about what we could or should be doing and therefore missing all the real-life opportunities happening all around us. Instead, we looked upwards, to find a higher, clearer, and more interesting view. We were impatient for excellence and just got on with actively doing it—designing and fine-tuning wonderful service with pace and momentum—from a higher place.

We applied a simple, powerful formula to every aspect of our service magic: add simplicity and grace to complexity and the result will be irresistibility.

I have lost count of how many times I've felt underwhelmed or disappointed as a customer. I love visiting and staying in hotels, experiencing the caring hospitality of restaurants, traveling through airports, visiting shopping centers, ordering coffee at a local coffee shop, even doing the weekly trip to the local supermarket. Whether I am mystery shopping for my clients or visiting personally, I am consistently hopeful to find and enjoy a vibrant and interesting experience, a meaningful and connected interaction. Sadly, and despite the impressive property, location, or facilities, the feeling is commonly underwhelming. Walking through the door often feels flat as a pancake, empty of soul, robotic, artificial, or hollow. The feeling is often stiff—with no hint of any fun, movement, or rhythm. As a customer, the disconnection is disappointing. Interestingly, I commonly observe businesses and operations like this who believe they are amazing and don't see or actually realize how far from the truth this is.

As a little boy, I distinctly remember the time spent with my grandparents, where courteous connection felt like a common way of life. I vividly remember the cheerful, whistling milkman who delivered fresh bottles of milk to their doorstep, the attentive and welcoming shopkeepers, and the pleasant conversations that everyone had with each other out and about on the street. Whilst I am not suggesting we head backward in time—our world has clearly evolved—I *am* encouraging an affectionate blend of our modern ways with the wonders from times gone by, to provide a future of glorious brightness with attentively connected service. Not just a kind of service that causes satisfaction—exciting service that effortlessly encourages everyone to keep coming back for more. Imagine the positivity that would happen if everyone realized this.

Curiosity vs. Conformity

The choice between curiosity and conformity has profound implications for the quality and effectiveness of service. Across any organization, team, or business, everyone has a role to play. When team members are encouraged to use their curiosity, space is created to transform ordinary service into irresistible experiences. Allowing everyone to practice curiosity ignites sparks that lead to all sorts of goodness. Being curious helps anticipate needs, adapt to changing preferences, and create a deeper connection with customers.

Curiosity encourages a mindset of exploration and a genuine desire to understand the unique needs of those being served. It fosters empathy, innovation, and a commitment to continuous improvement. Curious teams love to create personalized, meaningful, and tailored experiences that genuinely resonate with the people they serve. This leads to stronger relationships, increased trust, and more positive, impactful service outcomes.

On the other hand, if conformity is the guiding principle across a culture for employees, it will always limit the pursuit of positive service connections. By definition, conformity implies adhering to established norms, procedures, and standards without questioning or challenging them. While it can provide structure and efficiency, it can also stifle creativity, innovation, and the ability to adapt to the evolving expectations and preferences of those being served. Over-reliance on conformity leads to a one-size-fits-all approach, which can easily fail to meet the diverse and changing needs of customers.

To achieve service magic, it is crucial to strike the right balance between curiosity and conformity.

The Mirror Never Lies

I play here, as we were taught in hotels, with the analogy of the mirror—*the magic mirror*—because the reflection is always truthful. Smile at any mirror and it smiles back at you. Wave at it, and it always waves back. Pull faces, cry or shout, it's the same—the reflection is real. Placing the culture of your customer service in front of the mirror provides the same honesty.

To some, the view might be horrifying. To others, it would provide clear reassurance that they are on the right track and doing brilliantly well. Either way, many don't see it, nor look for it—the actual reflection through the eyes of their customers.

One of everyone's all-time favorite fairground amusements has to be the "Fun House Hall of Mirrors." Step in front of the variety of crazy mirrors and you'll be laughing within seconds (or at the very least cringing in disbelief and horror at your distorted reflection). They make you look short, long, thin, and any variety of peculiar shapes in between. You step away sideways, then back again to check if it's you. The view is real, and at the same time it isn't—it's distorted.

Here with *the magic mirror* and *the distorted mirror*, you have front row seats to consider all of the touches that provide a highly connected team, including their preparation, curiosity, and interactions to create wonderlicious customer experiences—service magic. Play along with my reflective examples and ponder how your sense of wonder looks, feels, and sounds to those you are serving, and what it takes to stand out with irresistible service. For this recipe I showcase one single theme—airplanes and airports, with, and without, wonder.

Airports (and airplanes) are similar in many ways to the complex organization and operation of a supermarket, hotel, and office skyscraper, a global corporate headquarters or high street restaurant. They stand out with one core ingredient: service.

PART 1: DISTORTED REFLECTIONS

The second I made it through security at a major airport on the US West Coast (I'm not going to say which one), I hastily grabbed a pen, sat down, and quickly wrote down the specific words I had just experienced in the preceding moments. I wondered if I was dreaming and wanted to capture the precise detail just in case.

I had been on one of my business trips in the States and checked in for my flight home to Sydney. With my boarding pass in hand, I joined the hundreds of passengers lining up to go through security. I instantly felt overwhelmed by the immensely unpleasant tension and chaotic noise echoing throughout the high-ceilinged departure hall.

In front of me was a Japanese family who accidently turned right instead of left through the confusing security queue system and headed in the opposite direction to where they should be going. A security guard sitting on a stool in her booth shouts down the hall, "Hey, where are you going? This is where you should be at." Then under her breath (but loud enough for everyone to hear) says, "Oh my god, someone needs to speak to these people."

In a dazed state, they placed their belongings into the tray.

"I told you three times already, don't push the tray! I do that," shouts another guard.

The Japanese family went through the security scanner, the next security guard pulled out a half empty water bottle from their bag, held it up and, highly agitated, shouted at the top of his voice "Whose is this? Whose is this?"

They didn't understand him at first, then instantly became terribly embarrassed, faces turning red.

"What's this huh?" as he asks again as he waves the bottle in front of them and shakes his head angrily. Then as their punishment, made them line up for a full bag search.

I know that things like this must be incredibly frustrating for an airport security team, but there was a language barrier in this instance, and it really was a simple, honest mistake.

The repeated dramatic shouting continues, over and over: "I want your belts and shoes off." As I reached the scanner for my turn, I was hit with the scent of travel ripe feet along with the sound of abrasive commotion.

"If you are listening to my instructions, your laptop is out of your bag and in the tray."

There was another family in the line behind me looking traumatized, with their two young children crying amongst the hideous and confronting chaos. Out of the corner of my eye, I noticed the person who looked in charge of this massive and complex security operation, like an orchestra conductor, leading his cattle-herding confrontation.

All I could smell was feet, ingrained in the strip of floor around the bag scanner from the previous thousands of shoeless passengers. Amongst the madness, I remember wondering why no one has ever stopped to not only consider a more courteous manner, but also a more hygienic way of processing hundreds of thousands of shoeless passengers daily.

Some will contest, "This is just how it is," or, "This is how it's always been" to the point of thinking it's normal. I realize airport security is an absolutely critical and paramount function for safety without compromise. Security teams are doing the same thing over and over, having to give the same repeated instruction hundreds, sometimes thousands of times a day.

And yet, is "How it's always been" normal? Is "Just how it is" necessary?

I've passed through many airports in my life, and I can tell you that you'll find the same security requirements and regime at Christchurch Airport in New Zealand, Changi Airport in Singapore or Nadi Airport in Fiji. But there's a big difference . . . Somehow—magically, one might say—Christchurch, Changi, and Nadi airports will do their job to secure airspace without the shouting, chaos, fear, belittlement, or confrontations. They ensure safety without sacrificing service. There is warmth and courtesy.

They have looked in the mirror.

Simplexity

The best hotels around the world also undertake necessary tasks over and over again every single day, but like Christchurch, Changi, and Nadi airports, they pause to look past the process and routine so that they can focus on tuning up the simplicity of the delivery.

Service magic comes to life when teams actively look beyond the mechanics and conformity of the processes before them. Airport security proves just how easy it is to lose sight of simplicity and miss opportunities for connection.

One of my favorite words of all time is *simplexity*, which means the subtle and fine art with service design of blending *simplicity* with *complexity*. In the hotel and hospitality teams I was a part of, we were masters at *simplexity*. We were in a never-ending pursuit of improvement and refinement, searching continuously for a better way without over-complicating the experience. It always began with care and humility, blended together to create efficient but calm and connected service.

Designing and Delivering Service Magic

There is a key question that can never be overlooked whenever designing and delivering service magic: "What does 'good' actually look like or mean?" Once this has been fully defined, the next step is to then explain to everyone what this means and how their personal contribution will help bring this to life. And the third step is to then show and encourage them how to blend this with operational efficiency.

On another occasion at the previously mentioned major US airport (again, not mentioning which one), with my shoes back on and the security nightmare behind me, I headed to the peace of the airport lounge to recuperate before my long flight home. Having a lounge pass is something I am always grateful for. More than something for my own comfort, I am always secretly excited to uncover new gems of service magic in action. If there's anywhere in the world where you are sure to be dazzled with a masterclass of service, it surely has to be an airport business lounge . . . Right?

I presented myself at the lounge reception desk only to feel my excitement disappear in a flash. My heart sank as I was "greeted" with a disinterested and unfriendly check-in. The interaction was emotionless, sparkle-less, eye-contact-less, and certainly missing any sense of welcome.

The lounge interiors were plush and impressive, in sharp contrast to their service. The disinterested bar team of three shared one common passion—chewing gum. They served my drink with no grace or enthusiasm, letting me know I didn't matter because I would be through the assembly line of their processes soon enough and on my way.

The hot and cold food display was as soulless as my arrival—a pile of dinner plates, wet from the dishwasher, followed by a disappointing line of food containers under heat lamps—a sad looking chicken stew, vegetarian noodles stuck together, a pot full of overcooked, broken new potatoes, and another pot with rice, crispy on the top from the heat lamps. All I could think was how has anyone decided this resembles *good*? There were plenty of knives and spoons, but no forks.

I sat back in annoyed fascination, watching the lounge manager (in his ill-fitting suit and unpolished shoes) walk around checking and inspecting everything. He went up and down the food display and seemed happy how it all looked. He went on and chatted with the bar team, obviously not minding the gum chewing, engaged with none of his guests, before then disappearing back of house, never to be seen again.

PART 2: MAGIC REFLECTIONS

Departing from Singapore's Changi Airport is always nothing short of exciting! It's one of the busiest airports in the world with sixty million passengers in 2019, and is renowned for its clockwork efficiency and unique, thoughtful services. It has also won every award under the sun for its unrivaled workplace and passenger experiences and is consistently rated as one of the world's cleanest, most beautiful, and most magical international airports. Changi Airport is also famed for being "Singapore's most attractive employer." They are role model ambassadors of *simplexity* and have a collective sense of wonder radiating on full beam.

As I stepped into the vast terminal, I immediately felt the vibrant difference. The sound of light jazz playing through the terminal sound system provided a calm atmosphere in comparison to the outside world. It was bustling and at the same time welcoming, with smiling "Changi Experience Agents" dotted around the vast departure hall, highly visible in their bright pink jackets. Playing a similar role to hotel lobby hosts, they greeted and guided everyone with an air of graceful hospitality.

I checked in for my flight home to Sydney, and with my boarding pass in hand, I didn't even realize I went through security. Everything was highly organized, and all happened without me noticing. Before I knew it, I was at the passport checkpoint with no queues. The officer checked my passport and concluded the interaction by pointing to his little bowl of candy on his desk, gesturing with a smile for me to take one—tiny individually wrapped "Changi Love Bites" sweets.

The thing that is clearer than anything else with their service magic—everything has been considered and you know they have painstakingly thought about every part of it and have done so with a shared sense of genuine pride and pleasure.

The business lounge was just as welcoming. It was immaculate. Each team member wore pristine white jackets, well-pressed white shirts, and neatly knotted black ties with the jacket button fastened.

Their calm smiles and air of elegance made it easy to relax and enjoy myself. Each walked around the lounge attending to and interacting with their guests. It was a wonderlicious theater of service magic!

The dinner selection exhibited the same touches of care. The starched white napkins were folded, the steamed broccoli was as perfectly fresh and crisp as the lounge team uniforms, and I found myself admiring how the lounge manager was gliding around the floor, guiding his team with subtle and encouraging gestures. We started a wonderful conversation together; he lit up when I explained my hotel background and how I was in awe of his service magic. He went on to explain that they had partnered with the hotel group Sofitel, who provide their training. I smiled as he relayed his pride to me, and I couldn't help but think to myself—what a stroke of genius.

Role Model Magic

To be crowned numerous times as the Best International Airport in the World and have over six hundred other prestigious awards to their name is an unparalleled accomplishment. I couldn't help but want to look deeper and uncover the secret touches that Changi Airport does so successfully, but which might be overlooked by other airports (and other sectors) trying to emulate their success.

For a first-time visitor to Changi Airport, one experiences a positive overload of both efficiency and wonder. You could quite happily miss your flight and be pleased to stay forever, left to marvel at the jaw-dropping attractions. The rooftop swimming pool, eight gardens (one with one thousand butterflies), and three spas could easily keep you fully occupied. There's not one, but two free twenty-four-hour movie theaters, in addition to Singapore's tallest slide, and over eighty restaurants, cafes, and bars.

But such ongoing investment to build features and architectures can only go so far to win the hearts of passengers (customers). There still has to be a positive connection overlaying everything.

What are the secrets that make Changi not just a world-class airport facility, but an irresistible attraction as well as a beloved workplace?

- **Customer Interaction:** Changi receives around two million clicks of feedback each month from passengers ranging from every subject you can think of. They go out of their way to make it extremely easy for passengers to provide their in-the-moment feedback and encourage their rating of everything from the restrooms and customer service agents to their facilities. On my way out of the sparkling, freshly scented restroom, a colorful touch screen displayed the name and picture of the janitor on duty, with a row of smiley face icons under the words: "Good evening. Please rate our toilet." The operational team monitors all feedback in real-time, and instantly deploys their janitors to any location that isn't rated highly.

- **Customer comfort:** Quality carpeting is something you normally expect at luxury hotels. Naturally, very few airports invest in carpeting, which comes with a higher cost of maintenance than tiling. But airside at Changi, you're welcomed with carpet—another deliberate touch of wonder that says, "We have thought about it, and we care." Not only do passengers subconsciously feel good as a result of being pampered like A-list celebrities, but such luxury also absorbs the acoustic sounds that otherwise would make the airport noisy and chaotic. A less-noisy airport means more relaxed passengers, which in turn produces a calmer environment that everyone actually loves spending time in.

- **Irresistible workplace:** the entire Changi Airport website is flavored with an inspiring, authentic, and graceful sentiment for the pride and heart of their people. This starts immediately at the top of the homepage with the proud opening statement: "The team behind the world's most awarded airport."

This messaging is followed by:

> *"Life at Changi—Find out what it's like to work at the world's most awarded airport. Come and make magic with us: At Changi Airport, we offer you the prestige and pride of working in a truly world-class environment, with abundant opportunities to learn and grow. Our Vision: To be a first-in-class, leading global aviation hub run by exceptional people, connecting lives and businesses, contributing to the economic growth of Singapore. Our Values: Our values and culture guide us in everything we do. They are the foundation for our decisions and the heart of our organization. Changi Airport Group is about world-class service, delivered through our passion and culture of excellence. We Work Hard and Play Harder: Terminal H (where H stands for the heart of the company) is the core of our people strategy to build deep engagement with and among our people. Some of the initiatives include "Fun Friday," where employees come*

together and bond over fun and thematic activities, such as art jamming sessions.
We also have an extensive workplace wellness programme to promote healthy
living, with complimentary fitness classes, cooking classes, and more."—Changi
Airport Group

More than anything, the vibrant workplace culture of Changi Airport is bursting with connection. They perform their craft of service amongst a highly competitive industry, yet they are consistently awarded as the world's number one. Yes, the airport architecture and amenities are truly magnificent—but beyond the concrete, steel, and glass is their rock-solid foundation of pride in doing whatever it takes to stand out with world-class service magic.

In our ultra-connected world, every solution and experience is at the control of our customers' fingertips. Searching online for flights, accommodations, and holidays can be done on their own. Their decision is sometimes made easy by price, sometimes by convenience, sometimes because the features and benefits stand out the brightest—but above all else, *they* get to choose.

It's a Matter of Choice

Another time, I had the daunting prospect of flying to London to visit family, just me and my boys. Traveling solo from Sydney for twenty-seven hours with a four- and six-year-old, was a disaster waiting to happen! I knew it would be the wildest nerve-testing roller coaster I'd had in a long time, so I was focused on one thing: survival.

Searching online for three economy tickets, a huge selection of flights flashed up from various airlines. One stood out brighter than all the others with one of my favorite airlines, Etihad. Not because it was $400 cheaper than everyone else, but because of their onboard *Flying Nanny*. We would have to go via Abu Dhabi and overall travel four hours longer. The cynical side of me wondered if it was just a cute marketing ploy or an empty gimmick. I am thankful that I was intrigued enough to find out!

At the gate waiting to board, Zac and Jake were already lively and in full action mode. I just started silently praying as we headed to the back of the plane, to my place of delirium—row 56, seats A, B and C. They started fighting over the window seat, but I managed to pull them apart like we were competing in a professional wrestling contest. As I pulled the seatbelt hard, restraining Jake in A, the same with Zac in C, with me in B, I noticed the look I was getting from nearby passengers. Their eyes said it all! "Glad I'm not you!" from some and, "I can't believe I have to sit this close to you," from others.

As we became airborne, the boys were restless, and I tried every technique to bring calm. Headphones did the trick at first, but that soon wore off.

Then *it* happened.

My vision went into extreme slow motion, like the scene of a movie as I looked down the length of the plane. The curtain in front of us separating economy from business class opens and all I can see, wearing a bright orange apron, is the imaginary image of Mary Poppins gliding toward *me*.

"Mr. Merrett, good afternoon! Do you need a break?"

"Is it that obvious?!" I eagerly replied with an expression of bursting relief.

"Off you go! Have a stretch, go for a walk. The crew in the galley have some refreshments waiting for you."

I get up out of B and am gobsmacked as she moves across into my seat, sitting between the boys and opens up one of their books to start reading to them. I curse to myself as I see how they instantly turn into silent, delightful angels.

Soon after she returned again with two little craft boxes filled with activities and coloring pens. The boys' dinner arrived inside party boxes with paper pirate hats. Zac squealed "Look, Daddy!" pointing to the label on his box that read "Zachary Merrett." It was just another touch that said, "We know you are here." Later she took them to the galley, they returned with their faces painted—Jake as a butterfly and Zac with the face of a tiger.

The business investment for Etihad to cause such a positive connection? Simply put, it's mainly the cost of the orange apron. The Flying Nanny is part of the crew. Once the safety briefing is complete and the plane is in the air, on goes the apron and they switch characters. Here lies another genius and classic example of *simplexity* at its best—simplifying complexity with something, an idea—that could so easily be tossed aside as too difficult.

Training is another part of this precious investment. Etihad sends a select group of cabin crew to a top nannying school in the UK to learn about childcare and how best to help parents. Then, as if by magic, one nanny (or more) appears on long haul flights to help families from the time of boarding until they exit.

It's a Matter of Grace

A close first place to Etihad, but hands down the best flight of my life, happened by pure and fortunate chance. I was transferred by my airline to Fiji Airways. My direct LA to Sydney flight was now three hours longer with a flight change in the Fiji port of Nadi. I was frustrated by the change, but I soon became thankful for it.

The plane was the same as any other—two wings, engines, and seats—but everything else felt extremely different—the air of warm grace and calm. I stepped into a friendly and eager welcome, which was exciting for me, and clearly the same for them too. I realize this came as no fluke. Fiji's national motto is, "Where happiness comes naturally." It has been forged for generations by their culture, environment, and faith. Fijians are known for having the "Bula Spirit," a desire to be kind and generous to everyone they meet.

I could see their smiles through their eyes. When they spoke, their words felt genuine. What made this even more special was them not even realizing their depth of authentic connection. Fijians are beautiful, soulful people and considered by many to be amongst the humblest on the planet. The same sentiment carried through during my short time in Nadi airport—going through security, passport control, the duty-free shops, all were effortlessly connected via service magic.

Even the inflight safety video had soul. Usually, the irritating piece of film on flights, whilst essential and of critical importance to safety, has a monotone and disconnected undercurrent. The vocal and visual of the Fiji Air film was clear and informative, but with a pleasant and soothing vocal tone that does nothing but captivate and draw you in.

In the outdoor tunnel leading to the connecting flight, we lined up for a final bag check before boarding. A dozen or more of the Fiji team were standing along one side of a long table. A young lady discreetly attended to the search of my bag as we chatted. Then she zipped it up, beamed the brightest smile, and said "It's been so nice meeting you today. Have a lovely flight."

I arrived in Sydney sixteen hours after leaving LA, and immediately began telling everyone about my happy flight. You see, happiness spreads. I contacted the senior Fiji Air team to say thank you and started sharing my love of their brand from the stage when I speak.

I think the favorite thing I found in my research since my flight is the authentic opening expression on their website; it sums everything up quite perfectly: *"Welcome to our home. When you board a Fiji Airways flight, you instantly feel like you've known us for a lifetime. You can expect the same care and warmth you naturally receive in the home of a loved one, because onboard Fiji airways, you're not just a seat number, you're part of our extended Fijian family."*

When customers find themselves connected with you for the right reasons and in an overwhelming state of admiration for your service magic, they want to tell the world about their newfound love . . . like I am trying to do here!

The most basic realization between the service a company believes they are providing, to the reality of what is being received by their customers is the reflection of truth. A mirror never lies and, when put to use, will always provide the actual opportunity to do whatever is necessary in closing the gap between distortion and magic. When you dare to look at the reflection, the truth always prevails.

Beyond all magnificent architecture, facilities, and amenities, it will always be the little things in service that cause the deepest connection.

Recipe 7 Recap:

SERVICE MAGIC

Service is usually one of two things: magic or distorted—i.e., excellent or disappointing, *wonderLICIOUS* or *wonderLESS*. You can get lost in complicated regimes "because that's just how it's done" or you can look in the mirror, see what your customers see, and find a fresh balance between conformity and creativity.

Ingredients:

★   A "magic mirror" for viewing your reflection of service through the eyes of your customers.

★   Simplexity: the subtle service design that blends *simplicity* with *complexity*.

★   Investment in innovative training, like Etihad and Fiji Airways, to inspire what "good" looks like.

★   Grace: make space to connect with customers personally, with heart and with care, through and beyond the transaction.

★   Curiosity: Whilst conformity can create service consistency, curiosity drives wondrous innovation. Mix both to spark innovation and produce connected, adored service magic.

Substitutions to Make this Recipe Your Own:

If your procedures and regimes are creating chaotic or complicated customer experiences, increase your curiosity and decrease your conformity. Look at things through your customers' eyes—the magic mirror. Rooftop swimming pools and rooms with 1000 butterflies are wonderful, but so are authentic, warm smiles, new connections, and freshly pressed napkins. The touches that will always make anyone feel welcome and valued.

Recipe 8:
DEVILS IN THE DETAILS

"

It's not about how much you do, but how much love you put into what you do
Mother Teresa

"**I**t's time to think bigger"—five words that strike exhaustion into the hearts and minds of everyone gathered around any boardroom table. When you ask people to keep reinventing "the next big thing," especially regarding service, they flinch in the anticipation of increased pressure from the enormity of the task. However, guide them with permission to playfully "think smaller," to have fun creating an ever-flowing cascade of service gestures, touches, and enhancements consisting of all the little things. They will run toward their new mission with groundbreaking greatness.

Once they feel how good it is to make a positive contribution or see the positive reaction from their leader, or from a customer to their unexpected gesture—they actively look for ways to do it again and try other things.

Gestures never have to be over the top, extraordinary, or complicated by design, and they don't have to happen by chance either. It takes warm encouragement to be present and imaginative, making everyone feel welcome to try and play with ideas, however small they may seem. This is what makes a company culture like switching on the Christmas tree lights. The only word that must be applied here, to bring this together with passionate momentum, is—consistency.

It was always down to me and my fellow hotel team leaders to do exactly this: lead by example and be role models of wonder with everyone around us. For us to expect our whole team to create unexpected moments of wonder, we knew it was down to us to walk the talk and consistently demonstrate it. We had to not only focus on the little things that made the biggest difference, but join in and be part of it.

The Devils in the Details

Hotel life taught us the importance of the little things. In other words, "the devil in the details." Throughout every part of our operation, our goal was to enhance everything. We had crystal clear sight of our daily business outcomes—to give our guests the reason to love their experience with us. Like flicking a switch over to auto-pilot, it became what we all did—as *good little devils*—automatically.

Everyone tends to overuse the phrase, "needing to have the right mindset." Whilst the sentiment is true, I choose to refine the expression with a slight turn of phrase. Instead of "needing to have the right mindset," we should put the importance on "keeping a clear and open mind."

Another commonly overused instruction is "having an attention to the details." My teams always took this further and lived a different version. To us, it was about having "an unconditional love of the details."

Does it even matter? For you to become a *good little devil*, it does!

Power Up the Passion

Everyone in the world is a master at charging their phones and devices when their batteries are running low. The same goes for *passion*. Passion on low power is lethargic and misses the beat. What if we kept our passion charged on a regular basis? Not just for big bursts of extra effort every now and again, but all the time? It would be like having your foot on the gas, gently revving the engine, like a permanent pilot light, always there to provide a slow simmer. As a leader, it's what people will love most about you.

Passion is contagious. It sparks the enthusiasm of everyone around you and inspires ongoing creativity with service. It is your passion that lifts people to navigate their biggest obstacles and overcome the most intractable challenges.

Yet, it is extremely easy to become tiresome with the monotony of service, sometimes doing exactly the same thing over and over again every day. Becoming a *good little devil* makes it a permanently invigorating ride, fueled by adding seemingly insignificant moments of unexpected wonder to anything and everything. The repetitiveness of life then dissolves, and instead of seeing gray, you get to stand back and marvel at the colorful reactions that come to life in front of your eyes.

Concentrate on the Icing

In a world that could benefit from far less seriousness and more uncomplicated joy, the personal touch has never been more necessary or important.

Imagine for a moment that your business, company, or organization made cakes. Even if your cakes are well made and delicious, they may also be similar to everyone else's cakes. Yours might appear to be fine as they are, but it will be down to the irresistible impression of your icing, decoration, and even candles (all the little touches) to stand out and capture the attention of your prospects, customers, and clients.

My mum knew, more than anyone else, how much I enjoyed pottery at school. Over the dinner table, my parents would ask me, "What's your dream when you leave school?" By then, I had started showing interest in becoming a chef, and that's what was in my heart, so I declared it.

"I think I want to be a chef!"

Mum asked, "Would you like to dip your toes in the water and see?"

She took me along to our local family-run bakery, Müller's Swiss Confectionery and Bakery Shop. She went about buying some bread and then asked if they had any vacancies for a Saturday job. She enthusiastically explained my pottery skills while I stood there blushing uncontrollably. "He's very creative," she insisted. Even as a sixteen-year-old, I thought to myself how stupidly unqualified I must have sounded.

Mrs. Müller asked with a big smile, "Would you like to start next weekend, as our junior baker?"

Let Me Show You the Way

Mr. and Mrs. Müller opened their prized little shop in 1959, and every day since then they have filled the window with intricate delicacies as if it were a scene from a fairy tale. I was enthralled watching the intense concentration of Mr. Müller going about his life's craft with passionate precision, just as his father and grandfather had done before him. He was one of the best *good little devils* I've ever seen. A proud and quiet man, only speaking occasionally just above a whisper. Amongst the sound of the mixing machines, bread ovens, and all the whisking, you had to really concentrate to hear his words. And he never repeated himself. All he wanted was your full and present attention.

The Müller family were famous in our area as the creator of *The Frog Cakes*, a small variety of fun and humble cupcake frogs. They looked so life-like as if they could jump out of the shop window. One day I was given the chance and responsibility of decorating them. Never did Mr. Müller just give instructions and leave us to figure it out.

Standing next to me he asked, "Do you know what the most important thing with our Frogs is?"

I shook my head.

"The way they look irresistible in the shop window!"

I thought of how amazing they usually looked in the display window.

He declared: "In this moment, the success of our frogs is in your hands! Don't decorate them with your piping bag—bring them to life!"

First, he would show me. I would just stare in awe as he moved his tiny piping bag of icing like a magic wand. "See their eyes? This way they become real!" he then turned away and left me to it.

Once I had finished the first large batch, he came back and spoke as if he was actually talking to the frogs. Maybe he was?

"Well, isn't this a marvelous sight! You all look amazing!" He was saying it to me but including *them* in it too. Never will I forget this moment of inclusive encouragement at its finest.

The Profound Influence of Permission

Mr. Müller's Swiss Confectionery and Bakery Shop, just like Singapore's Changi Airport or Disneyland or a big fancy hotel, was his "big thing." But never did he keep stopping to reinvent it; instead, he showed us how to consistently focus on the devil in the details—the small things that would produce continuous joy and wonder for our customers (and ourselves) every single day.

You can do this too. Anyone can. How? His influence on me to explore and play with detail is the same as the influence that you have on everyone around you.

Mr. Müller's shop window wouldn't have been such a jaw-dropping fairy tale if he hadn't encouraged himself and others to bring it to life with such precision.

Timing can be everything when you use wonder to create little touches of memorable delight, in particular through the practice of two very special words: *What else?* Tuck your napkin into your top for this part of the recipe—a wonderlicious selection of examples that can be adapted to just about any scenario to cause unforgettable connection.

GOOD LITTLE DEVILS

The Wonderliciousness of "What Else"

Jake, our youngest, was always fascinated each time he lost one of his baby teeth. Before he went to sleep, he put the tooth under his pillow for the tooth fairy (the role I always loved); to him, it's pure disbelief waking up to find the tooth gone and, in its place, a shiny coin. For one of his last baby teeth, I swapped the usual coin for a five-dollar note. "What else?" flashed through my mind. I went to our top kitchen drawer (which is full of accumulated junk) and found a ball of thin leftover gift ribbon. I quickly rolled up the five-dollar note, tied a short piece of the ribbon around it into a tiny bow, and popped the "miniature scroll" under his pillow.

Jake freaked out!

"Daddy look!" showing me his miniature magic scroll that the tooth fairy had left him. It took me all of seven seconds to do it. I could have saved seven seconds and just put the five-dollar note under his pillow. But it wasn't enough, I added a touch of wonder to the moment. At home, or in our work, wonder like this comes to life anywhere when we allow it and also ask ourselves, "What else?"

The Doughnut Moments

Hotel breakfasts are usually one of two things: average or amazing. The best hotel breakfast experience that I have ever seen was at the QT Hotel on the Gold Coast in Australia. It was a full theater-caliber production of spectacular simplicity, one of the most creatively interesting and well-thought-out breakfast displays I have seen. Breakfast buffets are usually quiet places, with people still waking up and conversation not yet in flow—un-caffeinated. That wasn't the case here. All I could hear was giggling, especially from the guests who were gathered in front of the doughnuts.

These weren't just fresh chocolate-filled doughnuts. These were fresh doughnuts with small plastic syringes full of liquid chocolate sticking into them. Guests were invited to be playful by squeezing their own shot of chocolate into their doughnuts. It was so awesome! The chocolate in the syringes was the experience, and each guest was put in charge of creating their own uncomplicated joy, inside a fully inclusive moment shared with complete strangers.

It was a strike of pure genius. I saw the young commis chef behind the buffet display, and I said, "This is amazing, how is this even possible?"

He beamed proudly, "This was my idea. I mentioned it to our head chef who told me to give it a try."

In your business, you probably don't have chocolate-filled syringes. But you could.

All of these seemingly little things make some people say, "It's all fluff—we haven't got time for this." So, they keep busy with the reinvention of the next big thing for tomorrow, and they miss it—the reality and opportunity of deep and memorable connection that's possible right now.

They are the *bad little devils*; they miss the details, and all goodwill (along with profitability and customer loyalty) disappears in a flash. Here are some more *doughnut moments* . . .

Magic Ink

I have sometimes arrived at a hotel to find a welcome card placed in the room from the general manager. Almost every time, although a nice enough touch and appreciated, they are generic pre-printed cards and provide little connection.

Unexpected magic happens whenever you take a moment to connect the tip of your pen, any kind of pen, to a piece of paper, and write a message for someone. Another time many years later in Australia we stayed at the Novotel Melbourne. Whilst making the reservation I excitedly mentioned it was the first time in a while that we weren't traveling with our children. On the bedroom table, we found a hand-written card: "Dear Mr. and Mrs. Merrett, wishing you a warm welcome to Novotel Melbourne South Wharf. We are delighted you are here—enjoy your time without the kids!"

This is a busy hotel operation with 347 guest rooms over twenty-six floors. All we could feel was how much they cared about us being there.

Soon after I was back in Melbourne speaking at an event at the 206-room city center Vibe Hotel. Within five minutes of stepping through the front door to check in, I felt deeply connected to the property. On my bedroom desk was a handwritten postcard: "Dear Mr. Merrett, Welcome to Vibe Melbourne! We're thrilled to have you here and hope that you have an awesome stay. Please don't hesitate to call us if you require any assistance." It was finished with a smiley face.

Here lies the irresistible difference—ink. It's a kind of magic!

Welcome Surprises

Just before we moved to Australia, when Zachary was two, we had a weekend break at Four Seasons, Canary Wharf in London. Imagine Zac's reaction stepping into our room to find a cupcake on the coffee table with *Hello Zachary* piped on top in icing. This wasn't just a cupcake, but a well-intended, carefully planned moment of wonder. In the bathroom, there was a little bag of mini-rubber ducks next to a line of small plastic toy letters around the bath: *Hello Zachary*. On the pillow of his bed, there was a little coloring book with crayons and a Post-it note stuck on the front, handwritten with *Hello Zachary*.

Hotels are masters at creating personalized welcome touches. Yet any business can create similar unexpected connections, at low to no cost. It doesn't take fancy bottles of free champagne to make customers feel special.

Virgin Mary

Often people judge the level of care of a hotel or restaurant by the cleanliness and presentation of the restrooms. I do too. However, my favorite wonderlicious ritual and test whenever I am dining out is to order a *Virgin Mary* (Bloody Mary without the vodka). It is one of the most widely known cocktails in the world. Everywhere I go, I quietly wait in hope for something exciting—it's my fastest way to see if they are *good little devils*, or not. The attentive mix of ingredients, garnishing, the glass—and the delivery. This is a cocktail that gives an establishment every chance to fully let go and express the vibrancy of their personality. It comes with the chance for them to consider *what else* they can do with every part of it. I have experienced every variation of Virgin Mary drinks, with the most common being the *bad little devils* version— tomato juice, slice of lemon, and a squirt of Tabasco sauce.

Our favorite local foodie hotspot is Jenson's. Everyone across our whole community loves the place, a beautiful, large, open-concept Modern Australian restaurant, owned and run by legendary chef Carl Jensen and his wife Brooke. This is consistently the best Virgin Mary I have experienced from anywhere around the world. It makes me close my eyes with pleasure as I sip on it. You just know that they have thought about, played with, experimented with, and considered every single detail of it.

It's consistently delivered with pride in a tall, heavy-patterned glass, the rim dipped in black charcoal salt, always elegantly garnished, and the taste—irresistible. They said their ingredients were secret when I asked, but they did lean in and whisper "We use chipotle, Worcestershire, Tabasco, celery bitters, and beetroot shrub. There's a couple of other little things in there, but we can't tell you everything!"

The beauty of this example is that it isn't restricted to a cocktail bar or restaurant business. You can apply this method—an unconditional love of the details—to anything.

Indian Takeaway

One of my favorite places to visit back home in England is the city of Winchester. It's a long-standing custom on trips that while staying there with my sister and her family, we have a big celebratory reunion around the kitchen table with an Indian takeaway dinner. Gandhi Restaurant is our favorite place. Their food is an exciting pleasure— especially the *Railway Lamb*, which is outrageously delicious—but that's another story for another time. We sometimes end up with a dozen containers of various curries and side dishes; apart from the rice, everything looks similar. Not being Indian ourselves, it's often a challenge to distinguish what's what. That's another thing we love about

Gandhi—they know this too! So, they put little printed stickers on each food container. A touch of delicious simplicity by a highly passionate team of *good little devils*.

Sunglasses

On a speaking trip in Dubai, I was lost in bewildered amazement by the awe-inspiring architecture, towering skyscrapers, flashy sports cars, and gigantic shopping malls. My memory, however, goes way beyond all the glitz and glam of this extravagantly mind-boggling place. I remember clearer than anything else the hotel where I stayed and how it made me feel. Their level of invisible anticipation was breathtaking. Returning to my freshly serviced room, my sunglasses had been placed on top of a neatly wrapped cleaning cloth for glasses. A simple touch that happened eight years ago, yet I still remember the feeling from the gesture. A tiny and fun surprise touch that said, "We noticed." More than this, it said to me, "We thought about it before you realized you needed it!"

Supermarket

Whenever I speak internationally, as a habit I always visit the local supermarket. I love to look for differences in fresh produce and service. I was speaking in Arizona and popped into the nearby Whole Foods superstore. The first thing I noticed was how clean the place was and how interesting the store looked. It felt exciting. The fresh vegetables were all arranged neatly and the whole place was beaming with pride.

As I was the only one wandering around without a basket or trolley, I must have stood out from the actual customers. One of the team came up to me and with a smile asked, "Hi there. Are you okay, sir?"

I replied, "I'm great, thanks. This place is amazing!"

He agreed with a smile, "Yep! It's pretty cool, isn't it?"

Pointing to the corn on the cob and fresh coconuts on a big bed of crushed ice, I asked, "Who comes up with ideas like this?"

Without skipping a beat he replies, "We all do!" He then cheekily asked, "Have you seen the asparagus?!"

He proudly takes me over to the dozens of asparagus bunches, beautifully arranged and lined up, standing at attention in stainless steel trays of iced water. "This was my idea," he proudly announces. "I suggested it in our team huddle." Sensing my excitement, he went on to explain that every morning they have their ten-minute team huddle and high-five each other to celebrate the ideas that worked the best yesterday. After which they then challenge each other to see who can come up with the best idea for today.

Even if you are not in the business of asparagus, creating moments of unexpected wonder works with anything. It just requires an environment where this is not only allowed and encouraged, but also wholeheartedly celebrated, like at Whole Foods—all from a ten-minute morning team huddle.

BAD LITTLE DEVILS

Cheese

On a trip to Los Angeles with my US Manager, we were encouraged to try the smart new Italian restaurant near where we were staying. It had a large warehouse industrial style of finish, rustic bare brick walls with elaborate fittings and furnishings. Everything about the place had a huge visual "Wow," the investment must have cost a fortune. The place was packed and the open-plan kitchen in the heart of the dining room gave a vibrant feel of theater. That's where the magic stopped. It was absent of all grace and detail. As they served our pasta entrees we asked for some Parmesan cheese. That's normally the exciting part of Italian hospitality, where the host proudly brings the block of Parmesan and theatrically grates it over your plate at the table. In this case, the server came back with a small plastic tube of dried processed Parmesan that you get in the supermarket, put it down on the table, and walked off. We realized they had focused on getting the furniture right and filling the place—but hadn't thought about any of the small touches.

Ice Cream

South of Sydney, down by one of our local beaches, there is a small line of shops and restaurants. A nice looking new little ice cream parlor opened there recently. You can see that a lot of care and expense had gone into setting up the shop. Within a couple of minutes' walk, there are two other ice cream shops. It was empty and the kids begged us to try it. A young team of three were standing behind the counter, scrolling on their phones.

The kids were glued to the big cabinet trying to decide which of the twenty flavors of ice cream they wanted.

"Which one is your favorite?" we asked one of the team.

"I don't know actually, I haven't been here very long," he replied, followed by a long (uncomfortable) pause.

"Oh! When did you start?" I asked.

"About three weeks ago," he said.

Plenty of time to learn the flavors, I thought.

The ice cream was delicious, but there was no one in charge. The shop was empty and silent. Afterward, we walked a few doors down past two other ice cream shops that were both packed. Each had the same amount of ice creams on display, both with music playing and a long line leading up to their counters, one with the person in charge standing at the front door welcoming everyone, the other behind the counter enthusiastically revving up the team. Small touches caused significant differences in customer popularity.

Tech

Everyone in our local area had been raving about a new pub that had opened down by the coast, a stunning one-hundred-year-old historical gem that has been brought back to life with a massive renovation. We went with friends for lunch around my wife Suzy's fiftieth birthday and stepped into a complicated mess.

Each table had a QR code for the menu, to send orders directly from your phone to the kitchen. I wanted to talk to someone to get a feel for the menu or hear about the specials, but we were on our own. The role of the team was to deliver the food and clear the tables, nothing else. You had to line up at the bar to get your own drinks, so the second we sat down we became instantly disconnected, with everyone either on their phones trying to navigate what to do, or worse, were off standing in a line at the bar. Zac and Jake love burgers, but we needed one with no onion and the other with no sauce. Nowhere on the app could you personalize your order or make special requests, so I had to walk around to find someone to explain it to.

Some of our main courses started coming out, along with some of our starters. Suzy got her pot-of-steamed-mussels main course together with her half-dozen-oyster appetizer. Within minutes our table of eight had the entire order of both courses on the table. I was instantly disappointed, also highly frustrated, but at the same time I didn't want to make a scene on such a special occasion.

"You have to order starters and mains separately on the app. We told you this when you sat down," one of the servers said dismissively.

They definitely didn't tell us this; even if they had, it wouldn't have made sense either, just added further complication.

Their intention for creating efficiency through the app had stripped away all connection, removing all remnants of true hospitality. All I could see across the packed dining room was highly frustrated customers. At no point had the team of the establishment thought, "What else can we do to make every part of this experience special for our customers?"

Four Ingredients For a Good Little Devil!

The four wonder ingredients for becoming a *good little devil*—to spread uncomplicated joy and make your customers go dizzy with delight, are exactly this—uncomplicated.

You don't need a big textbook explanation, weighty strategy, complex planning, or financial investment to bring wonder to life. You will, however, need to have—and encourage everyone around you to have—*present consciousness, extreme thoughtfulness, playful curiosity, and a little touch of mischief!*

These special little ingredients should be used regularly, not on and off like a light switch, but as a constant way of life. Being in a fully conscious and generous state of mischievousness, ever restless and with a constant eagerness to play with the detail.

No one will ever think badly of you being a thoughtful, big-hearted, playful expert. We were all born with a special sense of mischief. As children, it was our way—our great skill. Nobody ever had to tell us to be mischievous. It came naturally. And it still can.

Come to Life

How do we hard-wire the little things into, well, everything? It is virtually impossible to sit around a boardroom table to force creativity. I let it come to me and allow ideas to flow through me. My heart and mind are always switched on and open to mischief. With all my teams throughout my career, even during moments of pressure, this was what I encouraged with full consciousness, more than anything else.

As a personal habit, I don't switch my phone on for at least thirty minutes after waking each morning. This is my personal space to climb into my consciousness, to allow myself to reach room temperature, to allow my mind to daydream and gather clarity at my pace—to step into my character of being a good little devil before starting each day.

More Fun Please

Anyone who knows me knows I hate swearing, it's just something I don't get involved in. It therefore seems wrong for me to throw in the biggest F-word here—like kryptonite to Superman, one of the largest swear words of company cultures the world over—*Fun*.

One of the single most essential elements in creating a culture of service detail is fun and play. In our go-go-go world, we've become exceptionally clever at turning our back on it, but why? Some might label it as time-wasting silliness, some might brush it off as unprofessional, and others might have simply forgotten.

Fun and play help to deepen our learning and ability to be creative. They nurture critical thinking and adaptive pathways for us in childhood. It's the same for adults playing—not only is fun essential in our hectic modern lives, but it also releases endorphins, improves brain functionality, and stimulates creativity. I've had front row seats throughout my career for possibly one of the most important lessons of all—that the most significant way adults (yes, I did say adults—not just children!) learn is through play!

But the bad news is we stop our children playing. We tranquilize them with iPhones, iPads and Xboxes because we want them to be quiet. Where's the play? All the child psychologists share the research that children must play, it's how they learn. The same is for adults who play, they function better and perform better.

How many of us wake up in the morning wishing we could be more serious, more intense, or more focused on work today? I can't imagine it would be that many. There are a million ways you can help bring uncomplicated joy and fun into your life and other people's lives.

Children love playgrounds. What about playgrounds for adults to bring fun and laughter back to our work? I am not suggesting you put on a circus in your business and start wearing costumes. There are obviously moments where play isn't appropriate. But most of the time, play is appreciated—life is serious, and we are all overwhelmed. Just by adding a sense of fun to the air we breathe, we can turbocharge our curiosity. Here's what happens when you do . . .

Why So Serious?

I love exploring the heart (and soul) of organizations. One company that walks the talk with fun and play is Zappos. They are amongst my all-time favorite *good little devils*.

I have long admired their unique approach to "Delivering WOW through service." And I love their public statement:

> *"Zappos was founded in 1999 as a shoe retailer. And we sure have come a long way. We still sell shoes—as well as clothing, handbags, accessories, and *more.*
>
> **More is where we provide the very best customer service, customer experience, and company culture. We aim to inspire the world by showing it's possible to simultaneously deliver happiness to customers, employees, vendors, shareholders, partners, and the community in a long-term, sustainable way."*

The Zappos HQ is in downtown Las Vegas and on one of my trips to the US I had the exciting chance to spend time with the Zappos CEO Tony Hsieh. I heard back from them with a message that said, "We can't wait to see you on Tuesday at 10 a.m., Sarah will meet you in the lobby."

As I walked into the foyer everything changed. One of the *Zaponians* as they are known was there playing a ukulele. The first thing I noticed was the enormous sign that said, "Welcome to The Zappos Family." I instantly knew just through the feeling of the entrance foyer that it wasn't just a sign. This was a family.

I didn't have a chance to say that I was there, as within seconds of stepping through the door a chirpy character immediately came up to me. "Good morning, Peter, I'm Sarah, I'm the FNG. Welcome to Zappos!" She was enthusiastic and friendly. "We have so much for you to see!"

As she practically skipped down the hall, I asked what an FNG was.

"Oh! I'm the Fantastic New Girl! I only started recently, but who knows? There might be an FNB next week—the Fantastic New Boy."

All I could think was how brilliant this was, a stroke of genius from Zappos, a $1 billion business with one phrase that changes everything. Here was their newest recruit representing them at the front door, instead of being badged as the "trainee" and put in the corner.

The whole atmosphere exuded playfulness, not seriousness, even though Zappos is a serious business. Their way is to be extremely professional and do it with fun. To them, playing is an essential part of being professional.

Everywhere we went I kept spotting lots of other wall signs with their tagline, "Why so serious?" I am very aware that this would be a very silly story to share if Zappos was a small company that sold three pairs of shoes and had zero reputation. They have built a $1 billion business through better customer service and have virtually zero employee turnover. In fact, their CEO wrote the best-selling book *Delivering Happiness*. I wonder what it would be like if we all put up a sign like "Why so serious?"

We become and stay serious because business is serious. It is, but we can also be professional with play. What do the posted signs in your business say? Better yet, what are the invisible signs? What does the sense of energy in your foyer say to someone?

I met Tony and visited the Human Resources department, themed as a tropical jungle, and went past life-size gorillas, tigers, and pandas. Amongst it all were a series of large child-like ball pools. "What are these for?" I excitedly asked.

"Well! When you have your performance review with your leader, you get in and sit together in the ball pool while you have your review."

Now, before you judge this, before you think that's not very professional and that's not serious, or that's not the way HR is supposed to be done—Zappos is an extraordinarily successful company. This is a serious business full of happy people! People buy their shoes from Zappos just because they want to be happy.

And before you go, "Well that's never going to happen in our business," I wonder what would happen if you did? I wonder what would happen if all corporate cultures started to introduce some playfulness. Before you bag this idea, try it!

Human beings, by default, refuse to try new things that might make us look silly because of how others might judge us. If you're thinking this is silly and it would destroy your reputation, consider that it didn't seem so at Zappos!

You might think this is the best idea since sliced bread, or you might say "He's a moron!" Somewhere in between is fine. Just look at who you are, look at how you can bring some lightness into your world. I left Zappos feeling on top of the world with a copy of their beautiful hardback *Culture Book* from Tony. The book is published each year with only words and pictures from the Zaponians—292 pages on why they so love working there.

Beyond it all, *Zappos makes it clear what their values are* and there isn't anyone there who doesn't know them!

Our 10 Core Values are more than just words; they're our way of life.

1. *Deliver WOW Through Service*
2. *Embrace and Drive Change*
3. *Create Fun and a Little Weirdness*
4. *Be Adventurous, Creative, and Open-Minded*
5. *Pursue Growth and Learning*
6. *Build Open and Honest Relationships with Communication*
7. *Build a Positive Team and Family Spirit*
8. *Do More with Less*
9. *Be Passionate and Determined*
10. *Be Humble*

Just Try?

Tomorrow will be important—but we aren't there yet.

Today matters. Take a look around you. See and notice the endless possibilities. I encourage you to create moments of joy and wonder and forget about only chasing the next big thing. Take time to find and lead with some fun today.

Do one little thing.

Do ten.

Do a hundred.

Don't even count.

Just give it a try—be excited to play and experiment. If it doesn't work, try something else, take baby steps. Just try.

Timing is everything in life. The unexpected moments of wonder are always there, ready and waiting to be brought to life, through your touch.

DEVILS IN THE DETAILS

Providing memorable service often comes from sharing the smallest unexpected gestures. Allowing passion and presence to be your constant companion, you can inspire profound delight and loyalty among both your team and customers.

Ingredients:

- ★ The creation of little, unexpected moments of joy, no matter how seemingly insignificant.
- ★ Passion: let your passion shine so that it may inspire surprising creativity.
- ★ Be a "good little devil" by finding and loving the opportunity in the details.
- ★ Take fun seriously to create lightness and space for imagination.
- ★ Allow yourself to be playfully mischievous by adding wonder touches to anything and everything.

Substitutions to Make this Recipe Your Own:

When the devils are in the details, you will find yourself looking for new opportunities for wonder, even in the smallest places. This is true no matter what the circumstance, company, or job at hand may be. By embodying the spirit of a *Good Little Devil*, you will transform mundane or insignificant moments into memorable delights. Play with ideas and give new things a try. Then invite everyone else to do the same . . .

Recipe 9:
MAKING IT RIGHT

"

Well, here's another nice mess you've gotten me into
Oliver Hardy

Positive reviews from customers and consumers are one of the most fulfilling moments for any business. There isn't anyone who doesn't love an enthusiastic online review, glowing feedback, or a top-star rating. How about when things go wrong?

Service recovery and problem solving is a simple art. When done efficiently, promptly, and with sincerity, it can not only produce customer appreciation but also cultivate trust, loyalty, and opportunities for growth. It's that straightforward, and that uncomplicated. Otherwise, an unresolved mess just gets messier. It becomes an unnecessary pickle—a magnificent pickle of all pickles.

Hiding from a problem only deepens a customer's frustration. There is uncomplicated simplicity behind the formula for turning the greatest of blunders and customer dissatisfaction into extreme loyalty. There is abundant opportunity to grow, improve, learn, and create wonder from our mistakes. The way we creatively and compassionately find the solution through our reaction will always matter the most.

Well, Here's Another Fine Mess You've Gotten Me Into!

Talking of famous pickles, Stan Laurel and Oliver Hardy were widely adored and fondly regarded as one of the greatest comedy duos in film history. They made over one hundred films together during the early 1900s Classical Hollywood era of American cinema, with Laurel playing the bumbling and innocent foil to the wonderfully pompous Hardy.

Whenever Stan would get Oliver into some kind of trouble (which was all the time), Oliver would impatiently utter his classic catchphrase in desperate and frustrated disbelief, "Well, here's another nice mess you've gotten me into!" Stan's frequent and iconic response was to start to cry, lift his hat to ruffle his hair upwards with his fingertips, and exclaim with a squeal, "Well, I couldn't help it," then whimper and bumble away in gibberish.

Oliver would then exclaim sternly in desperation, "So why don't you do something to help me?!" Stan would stand helplessly fumbling and not knowing what to do next.

Oliver's frustration would always intensify and boil over to the point of steam coming out of his ears, because Stan never knew what to do next. He never had a solution, or any idea how to find one, which always made matters worse, and the situation would always spiral into an outrageously disastrous calamity.

The beauty of any good catchphrase is that it's catchy, and since I was a young boy, this one has been one of my all-time favorites. Almost a century has passed since Oliver Hardy first said "Well, here's another nice mess you've gotten me into!" back in the 1930s. Whilst I realize this is classic TV comedy at its best, I fondly use this example because this is a phrase that we all might be able to learn from and put to good use in our work today, either when we find ourselves solving a problem or situation, feeling burdened with a customer complaint, or when something simply goes wrong and we find ourselves handling a mess.

More important is Oliver's reaction to Stan, "So why don't you do something to help me?" Here lies the key to effective problem solving. While an apology is crucial in addressing an aggrieved customer, it is the solution that ultimately holds the greatest significance.

More Than Saying Sorry

Transforming a customer's dissatisfaction into delight is a key philosophy of any business. Imagine for a moment that your customers were actually made of water. When you handle their problems quickly, smoothly, and efficiently to provide a solution, it would be like pouring water into a highly polished sealed silver container. Getting your reaction wrong or providing no resolution is the same as pouring water through a sieve. Your customers leave you at the speed of the water pouring through the holes. They run away from you, with no intention of looking back.

To our downfall, we can get tangled up in creating highly complex processes with often disempowering systems; the layers of complication are easy to hold us back in effectively handling problems. Bringing our mind and heart together in sequence and reacting promptly is the most powerful way of turning a frustrated customer into an appreciated loyal fan. But it takes more than saying "sorry."

Three Mighty Words

In hotels, we were warmly encouraged, carefully trained, and guided on how to face (not fear) problems or shy away from our mistakes and not get defensive in response whenever problems occurred, with each other or with our guests. Whilst we weren't weighed down with formal black-and-white instructions or rigorous processes, we were loaded up with encouragement to find imaginative answers to service problems—with one goal that was consistently front of mind . . .

Make it right.

Everything lived within these three words and whatever our rank, role, or position, we clearly knew that we had the backing to react, respond, and deal with a situation as much as we could. We had support to sort it out and, wherever possible, solve it in the first instance and make it right.

Things undoubtedly went wrong or didn't go to plan from time to time, but it is how we were supported and encouraged to react to it, learn from it, and wherever possible, prevent it from recurring. Driving consistent satisfaction was our shared motivation.

Hotels don't tend to have a complaints department. It is a shared (and proud) role for everyone. With my hotel teams, it was always down to all of us to creatively and proactively solve a customer's problem and find a solution that makes it right.

THE GOOD, THE BAD, AND THE UGLY

With handling of customer complaints in mind, and more importantly the response to make it right, my thoughts flash from Laurel & Hardy to Clint Eastwood.

I have always felt that complaint handling and problem solving tends to fall into three extremely basic categories: Good, Bad, and Ugly. The 1966 film of the same name was hailed as a Western Masterpiece and received critical acclaim as one of the greatest films ever made. Its massive success at the worldwide box office is credited as the career-defining moment that catapulted Clint Eastwood into stardom.

Turning problems into defining moments is what it's all about. So, indulge me, if you will, in my version of The Good, The Bad, and The Ugly of complaint handling.

The Good—Make It Right

My Good category turns an aggrieved, frustrated, or upset customer into a thankful loyal fan. The positive interaction, apology, and solution not only ensure a full recovery, but cause your customer to go out of their way to tell everyone how much they love you.

International Coffee Specialist

I didn't have the time or strength to deal with it.

I have been a happy and loyal Nespresso coffee customer for several years. I treated myself to one of their smart new coffee machines for my home office and was in love with it from day one, especially the effortless convenience of their magic coffee pods. For several years it had served me well as my trusted companion, but then broke down. It was out of warranty by a few months. The burden of the immediate inconvenience hit me. It was bound to be a long and complicated process. The last thing I had was time to sort it out.

I called their Customer Care helpline and a friendly voice promptly answered. I forlornly explained my predicament.

The first words back to me, "Oh no! I am so sorry to hear this. I understand how you must be feeling. Okay, let me take care of this for you."

Not once did they put me on hold or transfer me to someone else. Nor did I have to fill in any complicated forms. It was caring and effortless.

After unsuccessfully troubleshooting the fault over the phone, they agreed to take my machine in for repair, which I begrudgingly accepted would take up to ten working days. I was therefore ecstatic when it was delivered back four days later! I excitedly opened the branded cardboard box that was filled with care—all the machine components had been carefully and neatly bubble-wrapped. There was no invoice or bill for repair charges, just a little card with a friendly message: "The repair is on us and please enjoy this little gift box tasting pack with our compliments." Inside was a selection of twelve coffee sample capsules to try.

I immediately sensed that behind the sophisticated elegance of this huge global brand was heart.

Several months later, I purchased a new and upgraded coffee machine. Upon setting it up, the water chamber started leaking.

I received an identical compassionate response from the Customer Care helpline. This time they asked me to allow up to five days for a replacement machine and finished the call by asking, "What is your favorite Nespresso coffee blend?"

The new machine arrived within twenty-four hours, along with three tubes of ten coffee capsules. The new machine was a dream and worked perfectly, but I certainly didn't expect to receive the generosity of thirty complimentary capsules. They were making a connection with goodwill that said, "We actually care." It felt like the icing on the cake, and I sincerely appreciated the gesture.

THE RESULT: PLEASURE

Nespresso has millions of customers globally, but at that moment they made me personally feel valued. I am a loyal Nespresso customer and love their product, with all the good intentions that the brand stands for.

What I love most is how they go so deep into uncovering the true sense of the word "uncomplicated."

On their website is a phone number and this simplicity:

Customer Care

Expert advice and machine troubleshooting 24/7

Speak to our Coffee Specialists anytime, 24 hours a day, 7 days a week.

I love that their motto is real: "Made with care." Beyond their products is the feeling that lives deep inside their culture. "We come together as coffee artists and coffee lovers to launch a movement devoted to coffee and to show that when care comes first, everything is possible."

Whilst things go wrong from time to time—on both occasions they provided a painless, effortless, prompt solution, along with an authentic apology. They clearly make it a practice to over-deliver and the unexpected goodwill gestures were appreciated.

What made my pleasure more acute is knowing they pride themselves on being a global brand with local presence, creating products that inspire the world. They are a massive business, yet it feels like they are connected to me personally.

So, rather than ever ordering my coffee capsules online for fast convenience, I always prefer to visit their high street boutiques. Because it's fun. They are always friendly, pleased to see me, proud to explain their products, and I enjoy the feeling of the experience.

The Bad—Make It Worse

The Bad category often causes unbearable migraine pain. This is problem-solving with defensive ignorance and arrogance. Customers are provided with no apology or solution, causing them to run away.

Fish & Chip Shop Owner

This gave me a whole new meaning to the word "disappointed." I was miserable.

We have a small and wonderful new shopping village close to home that serves our local community. The architects did a stunning job arranging this boutique and convenient amenity. It's a smart-looking place with an open-air courtyard and well laid out with around twenty retailers. There are a handful of nice outdoor shops, restaurants, beauty salons, a doctor, a dentist, a gym, a supermarket, and a children's playground. All sitting on top of four levels of free underground car parking. Everything you could need or want and all under one roof.

Amongst it all was a nicely designed fish and chip shop, with indoor seating and a huge fresh fish counter. It's a large unit and expensive-looking fit-out, which no doubt comes with a heavy rental commitment.

One Friday night and as a special family treat, we telephone-ordered fish and chips. I flew down in the car to pick it up. The boys started singing with excitement as I walked in the door and eagerly stood around me as I opened the bags of "freshly cooked fish and chips," and that's where the joy ended. Instantly I had a new meaning for the word "disappointed."

The chips were clearly cooked a while earlier and were lukewarm at best. The pieces of fish were whatever the temperature is between tepid and cold, in a soft and undercooked batter. Why would they do this and also think it's okay? Why would they be happy to send this out? Why were they happy to show such low care? I was angry and frustrated.

I called the phone number on their website ready to go into combat. No one answered and there was no message service. It just kept ringing. So, I emailed from the link on their website (that you can use to place an order) and had no response. The silence was deafening.

Now I was carrying heavy resentment for my family's ruined dinnertime treat. I took my little boy Jake with me the following day to visit the shop. I was in a calmer mood but had to say something. I played the story through as if I was in their shoes and what I might say to me! Firstly, I would be mortified and go straight into a heartfelt apology. To make it right I would then offer to remake the order then and there or at a future time. Failing that, as a token gesture, I might offer to refund the bad experience. I might also say to little Jake, "Would you like a fresh scoop of chips? They just came out of the fryer."

This is not exactly what happened. I didn't want to embarrass them or cause a dramatic scene, so I discreetly waited until there were no customers in the shop. I (politely) explained the situation. They defensively shrugged, turned their back, and walked away.

Jake needed the restroom, so we walked across the courtyard. One of the cooks from the fish and chip shop walked in behind us and proceeded to use the urinal—still wearing his blue disposable hygiene gloves. Then walked straight past the hand basins, and back out to the shop. Jake saw it too and piped up in distress, "Daddy he didn't wash his hands!" He then imitated the expression of someone vomiting.

I had to say something and went immediately back to the shop and asked him, "Are you actually serious?"

Again, he walked away, only this time waving his arms gesturing to me to leave.

THE RESULT: INTENSE PAIN

As an urgent duty of care and for the health of my fellow community—I sent an assertive but polite email to the on-site center management office. Remarkably, I never received any response. This only fanned the flames in my fire, so I started warning all our friends and telling them about the cold food and toilet experience. (Interestingly, everyone also imitated a vomiting expression, the same as Jake had done.)

I realize that it's unlikely you are in the business of fish and chips. But the heart of this simple and ridiculous example has played out in countless business environments. Sadly, though, are how common stories like this are and ultimately how profoundly damaging they are for a business.

In case you're wondering how things turned out, they were swamped with disappointed online reviews and have since closed.

The Ugly—Make It Evil

My Ugly category contains hand-grenades, explosives, and calamity. It causes permanent damage that makes your customers run away—forever. They won't look back and will warn everyone to do the same.

International Airline

The plane rattled and shook as we hit the turbulent evening storm.

There were waves of spontaneous frantic shouts and screams through the cabin as we bounced around like limp rag dolls, each trying to breathe through the anxiety. I was on my way home to Australia from the United States with two work colleagues after speaking at a spectacular conference. We had boarded the flight in Phoenix with a sense of excitement to be returning home to Sydney. Little did we know, this terrifying moment was just the beginning of the actual nightmare that was about to unravel before us.

As we said our fond farewells to our American friends after the conference ended, none of them could quite comprehend how we were about to travel for sixteen hours. Little did we know that this was about to become fifty-five hours and a traumatic nightmare that would still haunt us today.

The flight had already been delayed, but the worst was yet to come. We had sat on the runway for two long hours, waiting for takeoff clearance because of the incoming storm. The air conditioning "had a fault they were trying to fix" as we all sat there damp and sweating pathetically. By the time we were in the air, we knew that we were going to miss our connecting flight in Dallas. Panic set in as we tried to calculate how we were going to get home.

Abandoned

We landed in Dallas just after 10 p.m. and frantically ran to the gate in the next terminal building where our connecting flight was departing from. (Anyone who noticed us would have wondered if we were perhaps making the finest comedy sketch, watching the commotion of our racing effort.) But it was too late, the plane had already left.

Then it hit us. It was late and Dallas airport was completely empty. It was only us and a few others, along with a night cleaner driving his polishing machine across the marble floors. No airline staff, no security, nobody. The announcement eerily echoed around the ghost town terminal that the airport was about to close. Out of desperation, we called our airline back in Australia, who dismissively said they couldn't do anything and that we had to take it up with their partner airline who had delayed us. The real horror then began when we realized that the problem was ours to solve.

We were abandoned, and on our own to figure it out.

Thankfully by pure chance, we met a handful of fellow traumatized passengers in the same predicament. They had managed to get the partner airline to book them into a hotel and gave us the number to call. We got three rooms, with instructions to come back at 6 a.m. when the airport opened for assistance.

Into the Darkness

We were driven for miles into the darkness and left at the hotel entrance. It felt like a place where people went to disappear, maybe without a trace. We felt a sense of unease stepping into the lobby, but we were too tired to care. Yet there we were at midnight in the middle of nowhere, with our laptop computer cases and no luggage. No one knew we were there, and we wondered if this was where it would end. Standing in line to check in behind the handful of our other lost passengers, it was clear the night receptionist had been sleeping in the back office and was only awoken by our arrival. His mobile phone kept continuously ringing loudly, presumably with other lost souls who'd been given the special rescue number, but it was his "dog barking" ringtone echoing through the lobby that perfectly sealed our state of delirium. To us, it was as if we had literally stepped inside the set of a horror movie. By this stage, we had no will and simply didn't care.

On the positive, we each received a "Care Pack" with miniature toiletries as if they were made for a young child's doll house. One full squeeze of the toothpaste tube gave me a blob of paste the size of a pea (I saved half my pea for the morning), a bar of soap the size you might find in a Christmas Cracker, and little sachet of shampoo with enough to wash half your head, left or right side—it was entirely your choice.

We were also gifted with a "Care Meal Voucher" from the airline, which was enough to purchase one of the frozen sausage rolls and a bag of crisps from the hotel kiosk.

Five hours later, at 5 a.m., the three of us met in the lobby for our run back to the airport and deliriously shared our fresh nighttime stories—full credit to one of my colleagues who admitted that he'd creatively used his shampoo ration to wash his socks and then dried them on the heater. A genius move that we celebrated together and wondered if we should have done the same.

The proceeding hours were a blur of confusion and desperation. The partner airline had no record or knowledge of our plight, so we had to explain everything blow by blow. The next and only Dallas-to-Sydney flight that day was full, so they arranged to fly us up to San Francisco for the late-night connection from there in fifteen hours. We were grateful for this solution, nonetheless. Check-in would open three hours before our Sydney flight later that evening, so we spent the entire day in the departure hall. We were ecstatic when our airline opened check-in, but interestingly they also had no record or knowledge of what we had just been through, nor did they offer any sympathetic acknowledgment.

We were now zombie-numb and barely noticed being herded like cattle and shouted at through the confronting security process. We simply didn't care; we had lost all connection with the present moment.

"Sorry, We Can't Help You"

But all our angst was about to disappear; my colleague had a membership with our airline for their business lounge. We had marveled about it all day. They had showers, we could have dinner and some comfortable rest before our sixteen-hour flight home.

We excitedly presented ourselves at the Business Lounge entrance. It was a glorious sight and triumphant moment—like we had made it to the finish line! Their reaction literally felt like the roof caved in. Again, they had no idea what had happened to us (we were staggered that no one from check-in moments earlier hadn't mentioned it either). We explained it all over again, and they dismissively said, "Sorry, we can't help you."

"You can bring in one guest, but not two."

We couldn't breathe or think quickly enough. We felt devastated.

We fully appreciate that rules are important, and they can't diminish the exclusivity of their lounge membership by letting anyone in. However, they could have so easily shown some simple compassion and humble discretion. Three of their (loyal) passengers were in front of them, visibly disheveled. Our pain would have all gone away in a flash with a simple gesture and moment of empathy. They repeated, "One guest, not two—these are the rules."

I encouraged my colleagues to go in, and that I would be okay, and I would see them at the gate later. But in a moment of inspiring togetherness, almost like a line from the movie The Three Musketeers, they responded by proudly saying no, "If the three of us can't go in together, then none of us will."

THE RESULT: HORROR MOVIE

We sat near the departure gate for three hours feeling exhausted and let down. We hadn't made a fuss to anyone, or caused any commotion, or showed any bitterness. Our conversation turned into how much we hated our airline at that moment. We carried this resentment the whole flight home.

After leaving our conference in Phoenix, we each arrived home in Sydney fifty-five hours later, like horror movie zombies and still without luggage. We had to cancel work meetings, appointments, and other commitments.

We acknowledged that things go wrong from time to time, flights get delayed, and connections get missed—but what an epic shambles this had been.

On reflection, there were simple touches that could have very easily transformed our pain. Yet, we wondered how two major airlines working together in "partnership" could be so disconnected, especially with lines of communication between each other.

Had they created a straightforward method, system, or even just a simple desire to share information about our plight with each other, it would have provided an effortless sense of understanding at each of the touchpoints throughout our journey.

Instead, the broken links of communication were devastating. They had no idea what happened to us, nor did it feel that they actually cared. Whilst we ultimately received a solution—we had made it home—it was the sense of connection and apology that was missing. In the end, it's all we craved for most—some compassionate understanding.

We wrote to express the bitterness of our experience and received a cut-and-paste standard copy reply, along with some frequent flier points, to cover up the nightmare we had endured.

More Than Sorry

It is impossible to avoid the occasional upset customer. Rather than hiding away from a problem when things go wrong or becoming lost in a spiral of complicated processes and blame, you can quickly and efficiently smooth things over by being ready, open-hearted, and nimble in providing a positive reaction to turn a situation around. Your customer or consumer came to you for your product or service, and only you can do whatever is necessary to make it right—and you must.

Whenever you are faced with turning a pickle into pleasure, it is important to remember that problems, failures, and mistakes are definitely not end-of-the-world catastrophes. Yet they create an opening to our best learning and provide supreme fuel for improvement. Problems serve as our guide to positive refinement and open up the path to further greatness. By consistently embracing pickles as opportunities, rather than ever treating them as an inconvenience, we become fully present with operational progress—entirely in tune and in pole position for ongoing lasting success.

Customers who have had their dissatisfaction addressed in a positive way can become incredibly loyal advocates.

They will tell their friends, family, and even strangers about the exceptional service they received, and will keep coming back for more.

Recipe 9 Recap:
MAKING IT RIGHT

Positive customer reviews are fulfilling, but what about when things go wrong? Service recovery is a wonderful art, and when done well to make it right cultivates trust, loyalty, and growth. Whatever the type or size of a pickle—good, bad, or ugly—great pleasure can be made through your response.

Ingredients:

- ★ *Acknowledgment:* Show understanding and listen with sincerity to customer issues. Apologize appropriately and demonstrate promptness in finding the solution.
- ★ *Ownership:* Connect personally and acknowledge the situation with genuine care and validation. Make customers feel seen, heard, and understood.
- ★ *Making it right:* Get to the solution quickly, then proactively apply the lessons to create improvement and prevent repetition.

Substitutions to Make this Recipe Your Own:

When problem-solving, remember that fixing a pickle isn't just about saying sorry, it's about doing what it takes to *make it right*. Whilst a sincere and empathetic apology plays an important part when faced with an aggrieved customer, it is the solution that always matters most.

SIDE DISHES

—

EXPRESSION

"

Food, glorious food,
Hot sausage and mustard!
While we're in the mood,
Cold jelly and custard!

Lionel Bart, *Oliver!*

WORDS GLORIOUS WORDS

"**P**lease sir, I want some more?"

For some unknown reason, the song "Food Glorious Food" from the musical *Oliver!* entered my mind when creating this part of the menu. It was one of my favorite movies from my childhood. It plays during the scene when orphan Oliver Twist returns to the front of the big hall with his bowl of gruel and says to Mr. Bumble, the master, "Please Sir, I want some more?"

"More?" shouts Mr. Brumble in shocked disbelief.

I remember staring out of the window with this phrase running through my imagination and the idea came to me. *This is it!* I took a moment to think and switched the word "Food" to "Words" and this is exactly what I am excitedly bringing to life here—an extra serving of linguistic refreshment with Words Glorious Words.

Words have the power to turn an ordinary moment into joy or irritation, intrigue or dismay. And with no shortage of words to choose from—there are 171,476 of them, according to the Oxford English Dictionary—and let's not forget the languages of the world as well! It is entirely up to us to determine which emotion we want to inspire.

Think about the sheer volume of words we use daily, whether in emails, letters, business reports, or presentations. When used creatively or with subtlety, words can have the power to dramatically transform a product, brand, service, or experience. Some of us choose words without a second thought, while others carefully craft each phrase like a conductor orchestrating a linguistic symphony.

I have always been fascinated by the ability of words to connect and capture attention. Not only the words we choose, but also the intonation and cadence with which we say them. Used well, they have limitless powers to inspire emotion, create enchantment, and connect hearts, minds, and souls.

Throughout my career, I have encouraged my teams to play with their words. Our goal was to ensure customers felt our excitement, to know we were on their side.

I candidly admit that my enjoyment and enthusiasm with words in fact feels quite bizarre because English was one of my weakest subjects at school. I would always sit at the back of the class in hopes my teacher wouldn't pick me to stand up and read out loud in front of everyone. But of course, he did.

"Merrett, take it from the top of page twenty-three," he would bellow from the front of the class as my face always went bright red while I stood in blind panic to read, when all I wanted to do was just dissolve into the floor.

My mum was a speech and language therapist who specialized in helping children with Down's Syndrome. I was fascinated by her eagerness to help so many people find their voice. Mum wasn't only my mum; she was also my language coach. I am grateful that she encouraged me to not only explore and experiment with my choice of words, but to be highly present and precise with my expression. She would often sit across the table from me at home with her pile of picture cards and ask me to describe what I could see.

"Butter!" I would announce.

"Yes!" she confirmed. Then she emphasized the importance of the double-letter *t* in butter. We would make the tutting sound for *t* over and over. "With words like this, *t* is never *d*," she would say. "Butter is *never* budder."

I loved this word game she played with me. "It's the same as saying *water*. Never is it pronounced *warder*. The *t* is there for a reason."

Words have gone on to become one of my greatest curiosities and I adore causing different reactions with them. I am intrigued by how words never cost anything, yet they can elevate average business products to brilliant ones, transform mundane customer experiences to engaging interactions, and turn tedious work environments into uplifting, exciting adventures.

Let's stir up some glorious words together, shall we?

Recipe 10:
MAGNETIC EXPRESSION

"

What makes someone irresistible, is not their looks,
but the way they can make your mind tickle,
your heart race and your soul smile, all at once

Drishti Bablani

"Fully booked."

That's all she said. Nothing else. Just those two words—abrupt and confronting. Then came the uncomfortable silence, and it was down to me to awkwardly turn around and walk away.

For a couple of years, it was my favorite place in Sydney to go for a haircut. I visited every month as a loyal customer and told everyone about it too. This wasn't just a barbershop; it wasn't just a haircut. It was an occasion, an escape. It's a funky little place with four barber chairs and a tagline: "We provide a cool, comfortable place for men to get a great premium haircut." A cleverly designed, wonderFULL business that truly connected with its clients. In the window were big bold letters reading, "Free beer, free PlayStation, and free Fox Sports."

They had a small lounge area in the corner to relax with big screens—one showing live sports and the other hooked up to a PlayStation for Formula One racing—all while enjoying a free frosty cold beer as you waited your turn. There was never a rush, and in fact, no one ever seemed to care if they had to wait a while.

I popped in that afternoon as I did every month, walked up to the desk, and cheerfully said my usual line: "Hi! Could I get a quick haircut, please?"

The woman at the reception looked up at me. Her facial expression and body language said, "Can't you see we're busy?" followed quickly by those two killer words: "Fully booked."

Her tone told me I was an inconvenient interruption.

She could have said pretty much anything else, such as, "I'm so sorry, we are really busy at the moment. Can you pop back later?" or, "How does your schedule look tomorrow?" or, "Do you have time to come in and relax with a cold beer? There's a great game on Fox Sports right now, and we'll squeeze you in when we can?" But she didn't.

Those two words caused all of their hard-earned goodwill to unravel with terrifying speed. Have I been back since? No. Are they still open for business? No.

The Terrifying Power of Expression

You might remember the scene in the movie *The Wizard of Oz* when Dorothy threw a bucket of water over the Wicked Witch. With her bright green face she screeches in panic as she dissolves into the floor and disappears forever. The bucket of water in this instance has the exact same power and effect as the words we use and the way we use them when speaking with others.

Words can make or break any given moment, with the ability to uplift, transform, and connect, or disengage, destroy, and destruct. We can use them to delight and excite, irritate or frustrate. The list of emotional reactions that is caused by whatever words we select is endless. When we use words that are crisp, different, and interesting, we evoke positive responses from people. Likewise, commonly used gray, cold, or unattractive words create disconnected reactions.

Words can be whispered, spoken, even sung! Chosen well, words have magnetic powers; more so, they have the strength to make you melt—for the wrong and right reasons.

Words that Destroy the Good

My general daily character is usually pretty calm, and it takes a lot for me to lose my temper. This particular day was different.

One of the most joyful moments nearly any parent can witness takes place on Christmas Eve, with the unreserved excitement of a young child on the night that Santa comes. When Jake was seven and Zac was nine, they had been begging me to take them to our local shopping mall. They had heard all their friends on the school playground comparing stories of how they had been there and met Santa. So, I loaded them into the car, and we headed to the mall.

The boys raced frantically through the busy rows of shops. When they spotted Santa, they screamed, "He's there!" and pointed over to the jolly looking man in red, sitting in his oversized chair.

The first thing I noticed was the length of the line and there we stood, shuffling forward for twenty-five minutes. The closer we got, the more vocally excited Jake and Zac became. Finally, we reached the front and with no one else behind us, we were Santa's final visitors for the day.

Jake could hardly contain himself and proudly announced to Santa's helpers "I'm here to see Santa!" The first words from the young assistant, who turned her reply to me:

"You're in the wrong line," followed by a long pause as I just stared at her in confusion. She then sighed and pointed to the "Photo Collection Point" sign on my side of the counter, which nobody could see while everyone was lined up and standing in front of it.

This was followed by, "And we're closing now." Nothing else said. It was 4 p.m. on the dot and I could see out of the corner of my eye that Santa was about to walk away. I had a split second to decide what was about to come out of my mouth. I instantly decided that I mustn't say anything. I was devastated but discreetly threw her the strongest, most pleading expressions of desperation I could.

Jake, thankfully, seemed oblivious to what was happening, whereas Zac was very aware.

She then begrudgingly asked, "What package are you after?" She pointed to the laminated sheet of price options. Exploding inside my thoughts, all I could think to myself was, "Shame on you." But I somehow managed to not show it.

In the end, the boys got their visit with Santa and my wallet got a few notes lighter. Santa was authentically wonderful as he sat talking playfully with the boys about their dreams for Christmas.

Where Is the Joy?

Apart from Santa himself, nobody else was in the moment. It made me angry, wondering why on earth no one had thought about making the Santa experience smoother and more satisfyingly real through their word choice and action.

Santa's helpers have been employed and given instructions to stand behind the counter and process the photo package payments. In fairness to them, at no point has anyone encouraged them with what they should say (or how they should say it) to every single excited child who visits during their shift. The message shared with this team at their induction or at the start of each shift could have included how it is essential that they are fully present in the moment. That is what excellent leaders do to craft excellent customer experiences. They continuously guide operational efficiency with heart and with wonder. They also consider and share a layer of detail that is commonly overlooked—the use of words to create engaging customer experiences.

Additionally, they carefully choose the tone with which they guide their team, based on the circumstance—whether it be assertive, authoritative, gentle, exciting, teasing, happy or discreet, or something else. These are the leaders who know that their team won't always realize the tonality for specific instances and go out of their way to inspire this.

I guess that around five hundred children visit this "Photo with Santa Experience" on an average day. What if the manager, leader, or owner had simply highlighted to Santa's helpers the importance of "excitedly" welcoming each and every child. Along with using specific words like, "Santa has been so excited to see you!" or "Santa has been waiting for you all day!" That's all it would have taken. How different would each child have felt as a result? But no one here had thought of this kind of detail, only the volume of sales.

The leaders of any business must place great trust in their employees—trust that they will use the right word choice and expression. In almost every instance, hoping the team will figure it out themselves is the wrong path. No one will ever know what is expected if it hasn't been explained and encouraged, not to mention demonstrated personally.

Expression Over Process

Whilst this was a story of Father Christmas, it is a lesson that can apply to every interaction in every business: the way everyone answers the telephone, the words and tone that are used in emails and company reports, the way customers are greeted at reception . . . Anything and everything can be dramatically altered through word choice and tone.

Santa's helpers here were comparable in many ways to hotel receptionists the world over. There is so much that can be expressed in that precious short moment of first impression.

A few years ago, I was excited to have the chance to speak at a conference in Orlando. From Sydney it was twenty-two hours of flying and from leaving home to arriving at the hotel was twenty-nine hours of traveling—and that is before you consider the backward sixteen-hour time difference.

I was dazed, numb, and relieved by the time I finally walked through the hotel front doors into the tranquility of the grand lobby. I had never stood in an entrance hall quite like this, with a hotel in front of me that housed 1400 rooms. I enjoyed how my shoes effortlessly squeaked with every step across the immaculately polished marble floor as I closed the long distance between the entrance and the huge reception desk to speak with the immaculately dressed reception team in front of me.

Did I get some kind of friendly greeting such as "Good morning!" or "Welcome!"? No. The first words the receptionist asked without taking her eyes off her screen were, "Checking in?" This was followed by, "Can I get your photo ID and credit card?"

When my reservation popped up on her computer, revealing my Australian address that she diligently cross checked with my ID, did it prompt some sort of human exchange? Did she ask, "How was your journey from Australia?" No. Did she say, "Welcome to Orlando."? Also no.

I quickly realized she was simply "processing" me as she did with all the other guests—following the script and procedure the hotel leadership had given her. She pointed me in the direction of my room, then turned to the next guest, and asked, "Checking in? Can I get your ID and credit card?"

The words we use (or don't use) tell everyone everything they need to know about us. Just as the receptionist could have easily added any kind of welcome or shown some interest in my arrival. When this doesn't occur, the words not said speak louder than those that were. The opportunity will always be lost.

Many single words have the power to change everything: imagination, creativity, thought, presence . . . And of course, amongst others, my favorite word of all: *wonder*. There are a million tiny ways to create huge magnetic reactions from the people you interact with, including consciously playing with the way you express the things you say. How adventurous or daring are you with your expression?

Using Magnetic Words to Create Wonderlicious Moments

Checking-in for my connecting flight to Orlando, there was a family with two very young, very excited children at the booth adjacent to me. I overheard them explaining how they were going to Disneyland. The crew member serving them came around from behind her booth and knelt down on one knee to be eye-level with the little girl and boy, and asked, "Are you going to meet Mickey Mouse?"

They nodded eagerly.

She handed them their boarding passes for the flight and said, "Well, you must hold on tight to your magic ticket to take you there!"

The crew member could have simply handed the parents all four boarding passes and said, "Have a nice flight," before turning to the line of waiting passengers and calling out, "Next!" Instead, she stepped fully inside the moment. It took her thirty seconds longer—thirty seconds that transformed the experience for these two little children. She created a moment of wonder. Her words utterly transfixed the children and I imagine they will never forget it.

During my flight, it came time for the coffee service. I asked if it was possible to have tea instead. Immediately the member of the crew replied, "Oh, it's my specialty!" She smiled and paused, watching for it to register with me. *Special-tea.* As her play on words sunk in, we both burst out laughing. She handed me my cup of English breakfast with a chirpy, "Enjoy!" Then, off she went, resuming her task of pouring her coffee.

Wonder is all around us in every moment when we allow it.

I purchased some new business shirts from one of my favorite retailers here in Australia, Peter Jackson. Their in-store service always comes with an air of pride and so I always love shopping there. As I paid for my shirts, the young man serving me finished by saying, "Now, let me find you a nice bag for these."

The fact that it went beyond the usual, "Do you need a bag? They are fifteen cents each," was wonderful. I like my Peter Jackson shirts, but I love the feeling of connection to the attentiveness of their brand.

Emotionally Connected Expression with Honesty

For any couple, a wedding day is unquestionably one of life's greatest, most cherished celebrations. For a hotel venue and team, hosting a wedding is an incredible privilege. During my earlier hotel career, I organized and managed several hundred wedding receptions. Commonly, around eighteen months go into meticulous preparation, organization, and planning for such an event.

Imagine you are the general manager of the Four Seasons Hotel in Bali. You are hosting a wedding reception tomorrow. You are reviewing the arrivals list for the following day with your front-office team as you do every day, and suddenly you realize an unfathomable disaster. It is brought to your attention that you have overbooked your hotel rooms—in particular the honeymoon suite. The unintended victims of this error are the bride and groom arriving tomorrow. This lands firmly on your shoulders to lead and handle the situation with your team. What on earth would you do? You review the correspondence that had been sent to the wedding couple, confirming everything and promising them the most memorable time of their lives.

You likely wouldn't sleep that night worrying about the horrendous situation you will face tomorrow.

The following story is one of my all-time favorites. It comes from my dear friend in the UK, Derek Williams, founder and CEO of The WOW! Awards—the only awards program of its kind in the world, based purely on customer nominations. This is one of the stories that was sent in to them:

> "My neighbors had just got married and went on their honeymoon to Bali and stayed at the Four Seasons, the finest hotel on the island. As a special treat, they booked the honeymoon suite. Upon arrival at the hotel, they were informed that the honeymoon suite was double booked for the first two nights and so they would have to stay in a regular bedroom.
>
> The general manager apologized profusely, but the couple were not only angry but also quite upset, as this was their honeymoon. The hotel offered a complimentary dinner, free excursions, and bottles of champagne by way of apology. The couple went to their room still slightly upset but pleased with the way the hotel had reacted to the problem.

On the second day the couple went on their excursion and returned to be informed that they could move to the honeymoon suite. They opened the door and looked into the luxury of the suite. The wife burst into tears.

On the bed, spelled out in rose petals, was the word, "SORRY."

We all have limitless power to create a positive emotional connection with others through our thoughtful expression. Especially in the midst of worst-possible-scenario moments.

The rose petals will have cost the hotel nothing but meant everything. The general manager and his team sat down together and talked through the problem with one focus in mind—the solution. They wanted to create emotional connection through authenticity. They would have discussed it as a team and prepared for the difficult conversation. The bride and groom's heavy disappointment dissolved in an instant—because they knew how much the hotel cared. They felt it and appreciated it, to the point of their next-door neighbor feeling compelled enough to write and tell The WOW! Awards about it, who in turn provided the hotel with award-winning recognition for their customer care!

Imagine if the hotel had just brushed it under the carpet by offering a discounted room rate upon check-out. The wedding couple would have left bitterly disappointed and surely would have told everyone of their upset. Instead, now they will be loyal fans and highly likely to recommend not just this specific hotel but Four Seasons Hotels anywhere in the world.

Clever Business Enhancement with a Simple Twist of Words

Another time, after delivering a training program in Washington DC, my clients generously invited me to dinner before my trip back to Australia. We went to the stunning 2941 Restaurant. It was one of the most celebrated restaurants in the area, surrounded by immaculate landscaping, ponds, and waterfalls. Everything about the place was lush and exciting, especially the warm welcome and proud hospitality. I sat reveling over the menu of Executive Chef Bertrand Chemel, with contemporary American cuisine, emphasized delightfully with bold French and Mediterranean twists. Beyond the excellent culinary treats that came from the kitchen, it was the discreet air of playfulness with the dining-room team and their choice of words that made the experience so very engaging and memorable.

Following the masterfully elegant clearing of our main course plates, the waitress returned and warmly asked, "May I tease you with something sweet to finish?"

We all unanimously and politely declined, saying we couldn't possibly, each rubbing our full tummies. But nonetheless she left the dessert menus on the table edge, so we couldn't help but look. We all ordered dessert!

In just about every restaurant around the world, the dessert menu is nearly always called "The Dessert Menu." But not here. At 2941 it was called, "Never Say Never."

A strike of simple, creative genius. It cost absolutely nothing to do this, but as I watched the other tables the rest of the evening, I noticed that almost everyone ordered dessert. The increase in revenue, repeated across every dinner service, must undoubtedly make a significant difference to this business income.

More than only playing with these three words, it was clear as day that they had also engaged as a team and thought about their expression for when they approach the dessert moment, to entice their guests with "May I tease you with something sweet to finish?" Using the words "May I," not "May we," and "tease" (which every member of the restaurant team used, with warmth and with personal ownership) made the irresistible difference.

What struck me most was how fully in the moment our server was. As she went around our table taking our dessert order, she acknowledged each request with comments such as, "I am so pleased you are ordering this," and "lovely choice."

When I ordered the crème brûlée, she said, "You are going to love how we make this."

I remember that never-say-never moment whenever I am asked if I would like to see the dessert menu.

Several months later we were having a family lunch at a beachside restaurant near where we live. At the end of lunch one of the team came over with the dessert menu and asked, whilst friendly enough, "Are we after any desserts today?"

Our instant reply: "No thank you, just the bill please."

As she left to prepare the bill, I noticed that hardly anyone had ordered dessert. It hadn't crossed their mind to stop and consider why.

When you consider both stories, you see how easily the words we choose to use can create experiences worth remembering, reasons to return over and over again. *Or not.*

Avoid Autopilot Expressions

The opportunity to create a magnetic connection inside of any moment is in our hands. Never did I formally dictate with any of my teams what they must strictly say in every single scenario. I did, however, take the time to highlight certain words I wanted them to use and which ones to stay away from, along with the reason why. Never did I preach but involved everyone with consistent encouragement.

The top expression I took with me from my time in hotels was to always avoid the phrase, "No problem."

Whenever a customer said, "Thank you," our response was never "no problem." It might appear friendly enough, but why would we ever suggest that providing wonderful customer service experiences could be a problem in the first place? A genuine "You're welcome," is always one of the warmest options. There are countless simple alternatives to the phrase, "No problem."

> *"You are more than welcome."*
> *"You are very welcome."*
> *"Don't mention it."*
> *"Anytime!"*
> *"It has been a pleasure."*

The list goes on.

"Not bad" is another autopilot expression in the same league as "No problem," that always makes me flinch! Whether you are face to face or on the phone, it is like saying, "Well, I'm kind of good, but maybe not that great."

I get it, you're probably busy or concentrating on something else, or it has become a simple habitual figure of speech. Regardless, there are a million better responses than "Not bad."

> *"I am very well, thank you."*
> *"I'm great, thanks, how about you?"*
> *"I'm doing well, thank you."*

Then there's the often misused "We." When used flippantly, "we" can create an especially peculiar or disconnecting feeling to all involved. For example, when "We" is used instead of saying "You" such as when opening a team meeting or addressing a group, it can feel odd for the recipients. "How are we all today?" may appear innocent enough, however "How are you today?" is always far more genuine and attractive. "You" makes it personal to everyone individually.

The Easiest Investment

Real, magnetic connection will never flourish within a stifled, distracted culture if little or no thought goes into the use of written and spoken words. Becoming more playful, experimental, and passionate with your words, especially in front of your customers, will only ever reap rewards.

The best part about playing with words is that they are completely free! Choose them well and they will not only make others melt for the right reasons, but also define you or your brand, create loyalty, growth, and influence profitability too.

On the other hand, making people melt for the wrong reasons—by being ordinary, disconnected, or dull with words—can end up costing you a fortune.

Whichever ones you choose to share with someone today might just change the course of your life and theirs.

MAGNETIC EXPRESSION

Words, tone, and expression possess the power to uplift and inspire—but also to destroy. They can create wonderlicious moments, magnetic connections, and experiences that others will always remember and share. The key lesson here is that words matter.

Ingredients:

- ★ Careful, curious, playful, empathetic word choices.
- ★ Avoidance of tired, generic, or disconnected phrases.
- ★ Tone and expression that are carefully chosen to differentiate your brand and presence.
- ★ Foster an encouraging environment for your team to express themselves clearly.

Substitutions to Make this Recipe Your Own:

The wonder of words is that there are countless substitutions and choices to set the tone in your life, leadership, and business. Lead by example and start to play with words. With 171,476 words in the Oxford English Dictionary at your disposal, there are limitless possibilities, and they don't cost a cent!

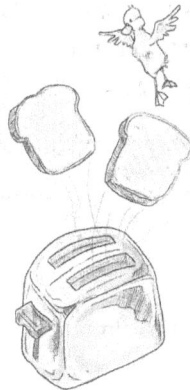

Recipe 11:
WORD WIZARDRY

"

No one cares how much you know, until they know how much you care

Theodore Roosevelt

I magine you put on a blindfold and spin around several times . . .

That is often how companies feel as they try to make contact with the outside world—with potential customers, clients, and consumers. And sometimes, that's also how customers feel when trying to find you.

We have never had so many options at our fingertips, so many ways to get everything and anything we need. If you're a business, that means it's easy to get lost in noise.

It doesn't matter how clever, sophisticated, or unique your products and services are if your messaging is off. The way you express yourself in your marketing and inter-actions are what will make you either wonderfully irresistible or miserably invisible. You have only the blink of an eye to catch people's attention and make them want to find out more.

For any establishment, department store, business, or product, the easiest way to cap-ture attention is to do something different. That is often accomplished through simple descriptive words that activate a desire.

Finding the Way Past Sameness

The next time you go out, take a look at shop windows. You will see a variety of words on display that are meant to entice you inside:

> "Half price sale"
> "Clearance prices today"
> "50% discount"
> "Price freeze"
> "All prices reduced"

There are so many variations that this almost becomes invisible, and you don't think twice about walking right by.

Priceline is one of Australia's favorite national pharmacy, health, and beauty chains with high-street stores all around the country. They created their own unique spark through their words: "Paying less is a beautiful thing." Another gem comes from Australia's national DIY superstore chain Bunnings, with their well-known tagline: "Lowest prices are just the beginning."

People may notice your website, hear about your new offering, or be interested in something they spotted in your marketing. That is an important stepping stone. However, capturing their attention with words that are interesting, different, or full of heart gives them no choice but to jump right in.

We love visiting our local greengrocer shop to buy our fresh vegetables and fruit. There are hundreds of other places close by where we could purchase similar products, but we go to our greengrocer instead. We are connected to the way they have put their heart into bringing their products alive with descriptive words. They have *juicy blueberries* whereas the next-door supermarket sells blueberries—same product and price, except our greengrocers have added a personality and a feeling. They have created a touch of irresistibility that draws us in on autopilot, along with all their other loyal customers.

A Split Second to Capture Attention

We all know that breweries produce beer, hotels provide bedrooms, retailers sell products, winemakers produce wine, baristas craft coffee, and the list goes on. Everyone in business has a product or service and a brand, as do organizations trying to create an excellent business culture for their employees.

There is a plentiful array of commonality across the world, and many often fall into the default of going with the flow and describing things the same that everyone else does—i.e., Beer = Beer; Concierge = Concierge; Shiraz = Shiraz; Socks = Socks; Tea Bags = Tea Bags, etc. Yet out there amongst us all are the wizards, like my greengrocers—the companies and brands that take additional steps to stand out and capture attention with a loyal fan base, their customers, by daring to be adventurous with their descriptive words.

It starts with applying an uncommon belief that it is important to follow your heart and dare to be different. You may well not believe you are a creative wordsmithing genius, but I bet you will be surprised by what comes out of you when you allow it. Throughout my working life I have consistently given my teams an open invitation, inside a no-judgment environment, to play and have fun with creativity. It's amazing what happens with people when you share permission to put forward their word ideas.

My Ten Favorite Wizardry Words of Adventurous Brands

Whilst I realize you may well not be in the same business or area of specialty as my personal Top 10 Word Wizards, playing with your words is easily transferable, no matter what your task, environment, or line of business might be.

My special showcase of *Wizards* comes from fascinating organizations and adventurous brands who have captured highly positive attention, abundant success, competitive edge, increased sales, business transformation and brand reputation—by daring to be different with their use of words. They have amplified their products, services, and profitability by simply (and courageously) casting a spell through their linguistic creativity . . .

1. Tea Bags & Chocolate Eggs

Whenever I go home to London, I always include a visit to my favorite address, Fortnum & Mason, the wonderful department store—it has been in Piccadilly since 1707 and is always brimming with authentic grace and wonder from times gone by.

Fortnum first started creating their hampers in the 1730s, after being asked by customers (traveling from London to their country estates) to prepare picnic baskets for the road. Founded as a grocery store, Fortnum's reputation was built on supplying quality food. As a result, they saw rapid growth throughout the Victorian era. Today, the store continues to focus on stocking a variety of specialty and basic provisions, all presented in the most splendid and joyful way possible.

I love how they continuously move with the times. Fortnum's often turns its iconic food products into other things. For example, their famous Chocolossus Biscuits, Rose & Violet Creams and Florentines are now all flavors in the ice cream parlor, and their Blanc de Blanc Champagne and Kir Royal have been turned into ice popsicles.

But amongst all the charm is their playfulness with their words that their loyal customers love. Fortnum's are famous for their tea—and of course, they don't just sell tea bags, they sell *silky* tea bags. Just by adding the word *silky*, they have created an enhanced feeling, desire and experience. This single word also highlights their quality, superiority, and difference. People faithfully go to Fortnum's for their tea and are happy to pay a tiny amount more for their *silky* tea bags.

There are a million types of enticing chocolate and old-fashioned confectionery. I love their chocolate hazelnut praline filled eggs. They look just like real eggs and are sold the same way, by the half-dozen in a traditional cardboard egg box. Except on the box, it doesn't say "Six Chocolate Eggs." This would be too obvious.

Can you remember what the goose laid in one of Aesop's Fables? There was once a countryman who possessed the most wonderful goose you can imagine, for every day when he visited the nest, the goose had laid a beautiful, glittering, golden egg.

And that's precisely what Fortnum's created for their customers; boxes of "Six Golden Eggs." By changing the word chocolate to *golden*, they have created an irresistible feeling of nostalgia and turned this product into a gorgeous piece of magic.

2. Ice-Cold Beer

On the way home to Australia from a family holiday, we had a stopover in Singapore. It was steaming hot outside, with wild humidity making it desperately impossible to maneuver through the lively, colorful alleyways of Chinatown. We practically threw ourselves into a tiny side street restaurant filled with locals sitting at little plastic tables and chairs. I guess we were a sight for sore eyes, as our pathetically hot, bright red faces and sweaty appearance soon became the talking point and entertainment of everyone. As we fanned ourselves frantically with the menu cards, all I urgently needed right then was an icy cold beer.

The grandmother of the family restaurant cheerfully brought me a frosted cold bottle of beer cleverly named *Snow* along with an unusual small plastic teacup. It was perfection! Simple brilliance in its one-word execution.

I have since found out that *Snow*, brewed by CR Snow in Shenyang, China, has been the best-selling beer in the world by volume since 2008. Snow is sold largely in China to the tune of an estimated one hundred million hectoliters each year. In comparison, fifty million hectoliters of Budweiser, the #2 brand in the world, were sold in the same period.

3. Government Charter

His Highness Sheikh Mohammed bin Rashid Al Maktoum, UAE Vice President, Prime Minister, and Ruler of Dubai, stunned the world in 2016, by announcing the creation of a "Ministry of Happiness" with the vision "To be among the happiest countries in the world." The UAE cabinet endorsed *The National Happiness and Positivity Charter*, which stipulates the UAE government's commitment to happiness at the core of public policy to provide an environment of happiness for the people of Dubai.

The government entity, Smart Dubai, launched the Happiness Agenda to fuel its city transformation to happiness by adopting a globally unique, science-based, and methodical approach to measure, impact, and sustain happiness for the whole city.

I was excited to have the chance to visit Dubai in 2015 for an international awards event, and before I flew home, I took the chance to visit one of the local government offices. Ordinarily, these are often unwelcoming, stand-in-a-long-line kinds of places.

The huge sign above the door with the words *Local Government Office* has been replaced with *Customer Happiness Center.* I had to step inside to see and yes, it was entirely real—warm, welcoming, and highly organized.

It didn't stop here. I jumped on one of the open-top tourist buses, to take in the sights before we left, and passed a giant roadside billboard promoting the local police service, with the proud hashtag *#YourSecurityOurHappiness.* We drove past *Happiness Street* and at breakfast in the hotel above the coffee machine was the sign *Happiness Brewed Here.*

More than a flimsy hollow word, it's real and it's everywhere! It comes from the top, and everyone is proudly following. Dubai and The United Arab Emirates are climbing the ranks of the World Happiness Report and reached twenty-sixth out of 149 countries in terms of happiness levels in 2023.

4. Tomato Ketchup

Do you know how much sugar is in your ketchup? Kids love to douse everything from their burgers to eggs in the red stuff, perhaps because of how sweet it tastes. There's no wonder it tastes sweet. A tablespoon-size serving has around four grams of sugar, which is more sugar than a typical chocolate chip cookie. But how many kids actually limit themselves to one tablespoon? My boys merrily squeeze and squirt two or three tablespoons onto their burgers, which means they are consuming about twelve grams of sugar, a whole day's worth for a child, just through a condiment.

Imagine taking sugar completely out of ketchup and children would surely hate it? Not so! What if there was a new healthy (and fun) ketchup that excited our kids and filled them with wonder? Could you come up with a single word that blends the words "wonder" and "ketchup"? One word that would not only capture attention, but also win the hearts of kids and grown-ups alike? A UK family-run "superhero food business" was determined to do something very different with ketchup. And in 2019, Wonderchup was born!

Wonderchup is a delicious and healthy tomato ketchup. It has no added sugar, salt, sweetener or fructose, just natural ingredients that include tomatoes, red and yellow peppers, beetroot, rosemary, and apple cider vinegar. They threw in some "brain health and wellbeing" too with "superhero vitamins" B6, B9, B12, D3, and E. And for extra goodness, they also added the antioxidant Lycopene, which is the natural flavoring of *umami* and *kokumi*—a Japanese word that roughly translates to "delicious" and is considered the sixth taste on the tongue.

So, I wonder, if you saw a plastic bottle of tomato ketchup next to the glass bottle of Wonderchup on the supermarket shelves—which one might make it into your shaping basket?

5. Unique Customer Experience Philosophy

For my fiftieth birthday, I was whisked away by surprise to experience the W Hotel in Brisbane. I use the word "experience" here quite intentionally because this is exactly what it was, every single part and moment of it.

W is an upscale lifestyle hotel chain owned by Marriott International, which as of 2020, operates sixty-six hotels in twenty-five countries with over sixteen thousand rooms. Their hospitality is sophisticated, vibrant, fun, soulful, exciting—and daringly attentive. W represents "wow service," and everyone is encouraged to provide an unassuming air of the extra special.

I noticed at check-in that they didn't have a concierge desk in the lobby. Strange I thought, but then I saw it. They have replaced the word concierge with two new words—proudly displayed on the desk adjacent to reception: "*Whatever Whenever.*" More than words, their entire culture and service philosophy is based on this principle, and it's completely real.

For W Hotels, this means doing the unexpected to deliver a service that is truly exceptional. Encapsulated in the *Whatever Whenever* promise: customers are at liberty to, within reason, ask for whatever they want, whenever they want it. Indeed, this might simply mean a different type of pillow, although W Hotels have put no limit on what they will try to deliver.

I forgot my phone charger, an often-irritating problem for hotels who rarely have a replacement for guests who need it. I called the *Whatever Whenever* number from my room and a real person picked up the phone almost instantly and their response was exciting, "Certainly Mr. Merrett, we will be with you in a flash." The spare phone charger arrived sixty seconds later, without any complicated paperwork to complete or any holding deposit to pay.

W Hotels' proficiency is rooted in its passionate and enthusiastic customer experience design, which strives to surprise and delight its guests in the most simple and unique ways. It was one of the best hotel experiences I've ever had.

6. Socks

Until the turn of the last decade or so, socks were still pretty much just socks—an everyday item that served a purpose and was never really considered a fashionable part of our wardrobe. But that was all about to change. In 2008 two friends in

Sweden, Mikael Söderlindh and Viktor Tell, had a vision: to spread happiness and bring color to every corner of the world by turning an everyday essential into a vibrant design statement.

They added the word "Happy" to their socks and quickly established a highly desirable and quality sock that combines unique designs and craftsmanship. Today, Happy Socks has reached ninety countries and every continent. With concept stores all around the world, from LA to Tokyo, Happy Socks can be found in over ten thousand top fashion apparel boutiques.

By playing with their words, they are indeed coloring the world by energetically introducing one single word . . . *Happy*!

7. Business Mission Tagline

Can you sum up your business purpose or culture and fully define it with three words? More than only this, three words that define the culture for both your employees and your customers?

Ovolo Hotels is one of my favorite hotel brands. It is an independent hospitality company, headquartered in Hong Kong, which owns and operates a small collection of individually designed lifestyle hotels there and around Australia. The company keeps in touch with the modern traveler through creative interiors, convenience-driven comforts, and focused all-inclusive services, all presented in a signature style of wonder.

It's their business tagline that everyone adores: "Shiny Happy People." And it's more than just three words. It is completely real. When you check in, you become a shiny, happy person, and every single member of the Ovolo team lives and breathes it.

It is their vibrant personality that I admire the most. They say:

"We set the stage for effortless living. Our Mission: Shiny Happy People. That is what we want to see, everywhere. Walking in and out of our hotels, sitting at our desks in the office, we want everyone to be happy, that is the ultimate achievement in life, after all.

"We're Ovolo. Young at heart, fun-loving and a little bit wild. We don't behave like other hotels . . . we do things differently. We say what we think, we don't hold back. We love to feel free, and hate being told that we can't do something. We believe that rules are there to bend."

Our Mission—Shiny Happy People

1. *Make our guests shine everyday!*
2. *Happy and productive workplace*
3. *Meaningful contributions to people and society*

They also say, "It's like absolutely nothing else out there," and I wholeheartedly agree!

8. Wine Maker

The Hunter Valley, north of Sydney in New South Wales, is one of Australia's major wine regions, with a viticultural history dating back to the early 1800s. With over 150 wineries, this is not only Australia's oldest wine region but a firm favorite with visitors each year who come to encounter the many varieties of cellar doors and exciting wines on offer. However, the ongoing success of each winemaker comes with relentless hard work to stand out. For example, how would you dare to be different so that your Shiraz stands out from the huge array of other Shirazes produced in the Hunter?

We always enjoy visiting the Piggs Peake winery. They describe themselves with the two words: *Unique Boutique*. It's an unusual place and it's fun. Each of their wines are proudly and playfully characterized in some way with pigs. In fundamental terms, it's a winery and their wines are divinely delicious. For me (and countless others), it was love at first sight.

I have been fascinated to learn how far they go all out to bend and twist the rules of winemaking. It's not uncommon when you are doing a tasting at Piggs to hear others using words like Heston Blumenthal and Willy Wonka to describe the environment.

They produce the classic wines, but also unusual varieties you've never experienced before. There are superb examples of Hunter Valley Sémillons and Shirazes made at Piggs. But it's things like Moree Pedro Ximenez and Orange Zinfandels that take you by surprise and make you stop and think. Their grapes are sourced from Moree, Mudgee, Orange, Young, McLaren Vale, and the Hunter Valley. Then as soon as the grapes arrive, this is when the fun starts . . .

Steve Langham (*Boss Hogg*) has been at the helm of the winery since the 2003 vintage. His early career as a chemical engineer shows itself through the wines and styles that Piggs Peake has become famous for. As the leader of this great little business, he breathes an air of play through his team.

Most cellar doors in the Hunter have little sherry-size tasting glasses. Not at Piggs. They have large glasses, like the ones you'd get out for a special occasion at home for your fanciest dinner party.

Each July, they hold a series of fancy dress themed release nights in the winery to showcase their new wines for their members. Obviously, the members of Piggs Peak aren't referred to, or treated as, "members." That would be far too ordinary. They are "Lucky Swines."

I can never choose between the three Shiraz varieties and end up buying one of each. Themed from *The Three Little Pigs*, there is: House of Straw; House of Sticks, and House of Bricks. But then there are the top shelf reds, their signature heavyweight big hitters that come out. Kevin (named after American actor Kevin Bacon) and not for the faint hearted—Big Pig, Werewolf, and Bushpig.

As you can imagine, their sparkling isn't called sparkling, but Sporkling, and their champagne—Ham Pain—is enchanting. Another favorite sparkling is Pig Juice—something easy to drink on a Sunday morning with pancakes or drizzle on scoops of ice-cream.

Then there's the Wiggly Tail Marsanne; the rose—Rosed Pork and the only red sweet dessert wine in the Hunter: Suckling Pig Shiraz, which is ridiculously brilliant with dark chocolate!

The wine is sensational, and they bring it all to life by playing with their words. But does this all sound too silly to be taken seriously?

In the early days, their 2005 Wolfie was written up as the greatest Zinfandel ever made in Australia. Then the 2005 Sémillon and the 2004 Cabernet Merlot were listed in Halliday's Best of the Best section. The 2006 Cabernet Merlot was written up as the best in Australia—and this little gem of a winery has never looked back since.

9. Chili Sauce

Type "Chili Sauce" into Google and you get 91,700,000 results. If you were in the business of chili sauce, what descriptive words would you apply to your product to create irresistible attention and a loyal customer base?

Through our local farmers markets, I have come to know The River Kitchen, south of Sydney and based down the road from us by the river in Woronora. It was started by John Slye in 2014 after being made redundant from his IT corporate job. He took some time out to think about what he really wanted to do for a living and pondered his relenting desire to share his love of cooking with others. And so, The River Kitchen was born.

John and his little team pride themselves on creating home-like sauces, using quality ingredients. They hand make, hand pour, and label their sauces in small batches using traditional methods. There is Lemon Curd (just like my Grandmother used to make), Chocolate Caramel (described as: This cheeky chocolate number is a bit like a melted Mars bar), Salted Caramel, Peanut Butter Caramel, and the big favorite and point to my example: Smoke 'n' Hot—their stunning chili sauce.

They have put their full hearts into the customer experience of their sauces and added a special ingredient. On the label it reads, "*Ingredients: red chili, apple vinegar, chipotle chili, ginger, garlic, and now with added happiness.*" Who could believe that this tiny, but hearty play with words has seen them crowned several times over at the Sydney Royal Fine Food Awards?

10. Delivery Service

Rather than uncovering a magic word—what if a single letter could change everything? I love simple brilliance and tiny touches of wonder that cause massive waves of positivity. The utter simplicity that's easily missed through our complicated ways.

Following a speaking engagement in Nashville, I spent several days exploring and walked several blocks out into the industrial area. My greatest find? The small business unit of The Little Blue Menu and their magic letter *S*. A new dining delivery concept with their tagline painted on the wall for all to see, "Delivery that goes the extra smile."

The Little Blue Menu is an online business and therefore people call in their orders. Customers didn't physically go there, but I couldn't resist seeing if "delivery with a smile" was real and popped my head in the door! They were surprised but pleased to see me and the first thing I noticed was their immaculate team uniforms. I asked a young team member, "What's the Little Blue Menu?"

Without skipping a beat, she proudly announces, "We make and deliver tasty wings, burgers, and other special treats!"

"And do I order the extra smile?" I asked playfully.

"No! You get that automatically!" she said beaming and we laughed together.

It was such a wonderful reminder that enhancing business with touches of wonder requires only the smallest and most humble of ideas.

Becoming a Word Wizard: What Else?

There is no formal application process to becoming a "Word Wizard." Blindfolds aren't required either. Just an open heart of inquisitiveness to consistently consider *what else*.

This is the starting point. *What else* could you do, say, or try to make something sound more irresistible through your choice of words?

Through all of our busyness, it will always be much easier to just copy what everyone else is doing. But why blend in with common word choices when there are numerous easy ways to stand out?

Recipe 11 Recap:
WORD WIZARDRY

In a world brimming with options, standing out is essential. By infusing your services, experiences, and brand with unique word choices, you can create an irresistible allure. Set yourself apart amongst a sea of sameness. Create brand magic by spinning descriptive words that captivate and invite people to stop, notice, and engage.

Ingredients:

- ★ A break-away from vocabulary norms to embrace words that evoke emotion and connection.
- ★ An injection of playfulness into the way you and your brand infuse personality into the messages you share with the world.
- ★ Unexpected, clever messaging designed to cause irresistible delight for customers at every turn.
- ★ An incorporation of new experiences and messaging for classic products.
- ★ Involvement and encouragement of your team to explore and suggest new word ideas.

Substitutions to Make this Recipe Your Own:

Think like some of the "Word Wizards" you've read about in this recipe. They haven't spent a fortune on gimmicks, but they have spent time to inject personality and connection into each message they put out into the world. How can you swap out the generic, boring messaging for something that sparks a smile, a laugh, or inspires the words, "I have to have that."

Recipe 12:
GOBBLEDYGOOK ALTERNATIVES

"

[Excerpt from memorandum sent to government employees 24 March 1944]
Stay off the gobbledygook language. It only fouls people up. For the
Lord's sake, be short, say what you're talking about and use plain English.

Maury Maverick
Chairman, Smaller War Plants Corporation

At some point in time, we have all undoubtedly encountered that meeting, overheard that conversation, or received that email in which someone offers to "*touch base offline*" before "*going on the journey*" for "*low hanging fruit.*"

You might have heard someone suggesting some "*blue sky thinking*" ahead of "*looking under the bonnet*" and then having a "*thought shower.*" Or possibly you received the request to "*run it up the flagpole*" before everyone gathers together to "*sing from the same hymn sheet*" so that you can "*move the needle.*" You might have even had the request to "*boil the ocean*" to assist "*getting on the same page.*"

Underneath the surface of corporate communication, through the corridors and meeting rooms of companies the world over, lurks something menacing. The tangled web of peculiar business jargon that has mesmerized the rank and file around the globe. It is possible, likely even, that you have heard these odd expressions, or at worst, you've fallen under the poisonous spell of the invisible linguistic monster spreading up the walls of businesses like black mold—*gobbledygook.*

In every good book or at every good party there's always a black sheep. This is the black sheep recipe, where for once, I'm going to suggest what not to do instead of what to do. The fastest way to destroy wonder in the workplace is by using sentences that are gobbledygook. Especially clichés, overused euphemisms, and expressions that serve no purpose, and actually don't mean much of anything at all.

Imagine what could be created if instead of gobbledygook, we used clear praise or precise recommendations, or plain language instead of trying to put it into some cliché nonsense. This is my one black sheep, my one faux pas, things that I see that sabotage wonder in the workplace.

The Uncontrollable Desire to Staple the Boss's Tongue to the Desk

I have sat through my fair share of corporate business meetings, conversations and presentations in my time. My memory is hazy from the numerous meetings I participated in, where I didn't always understand (and even questioned) the reason I was actually there.

It wouldn't be uncommon for me to walk away from office meetings feeling dazed, numb, or disconnected—or all three. The business jargon gobbledygook, peppered with a blended crossfire of confusing acronyms, made my head spin and eyes glaze over. It was a similar feeling to the sensation you experience when you come up to the surface from swimming in deep water and you find sound to be muffled until your ears clear. All I could hear through my trance was gobbledygook. If I ever caught the eye of others who shared my pain, they would secretly pull deranged faces at me across the meeting table.

In the corporate world—and please excuse my "gentle" sarcasm here—the jargon of gobbledygook business phrases and management lingo causes people to want to scream inside their heads. It fires up an uncontrollable desire to staple the boss's tongue to the desk. I was no exception.

Individuality Has Its Rightful Place

Every industry, organization, and company has its own individual style of expression with useful and familiar in-house phrases and technical statements. This comes with acronyms, in-house terminology, and references that everyone internally understands and serves a convenient and important purpose. This isn't gobbledygook.

Like I explained in Recipe 3 with chefs and their *mise en place*, this is an actual thing. In Recipe 8 Zappos with the *FNG—The Fantastic New Girl*, this is a genius differentiator inside the heart of their culture, showing the world what is possible with groundbreaking service innovation. This isn't gobbledygook either.

Different countries, too, have their own unique societal expressions. "Sweet as" is the common way in New Zealand to say something is great. In Australia, it is, "No worries." Gobbledygook isn't this.

It's the layer of mindless expression that festers beyond all of this. The invented "corporate jargon and business buzzwords" that clog the arteries of organizations functionality and spirit. The enemy of plain English that causes insanity, a language that uses a variety of words but at the same time doesn't say much or make much actual sense.

In an attempt to blend in with corporate culture and the "gobbledygook," everyone subconsciously follows the strange expressions, without any understanding or empowerment to change it. And so, we watch our language and stick to what has been prescribed instead of saying what we really feel.

Parlez-vous Gobbledygook? (Do You Speak Gobbledygook?)

Jargon is a bad habit—a common, growing infection within modern businesses around the globe. Everyone has become fixated with "moving the needle," yet why on earth are we trying to uplift our business cultures with such nauseating peculiarity? Is this even necessary?

The easy answer is, "No."

The expression "moving the needle" first appeared in England during the industrial revolution. The reference was for the gauge on steam engines. During World War II, it became a more common term in reference to aviation gauges. This makes such perfect sense for *that* purpose and *that* moment in time.

So, the next time someone tells you to "move the needle," perhaps ask where they want it moved to and then start looking for the steam engine in the room?

I sympathize with the people who go to work each day and find themselves embroiled in the pain of management jargon. If you've ever been at work and thought, *What on earth are you talking about?* Please let me assure you, you're not alone.

It's like people get to the office, put on their special top hat, and in a heartbeat become an entirely different character. They turn into the official business person who "pushes the envelope" and becomes the "blue sky thinking" promoter. They adopt an imaginary illusion of seniority over other people by using fancy leadership terms to sound smart in the boardroom, even though no one actually knows what on earth it all means. For them, nobody's going to "rain on their parade," they are going all out for "110%." They are the business person, and suggest you are not if you don't use these words.

I also wonder if it's actually a technique for keeping people down. If they don't speak the same way, they might not get the job or climb the career ladder, because they sound different. Every time someone goes in for an interview, if they don't speak it—if they don't use the cliche terms, do they get judged by HR and knocked back down a rung or two?

But that's not the whole dilemma. Corporate jargon spills over to their customers or clients, who probably have to put up with their own share of gobbledygook through their own offices. So, they're not going to be enamored when businesses are trying to engage them using the same kind of language that they too also quite possibly despise.

If we want to create wonder in connection, repeating corporate gobbledygook is not the way to do so. It does not make employees or clients feel wonderful. 99.9% of the time, it makes them feel like a number. Are you here to make somebody feel like a number or make somebody feel seen and heard—and wonderful?

Unpickling the Communication Jam

The simplest explanation behind the spread of business jargon is that it is highly contagious. If someone hears a phrase, let's say "hit the ground running" they might find themselves using it without even realizing it. Others then also catch the phrase and do the same, and before the "close of play," it will be "going on a journey" around the office before the "grass grows too long."

This said, it might well be time to make a fresh start and retire this peculiar gobbledygook language. It isn't getting anyone anywhere and it wastes time, sanity, and willpower. Instead, let's say what we mean and get to the point. As infectious as it is with the way it spreads, the same can be said for the organizations who avoid it and only practice clarity.

So, shall we "touch base" with this and "strike while the iron is hot"?

Argh . . . it's following me!

Some may think that ditching corporate jargon is a preposterous idea, whereas others may be more likely to dance in a circle singing hallelujah. My point is that change only happens when someone is brave enough to lead the charge against gobbledygook by speaking with clarity.

You can often find the gobbledygook talkers down at ground level in the space station (the boardroom) trying to help everyone figure out how to launch their rocket. Those free of its spell, living with wonder and clear of all gobbledygook, are already inside their rocket flying into orbit up to the moon!

Mindless or Mindful?

There are many inspiring and successful organizations around the world who avoid corporate jargon at all costs. In luxury hotels for example, never did it cross our lips. We expressed ourselves with care and clarity. The air around us was light and bright, free of the skin-peeling irritation.

Our meetings were open, engaging, and incredibly enjoyable. I learned first-hand the difference between excellent leaders and average ones because it was always their pleasure to host a meeting, speak at an event, or compose an email with engaging simplicity. They understood their audience—the individuals in the room (the recipients of their written messages) and used clear, recognizable words blended with mindful expression to connect with them. Excellent leaders were always present in the room and in the moment. It made everyone sit up and eagerly gravitate toward them.

Every day we are inundated with information and communication, leading to shorter attention spans. The modern workplace, devoid of physical barriers, challenges our privacy and concentration. Despite this, the impact of our words on others is profound, and often overlooked amidst the workplace buzzwords that symbolize our communication challenges.

GOBBLEDYGOOK TRANSLATIONS

As we navigate through the murky waters of gobbledygook my ambition is to not criticize, instead illuminate an easy path back to coherence. This is a call to arms for everyone, a rally against the forces that obscure meaning.

Please fasten up your linguistic armor here and prepare for a wordsmithing adventure to return to making sense with words that resonate, and phrases that bring clarity and comprehension back to the origins of our language:

TOUCH BASE = **Let's get together / meet / talk / connect**
One of the top most commonly hated pieces of jargon of all time. Yes, it is possible (and oh so good) to communicate with or meet someone—without finding a baseball pitch. Shall we go for a coffee?

GIVE IT 110% = **Give it 100%**
Whilst this suggests a lot of effort, everyone knows that the most you can give anything is 100%. Giving more than 100% is impossible. Football managers use this phrase a lot.

THE WAR ON TALENT = **Attracting and retaining brilliant people**
Everyone has declared the "long siege" with the "war for talent." Organizations are down in the trenches preparing for combat with a new "battle plan." The simple fact and let us never forget, people are people and have their own unique talents. Can't we just go back to calling people "people," rather than labeling them as "talent," let alone thinking there's a war on?

INTERROGATE THE DATA = **Thoroughly review the figures**
From war into interrogation . . . like we should try to torture the data into a confession? When deciding what advertising to do in the second quarter, just review the figures.

NOT ENOUGH BANDWIDTH = **I don't have the time or capacity**
I know my internet connection at home could probably benefit from better "bandwidth," but it's got nothing to do with my current personal capacity.

BALLS IN THE AIR = **Dealing with several things at the same time**
Instead of creating a circus act, simply say that you are busy or have several projects on the go.

HELICOPTER VIEW = **Take a broad overview**
Instead of making people think they have to get a pilot's license, can we take a broad overview?

SINGING FROM THE SAME HYMN SHEET = **Work together in harmony**
This is still widely used by those who remain unsure how to get everyone in harmony, so attempt to do this with music?

LOOK UNDER THE BONNET = **Analyze the situation**
Most people don't have any clue about their car engine and commonly just take it to the local garage for someone who does.

RUN IT UP THE FLAGPOLE = **Give it a go**
If you are sure, could I borrow your ladder please?

CLOSE OF PLAY = **End of the day**
Why business jargon is so prone to sporting metaphors is anyone's guess.

LOW-HANGING FRUIT = **The most easily achievable tasks, targets, goals, etc.**
This will obviously go nicely if you work in an orchard. Be clear and specific, i.e., let's go after the easiest sales targets first (not the apples).

DON'T LET THE GRASS GROW TOO LONG = **Seize the opportunity**
Just be respectful in saying get on with it and seize opportunities instead of waiting and missing out.

THOUGHT SHOWER = **Come up with some new ideas**
I was invited to one of these once for some creative thinking and although none of us had a shower, we did "create some superb ideas."

BOIL THE OCEAN = **To waste time**
This phrase is way less dramatic than its weird name suggests. Nonetheless this one does the rounds in corporate land. It conjures up devastation, calamity, and an ocean full of dead fish.

DEEP DIVE = **Look at something in detail**
"Could you explore, analyze or provide a more detailed explanation?" without needing to take a boat out to the coral reef in a wet suit and scuba gear.

GOING ON A JOURNEY = **Working together**
You hear the words, "We need to bring people on the journey with us," and everyone in corporate land is packing their backpacks for a trek through the mountains.

HOW ARE YOU TRAVELING? = **How are you getting on?**
The traveling continues with this one and is popular here in Australia. People will always prefer and feel much more valued and appreciated if we simply ask them, "Are you okay?" or, "How are you getting on?"

BLUE SKY THINKING = **Permission to be creative**
Anyone who announces this beauty should be avoided at all costs. It means creative ideas free from any practical constraints. It is used by people who are themselves constrained by creative imagination and have to use a fancy name to suggest otherwise.

CASCADING RELEVANT INFORMATION = **Communicating clearly with your colleagues**
This one is possibly worse than touching base. Every word in this phrase is complete gobbledygook.

PEEL THE ONION = **Examine in detail**
This one is a gem. Put your team in the boardroom with a big bag of French onions peeling away the skins and crying uncontrollably. It means to examine something in detail.

HIT THE GROUND RUNNING = **Move at a prompt, enthusiastic pace**
A classic common phrase that implies a painful accident. It is supposed to mean "starting something and proceeding at a prompt, enthusiastic pace." Why not just say this, rather than cause people to shudder at this lifeless jargon?

IN LIGHT OF THE FACT THAT = **Because**
Replace this peculiar expression with one of the most influential and persuasive words of business dialog, especially writing—because.

LASER FOCUS = **Focus**
When regular focus isn't enough, we bring out the machinery and fire up the laser to focus our focus. This one lives with 110%. Let's just focus.

MOVE THE NEEDLE = **To get meaningful results**
If we are seeking to get meaningful or measurable results why not just say one or the other? Before getting out the vinyl and powering up the turntable, or bringing out the steam engine, instead just stick with "improve a situation" or "get meaningful results."

GET ON THE SAME PAGE = **Let's agree**
Without heading to the library to find a book and share a page. It's easier to just simply say those two words, "let's agree."

PAIN POINT = **Specific problem**
Leave the pain point with the doctor to assist (after hitting the ground running). Replace pain with a specific challenge, frustration, problem, or difficulty.

RAISE THE BAR = **Set a higher standard**
It sounds a whole lot better, clearer, and more motivating to say "to set a higher standard" instead of practicing gymnastics.

MAKE HAY WHILE THE SUN SHINES = **Make the most of the opportunity**
If you're not a farmer collecting the low-hanging fruit, simply replace this phrase with "make the most of the opportunity."

STRIKE WHILE THE IRON IS HOT = **See "make hay while the sun shines"**

FORWARD PLANNING = **Planning**
Planning is always for the future so putting "forward" in front of it is entirely irrelevant.

TAKE IT TO THE NEXT LEVEL = **Make something better**
In theory this suggests "making something better." It is far easier to understand by

just saying this or to "aim higher" because nobody knows what the next level actually looks like or if they've reached it.

PUSH THE ENVELOPE = **Go further**
Perfect irony with this worn-out corporate gobbledygook gem. Someone will tell you to push the envelope in encouragement to "exceed the limits of what's possible." Have you ever pushed an envelope? It's as light as a feather. You'd understand if it was a helicopter but that's already taken.

And not forgetting the old favorite:

THINKING OUTSIDE THE BOX = **To think creatively**
Possibly the oldest and most tired saying. Who wants to go in and out of a box? This one not only makes people groan with pain and irritation, but many people find it belittling. If you are faced with tackling a situation or opportunity and want to inspire people to "think creatively and imaginatively," then forget the box and simply do just that—express your invitation to think creatively and imaginatively.

Shine a Bright Fresh Light of Respect and Influence

There are hundreds of other examples that I could have featured, and yes, I could have *peeled the onion* and taken a *helicopter view* to help you *take it to the next level*. I decided enough was enough, and *strike while the iron is hot* . . .

Are you asking yourself, *Why shouldn't I speak the gobbledygook? Why shouldn't I just follow everyone the same way? Why should I want to change this? What's in it for me to change it?*

The vivid lesson I learned from my career in hospitality is that plain expression is always appreciated. Why not lead by example and just speak clearly? Challenge the gobbledygook around you and become a pioneer in promoting communication clarity.

Your colleagues, customers, clients, friends, and family will appreciate you cutting through the gobbledygook from this point on. It will inspire others to embrace simplicity and become advocates for sharing understandable language that speaks from the heart.

Who knows? They might even celebrate your trendsetting ways with fireworks and by toasting marshmallows around the fire in your honor!

Recipe 12 Recap:

GOBBLEDYGOOK ALTERNATIVES

Gobbledygook is highly contagious! It's a linguistic monstrosity that spreads like mold in business workplaces and leaves a tangled mess that stifles clear communication. Although each organization has its unique style, it's crucial to avoid the trap of mindless jargon. What steps can you take to champion the power of plain speech? Could you be the one to lead the return to clarity?

Ingredients:

★ Recognition of the difference between useful in-house terms and gobbledygook.

★ A willingness to carefully remove the gobbledygook chip from your memory and toss it away.

★ Resistance to the pressure to conform. Courage to lead the charge with clarity of expression.

★ Conscious replacement of convoluted phrases with simple, clear language.

★ Inspire others around you to do the same by communicating clearly.

Substitutions to Make this Recipe Your Own:

Consider trading corporate jargon that makes your skin crawl with any of the translations and substitutions you read in this recipe. Replace it with what you really want to say. Recognize that there is little to no value in gobbledygook.

MAIN COURSE

—

RHYTHM

"

When hearts are high,
the time will fly,
so whistle while you work.

Snow White

HAPPY FEET

What if going to work didn't actually feel like work? *What if*, instead, it was a joyful part of your life that offered stimulation and fulfillment? Not a chore, but something that made you want to run in each day, to tap your feet and whistle while you work? A positive experience we subconsciously looked forward to?

Imagine if the land behind the wardrobe door in *The Lion, The Witch and The Wardrobe*, became true, or the Doorknob to the main entrance of Wonderland in Disney's 1951 film *Alice in Wonderland* was a real place. Both stories feature the importance of imagination. That, combined with Alice's vivid curiosity, is what allowed her to navigate the absurd and unpredictable world she found herself in. Childlike curiosity and imagination aren't just for storybook characters. We *all* possess the gift of imagination—the ability to see beyond what we think we know of the real world, look behind our life's wardrobe door, and bring it to life.

For every individual business filling our lives with wonder and joy, there are plenty of others fizzling out, dying off, and closing their doors because their imaginations saw the opening but failed to equip them to avoid the close. New and interesting brands come and go; the latest and greatest fancy customer service concepts pop up with great enthusiasm, then vanish. They might have shown plenty of positive intent and offered real promise with wonderful service at first—but as the eagerness and stamina faded, so did their reputation. Customers walk away in disappointment, saying, "That's a shame, they used to be good," as do the brand's employees.

Companies that stand the test of time are the ones who possess relentless determination in their pursuit of excellence. They are daring and playful and let nothing stand in their way. Ordinary bores them. They are driven in the pursuit of their own unique and positive rhythm.

They have pace and movement—a bounce in their step.

They have *Happy Feet*.

It goes way deeper than the nice sounding marketing words (such as "*people are our greatest asset*"), which are not much more than great copy on a company website. When you look behind the door, you find a neglected environment with hearts running on empty—all feet are motionless and hidden underneath desks.

Companies with *happy feet* thrive amongst the joyful rhythm of a big-hearted culture, caring for their employees as second nature.

Take a peek behind the scenes of a luxury hotel and you will notice the almost wizard-like practices of wonderlicious leadership at play. You will find leaders who are fascinated by possibility. They are masters at experimenting with an array of ingredients to produce a happy, connected workplace for their employees.

Back in early 1993, something truly wonderful happened deep in the heart of Ashdown Forest in Southeast England. Following a major renovation, an old mansion and former convent was returned to its original glory. Upon completion, Ashdown Park proudly opened its doors as one of England's finest country house hotels. As I write this, thirty years have passed since I helped open this incredible property, a special place that truly changed my life in so many ways. I struggle to find the words to express the monumental impact that this brought to me personally.

The following three recipes have been the hardest and most daunting for me to write, because I want to do them justice. I want to be sure my words are enough to express how Ashdown Park truly changed my world.

There is much wonder and determination that goes into opening a magnificent country house hotel, and it requires painstaking passion to establish a finely tuned culture of excellence. We put the highest level of attention into not only sharing our own individual sense of wonder, but also how we created a multi-award-winning culture that would be loved by all our employees and, just as enthusiastically, by our loyal guests. The wonder created within Ashdown Park led to a momentous hotel opening and a business that has stood the test of time over the past three decades.

Surrounded by 186 acres of peaceful gardens and parkland, the sprawling property features 106 individually designed guest rooms and suites, and a beautiful restaurant. The former chapel provides a unique venue to complement the sixteen conference and banqueting suites, country club, beauty spa, and golf course.

Beyond the sandstone walls and glorious architecture of Ashdown Park radiates wonder. If there was ever an example of the mesmerizing effect of a culture of *Happy Feet*, Ashdown Park was it.

I've never seen anything like it since . . .

Recipe 13:
THE CRAFTSMANSHIP OF CARE

"

It's amazing what people will accomplish,
when they know you believe in them

Jon Gordon

Imagine how it would feel to lead a workplace and business culture your employees loved so fully that they still spoke of it years after they have departed?

I vividly remember apprehensively approaching the entrance of Ashdown Park, overwhelmed by the grandeur of its architecture, which dated back to 1815. My mind raced, wondering, *Am I good enough to work somewhere like this?* I was there to interview for the position of assistant to the general manager.

Although three decades have passed since that moment, spring of 1993 feels like yesterday. I knew at that moment how *Alice in Wonderland* must have felt as I walked down the long winding driveway past countless deer roaming peacefully around the grounds and a thousand birds singing in the trees. It was as if I had stepped into another world and was a day that will live on with me through all time.

Creating First Impressions That Last a Lifetime

I clearly recall how my anxiousness evaporated in a flash when I first met General Manager Graeme Bateman (who I think of now as Graeme, but at the time, formality—and of course respect—certainly had us all calling him Mr. Bateman). He awaited me at the front door of Ashdown Park. As I approached the entrance, he stepped forward and shook my hand, with a warm and friendly "Good morning Mr. Merrett, welcome to Ashdown Park!"

It was my first lesson learned at Ashdown—that considerate first impressions like this wouldn't ever be reserved exclusively for customers and guests. I had no idea at the time that the lesson would go on to inspire my entire professional working life: creating a welcoming atmosphere for potential employees during interviews is always equally, if not more important, than anything else.

In the exhilarating moments it took to get to his office, chatting informally along the route, I already knew . . . I really wanted this role.

"So, why did you come here today?" Graeme asked with a smile and then sat back in his chair to listen intently to my response. It was clear that he was making the moment all about the person in front of him. Not about himself.

How's Your Shoes?

After I answered most of the interview questions, one stands out in my mind to this day: "How's your shoes?" Graeme asked.

"I think they're fine . . ." I replied, knowing I had given them an extra polish for the occasion, but wondering if I had missed something.

"Joining the management team, there will be a lot of time on your feet," he explained. "The success of your role will come from the way you lead the operation from the floor."

Finding and retaining wonderful people is a hot recruitment challenge that is faced by businesses the world over. Graeme's interviews were a leadership masterclass demonstrating the aspirations of Ashdown's quality standards to every oncoming member of the hotel management team. It wasn't just an interview or a recruitment process; he was demonstrating the example of humility that we would all eagerly follow. We all went on to incorporate our personal interview experiences to become more present, to build rapport and values inside our team, and to create extra special moments for our guests and each other.

The Power of Love

This wasn't just a breathtaking historical property; it was a special place that we each cared for like our own. For many months leading up to the official opening, Ashdown Park was a building site. That means we were surrounded by a huge team of builders, carpenters, plasterers, painters, designers, carpet fitters, and representatives of every other type of specialist trade, each expertly and lovingly bringing the property back to its original splendor. It was exciting to watch 106 individually designed bedrooms come to life in front of our eyes. Whilst there were plenty of hair-raising moments, it was the pride of everyone working together that carried us through to our opening day.

For the following eight enriching years, I was excited to go to work each day at Ashdown Park, as were all my colleagues. This is a place that has a mesmerizing effect on anyone who has had the pleasure to work or stay there. It isn't only a beautiful country house hotel or prosperous business. Nor is it the consequence of the stunning architecture, the elegant fixtures and fittings, or the log fires, nor the beautiful fabrics, exquisite bone china, and plush carpets. It's a place of celebration, joy, and reunion. A place of love, indulgence, and rest, passed down through the generations so that new memories could be crafted.

Looking back, I realize that Ashdown Park was way ahead of its time.

It was an act of love.

A vibrant workplace worth celebrating.

A wonderlicious masterpiece that invited guests and team members alike to gloriously step back in time and yet also embrace the thrilling vitality of the present.

There was one crucial ingredient that stood out above all else: the entire estate, and business, was built on a solid foundation of caring leadership.

The vision was both ambitious and exquisitely simple: to uncover traditional and luxurious English-country-house hospitality, with reflections of a glorious bygone age. We wouldn't just be providing products and services—it went way beyond selling accommodation and convenience. We knew that our guests would expect more than just a solution—room and shelter.

In preparation for our hotel opening, we knew more than anything that to cause this level of guest and team attraction wouldn't happen by chance. Our hotel team and our guests had a choice whether to come to us—or not.

It was down to us to create a meaningful and bright experience—a deep, irresistible, emotional connection. We wanted to send this proud sentiment out to the world far and wide and become well known for the feeling we were providing.

Being the Heart of Humility

For the entire hotel team, Graeme wasn't just the general manager. He was more like the pied piper. His authenticity crafted a trusted bond with each of us individually and across the team as a whole. Never did he shine the spotlight on himself, nor was he distracted, desk-bound, or invisible. He didn't walk around with a clipboard, marking our performances, or try to catch us doing things wrong. Simply, he guided and showed us exactly what gracious hospitality looked like. His actions and presence showed how much he cared, and that he noticed our efforts.

The sense of leadership and consistently high standards he instilled ignited something special within us. Without hesitation, we energetically followed his lead. Our deep sense of belonging fueled our culture, inspiring us to aim higher, persevere, and strive harder.

None of us wanted to disappoint Graeme, so we were always on our toes, never knowing when he might appear. His unpredictable presence kept us consistently on our A-game, always in anticipation.

NON-NEGOTIABLE BASICS

I still have my notebook filled with scribbles from our pre-opening meetings, and after thirty years, the pages are now well worn from frequent reference. During one of our early planning meetings as we were defining our cultural values ahead of recruiting the team, I wrote six words and circled them in red pen:

- **Recruit wisely**
- **Develop thoroughly**
- **Respect equally**

Together we agreed that the values of our team and guest culture would be balanced evenly and with distinguishable clarity. To give us the best position, we set our sights high to establish excellent interview and hiring practices. Much more than only impressive sounding words—recruit wisely, develop thoroughly, and respect equally became our way.

To prepare us well for the imminent recruitment of our brand-new opening team, we wanted, more than anything, to show our heart and make sure it was a pleasurable experience for our undoubtedly nervous and apprehensive candidates. We had one chance to make the right impression with the people applying for our vacancies and never would we appear robotic.

We didn't score ourselves with things like one to ten ratings for our methods, apart from recruitment. Our approach to interviewing and team orientation included aiming for ten out of ten. A score that was about connection, not perfection. Anything lower would have held us back in creating a first-class culture. Getting either wrong or below average standards would have been against our vision and everything we stood for.

Across the whole management team, we were each faced with hosting many dozens of interviews every week in the months leading to our opening. To set us up for consistent success and establish a uniform approach to recruitment, Graeme organized a series of special refresher training days on interview techniques. We had all interviewed before, but we wanted to create a unique experience standard. To us they weren't only candidates; they were people—real people—and we had one chance to welcome them consistently.

Showing Care from the First Second

My initial responsibility was for Personnel & Training, and I loved it. One of my first tasks was to design our team welcome orientation. My focus was to create an experience that was refreshing, purposeful, and provided a reassuring feeling of warmth. It was something else in which we aimed for ten out of ten. We knew that anyone starting their first day would undoubtedly be nervous and probably feel quite overwhelmed. Ashdown Park had an intimidating effect on everyone!

There wouldn't be any hint of this being a tick-box process of necessity or have any uncomfortable formality. This was our opportunity to provide everyone with a generous serving of encouragement to how our new recruits contributed to our culture. Whilst we would include our safety and fire procedures, it was our chance to explain our hospitality traditions and quality standards, our values and culture foundations. Above all else, we would go all out to express how exciting it was to work at Ashdown Park.

There was more to it than this. We put careful thought into how we would choose and set the meeting room on each occasion—again, going for a relaxed and welcoming feel. We wanted new team members to feel comfortable and see that we had put care and thought into their first Ashdown Park moments. We'd have a fresh pot of tea and coffee ready, with some home baked chocolate chip cookies straight from the oven. Graeme would pop in at the start of every single team welcome, meet everyone individually, and provide the opening welcome message.

I presented the welcome induction every Monday morning at 9 a.m. Of the highest importance—no one started their role before receiving their team welcome experience, which came with good reason. Our head housekeeper, for example, would practically get on her knees and beg us to let her two new room attendants start on Thursday—as she "Urgently needs them right now and can't wait until Monday." We always steered everyone to the Monday start and welcome first. Without it, more harm than good would be caused. Our new recruits would have no sense of where they were, or who anyone was, or how we do things. Imagine if some guests bumped into the two new room attendants in the hallway and asked for directions to the restaurant and they didn't know where it was. Or how uncomfortable they would feel going to the team rest area for lunch and knowing absolutely no one.

Monday morning was our tradition, designed to consistently provide a fresh start, a fresh week, a fresh Monday. It was another part of the reason why our culture shone so brightly.

The Gift of Explicit Permission

We all shared the weighty task of leading, balancing, and influencing the intricate vision of our owner, and Graeme was the conductor. To build such great bonds of trust amongst each other, he encouraged us to be both brave and vulnerable in our work. He didn't want us to feel apprehensive in experimenting throughout our day if it meant enhancing the experience of our guests.

One of the most impactful things that we all received from him was presence. He showed each of us across the management team that a leader is a title one must earn. This came from understanding the difference between being reactive and proactive. He continuously reminded us of the distinct difference between process-driven reactive management and proactive visionary leadership. We performed the latter and also learned from his example that kindness reaches beyond everything else. It was down to us all to make sure everyone not only felt uniquely seen and understood, but also valued, and appreciated.

He showed us how to walk into any area of the hotel and simultaneously sense everything all around us in equal measure—sight with awareness and meaning—full peripheral vision switched on high beam. This supreme level of attention to detail became our superpower.

He also demonstrated the importance of truly listening. When he spoke, we listened intently. When we spoke, he did the same. It was that simple and that respectfully pure. We wouldn't interrupt or lose our eye contact between each other mid-conversation or talk over each other. Such was the level of our humility and purposeful connection in the moment, we were all free of any complicated and meaningless dialog between each other.

We lovingly provided every member of the hotel team with a meaningful job description, rather than issue uninspiring process-laden lists of tasks. These were documents that shone with life and also with permission for everyone to bring personality to their role. It went beyond the paperwork.

Take the duty managers for example: during our nominated shift we had responsibility for overseeing the overall running of the hotel each day. Graeme explained, "This is your hotel." He took us to the main front door of the hotel and said, "This is your front door." Inside the lobby he continued, "This is your reception." And he meant it. The culture of Ashdown Park encouraged ownership of the space from each and every member of the team, whatever their role. As a result, we worked hard to keep it pristine, beautiful and functional.

We then shared the same sentiment and encouragement with our housekeepers: "These are your bedrooms." With our ground staff: "These are your gardens."

Making Time for Rehearsals

We continuously organized many impactful "rehearsal" learning moments for the whole hotel team. Prior to opening day and to help bring the newly formed management team of twelve together, we were set a daunting but inspiring training challenge as part of our rehearsals. We were taken deep into the forest at the back of the property in the midafternoon and left there with a large tent in a big bag, a small gas camping stove, fifty pounds, and some simple instructions. *"You have five hours to prepare and serve a high-quality white-tablecloth three-course dining experience for some special VIP guests, including Mr. Bateman. The only rule is this: you're not allowed to go into the hotel for anything."*

The enormity of the challenge was clear as day—seeing as the hotel is literally in the middle of the vast Ashdown Forest, with the surrounding town and villages several miles away, this was an epic task.

We formed a plan and then proceeded to beg, borrow, and pilfer from the local area. It came together like poetry in motion. We found elaborate candelabras, beautiful, rustic flower arrangements, homemade menus and name cards, and an elegantly set table for sixteen that looked like something off a prestigious movie set. I forget what we actually cooked and served, but I remember it was impressive and can still, to this day, remember the feeling of our triumphant pride.

The countdown to the official opening flew by with adrenaline-fueled excitement. For days on end the newly formed team all helped to unload the never-ending line of lorries delivering the masses of individually selected furniture, the beds, mattresses, linen, lamps and art. We carried every single piece of furniture for the miles around the long hallways to each allocated guest bedroom.

We hosted a series of full-blown dress rehearsals with real, but pretend, guests. They would be our most willing guinea pigs and for the first time, we would put on our show. Our hearts were ready, as were our (happy) feet.

We attended to our first guest arrivals list; we excitedly prepared the restaurant and set the lounges for our first service of tea. It was all hands on deck and as our guinea pigs started arriving—although we were ready—nothing prepared us for the sound. Hearing laughter and joy echoing around the public areas and through the hallways for the first time was a deeply moving moment for us all. As part of our rehearsals, we even played with testing the fire alarms. We had been given a precise and incredibly short evacuation time from the local fire service and, like naughty children, we used our guinea pigs to experiment with some surprise tests.

To help celebrate the hotel opening, we welcomed American-British TV broadcaster Lloyd Grossman to provide the celebratory toast at our official opening dinner. Famed from presenting the popular TV shows *MasterChef* and *Through the Keyhole*, he gave a fascinating dinner speech. In his concluding words, he asked if we could bring all of our chefs out from the kitchen into the restaurant. He promptly proceeded to line them up in the dining room to face their eager audience and proudly initiated the most rapturous round of applause for them from our delighted guests.

This was clearly more than a token gesture and was such a poignant moment of realization for us to witness. He had just performed a moment that aligned quite perfectly with who and what we were becoming—a culture that radiated the purity of celebrated appreciation.

An Elixir of Emotional Connection

Shortly after the opening, we each found hand-written thank you messages on Ashdown Park letterhead in our pigeonholes (mail slots) from Graeme. I still have mine. I distinctly remember how it felt to read:

12 October 1993

Dear Peter,

Now that we have successfully opened our doors, I would like to take the opportunity to thank you personally for your commitment shown over the past few months.

It has been most encouraging to see the initiative and enthusiasm with which you have carried out your duties. You should be proud of what you have achieved to date. Keep up the good work.

Sincerely

Graeme Bateman

Had this been a group memo copied to everyone collectively—the impact would have been entirely different. But it was, instead, a hand-written letter—another example from Graeme demonstrating the influence of creating something unexpected. We ourselves learned from (and then shared) similar gestures of connection like this with everyone else.

Five Words That Change Everything

"Have you got a minute?"

Those five simple words propelled his position as our principal leader and continuously breathed fresh life through our culture. I loved it every single time he said these words.

Sometimes we would sit in his office with a fresh pot of tea, or we would walk the hotel floors together, or sit in one of the lounges. Never was there an agenda and often no talk of work. It was a simple "How are you?" or "Are you okay?" type of conversation. Sometimes it would turn into an idea-sharing moment, a reflection on a recent guest experience, or a moment of gratitude. Other times we might examine a particular challenge we were handling. He was consistent with everyone and for all of the team, "Have you got a minute?" wasn't only a moment that mattered the most but changed everything.

From this level of trusted connection, we all felt safe, encouraged, appreciated, and we carried it forward—sharing the same courtesy to everyone else across the broader team.

Through his leadership, we mastered two simple yet potent ingredients for success: *craftsmanship* and *care*—not one without the other, but a crucial blend that inspired our foundation. *Care* was never brushed aside as unnecessary and time-consuming fluff, and *craftsmanship* was the level of attentive pride and extreme detail with our work. These two nourishing ingredients built our team's trust and loyalty and encouraged them to stay and grow with us. It is also why our guests kept coming back.

Craftsmanship

At Ashdown Park, we didn't just arrive for our shift, do our tasks, and then go home. Such was our level of attentiveness, we subconsciously adapted the precise ways and approach of craftsmanship—the blacksmith, the swordsmith, the diamond cutter. We aimed as high as we could with everything. We approached the detail of our work like the masons responsible for building cathedrals, castles, and guildhalls.

It didn't cost us anything being so detail-focused, although it did provide another reason for our guests to decide to stay with us.

Care

Care is one of the most useful and important words of any language. It carries the strength to make the ground move. And it was our way of life—showing genuine kindness and concern for others in everything that we did. It was something that we could at no time do by halves, nor could we ever say we cared about something or someone unless we truly did. We knew that kindness cost us nothing—a priceless gift we could freely share with everyone we met.

Intoxicating things happen when you blend these two leadership ingredients together.

If *craftsmanship* and *care* were the two principal ingredients for a cookery recipe—for say a simple and imaginary sauce to smother all over your business—it would quite possibly be the champion of all sauces.

Recipe 13 Recap:

THE CRAFTSMANSHIP OF CARE

Gracious hospitality and caring leadership aren't limited to luxury hotels. For any workplace culture, people will always thrive when they feel appreciated, valued, and recognized.

Mix Together:

- ★ Craftsmanship: approach the detail of your work like the masons responsible for building cathedrals, castles, and guildhalls would.
- ★ Care: it costs you nothing and is a priceless gift you can freely share with everyone you meet.

Then Add:

- ★ Leadership by example: lead from the floor, not from behind your desk or meeting room tables.
- ★ Warm welcomes: anytime someone comes to you for an interview or to purchase your products or services, greet them at the front door.
- ★ A magic phrase: *"Have you got a minute?"* Make time to consistently offer these wonderlicious words.
- ★ Authenticity: let your team consistently see the real you. People (employees and customers alike) will always go to the moon and back for you when they know how much you care.

Substitutions to Make this Recipe Your Own:

Blend the above ingredients until care is spread evenly throughout the environment you are sharing with your team and your customers. Add visibility, authenticity, and presence to establish a business workplace that people adore. To radiate great trust and loyalty, be the role model of care. **Provide reassurance, guidance, and** heart-lead connection.

Recipe 14:
SYMPHONY NO. 8

"

No one can whistle a symphony.
It takes a whole orchestra to play it.

Halford Luccock

Together is such a handsome, exquisite little word.

The power and importance of its true meaning can easily go unnoticed. Although, when it is used and expressed with the right intention, it provides an electric current strong enough to inspire the team culture of a business up to the sky.

Hotels are never a one-person show. At Ashdown Park, the sense of *together* proudly guided our compass. It sparked our wonder engine to life and as the team began to grow in physical size, so did our spirit of belief.

All of our success came from this magic eight-letter word.

Symphony Strength Togetherness

We weren't just a group of people joining a team; we were equal, aligned, and intently focused on bringing this magnificent property to life, none of which happened by chance.

During one of our weekly heads-of-department meetings, there was a defining moment for our newly establishing culture. It was like an epiphany. Graeme was seated at the head of the grand old oval table in one of the side meeting rooms of the chapel with its huge, vaulted ceiling and stained-glass windows.

He sat forward and eagerly announced, "We aren't just a team."

Our antennas went up.

"This isn't just a hotel operation."

He continued, "We are more like an orchestra playing a symphony."

We waited to see what he meant.

"There's no 'I' or 'me' in an orchestra. Our success will come from the way *we* all play our instruments *together*, to play the perfect symphony for our guests. Our housekeepers, chefs, the restaurant team, reception, *everyone*. If *we* aren't all in rhythm, the music we play will be out of tune for our guests! If anyone is sitting by themselves, or hiding away, or does not feel included, none of this will work. The rhythm of our backstage has to match our onstage."

That was precisely what we needed to hear. In a flash, we went from being a magnificent team to an orchestra. We rather liked the idea.

We left the meeting giggling and teasing each other about who would be the violinists, the flutists or maybe the tuba players. "I'm on the drums," I think Kevin, our head gardener, announced. Whatever our instrument, it didn't matter—it was agreed. Working as an orchestra connected us. We would be going all out to play our symphony, in harmony and together.

PERFORMING A CULTURE OF TOGETHERNESS

For true success in the hospitality industry, you need to enjoy it, be passionate about it, truly love it. Hospitality is relentlessly demanding. You get used to continuously apologizing to your friends who invite you out to party with them on a Saturday night because you are working that day and expected back again at 7 a.m. on Sunday.

We all worked tirelessly but we did so willingly—because we felt appreciated. We worked hard, long, and unsociable hours—late nights, early mornings, weekends, public holidays, and every Christmas—yet it always felt worthwhile because our colleagues were also our friends and chosen families. It was so much more than a job for the whole team; it was a pleasure and massively fulfilling.

If we were not a hotel but, instead, a boat, Ashdown Park wouldn't be an inflatable dinghy, speedboat, noisy diesel liner, or a big modern tanker, but perhaps a beautiful old wooden sailing ship from times gone by. In any stormy or challenging waters, our crew worked together in harmony to keep her steady. Never did we capsize or run adrift. We weren't just performing "lead-er-ship." We took on our individual responsibility with pride and balanced tasks together with rhythm to "lead-the-ship." We had all hands and hearts on deck, with one clear focus on the horizon—excellence.

We did this by fostering an invisible camaraderie. We were bound by our focus on the horizon, our common goal: to provide unrivaled luxury, award-winning dining, and outstanding business and leisure facilities, all wrapped up and shared with heart.

We were able to achieve this level of team supremacy because there were no cliques, which was a direct result of Graeme's encouraging leadership. He showed us how *nothing* would or could ever get in the way of our guest experience.

Becoming Master Jugglers

"That's not my job" were words never said by anyone at Ashdown. It wouldn't have ever crossed our minds. If we had, our guest experience would have been very different. Instead, by having our ears to the ground and knowing what was going on outside of our own roles and departments, we were all able to perform genuinely and whole-heartedly as one team.

We were passionate about being the best in everything we did, and it was our culture of positivity that laid a solid foundation for success. Negativity would crush our flow, so we consistently avoided it.

We had no official term for the way we supported and assisted each other's departments. It was something that simply became second nature, and for any guest arriving, they would feel it stepping through the front door.

Across the whole team, any of us could step into any area of the hotel and immediately assist or support. None of it was a magic trick, nor was it a fluke. Like the skills of a master juggler, we could spin multiple things in the air, almost with our eyes closed . . .

To gain a crystal-clear understanding of everyone's operational methods and challenges, we learned how to perform each other's roles by spending time shadowing all departments. At no time would any task outside of our regular responsibility be considered beneath us, and within a split second any of us could (and would) assist putting the tablecloths and bedsheets through our laundry press, deliver a room service tray, step behind reception to assist checking in a guest, take a reservation, handle a wedding or conference enquiry, service a guest bedroom, or navigate the wine cellar.

Our head chef would perform duty management shifts, the duty managers spent time working in the kitchen, the reception team worked in housekeeping, and vice versa. The bar team understood the complexities of room service and could jump in at times of peak demand to assist. During a busy checkout, any of us could automatically step in to assist the reception team. If we noticed the switchboard ringing while a receptionist was attending to a guest, it was effortless for one of us to step in and handle the calls. The result was an unparalleled ability to provide uninterrupted guest experience.

Sunday morning breakfasts were an operational challenge and could have so easily backfired and been a disappointing experience. Service was open from 7 to 10 a.m. If we had two hundred guests in-house, one hundred would traditionally come down for breakfast at 9:45 a.m., creating an extreme 15-minute pressure point. It wouldn't be unusual for Terry, our deputy general manager, to magically appear in the kitchen stillroom and take charge of the conveyor belt toaster machine. His intuition gave the restaurant team an instant supply of hot toast inside those fleeting minutes. Graeme sometimes had his jacket off relaying tables. I would assist in replenishing the buffet. We weren't reacting to any weakness of the restaurant team, but to an operational reality. At no point did we take over running the restaurant; instead, we invisibly stepped in to assist, sometimes for only fifteen minutes. We adapted proactively and without being asked.

This left our amazing breakfast host, Jenny, to do what she did best—provide everyone with the warmest and undistracted welcome at the door.

This seamless all-hands-on-deck team approach to all tasks and positions within the hotel put us in the position to offer the highest standards of hospitality. We felt invincible. We could achieve anything together.

It was our way. It was our culture. It was everything.

Every Minute Counts

At Ashdown Park, we stayed in the present without losing sight of the future. We spent copious amounts of time planning, not only for the following month but also the next twelve months and beyond. Of the greatest importance, we put huge attention into what was happening each following hour, and every minute that made up each hour.

Going to work at Ashdown Park felt more like an ongoing adventure; none of it was ever a chore, or grueling. It was bright, healthy, uplifting, and massively motivating.

Our focus on providing excellent guest experiences remained clear as day. Creating special "wow moments" became our well-known way. Our reputation of gracious hospitality all came through the pace and momentum that we established through—our happy feet.

Involving Everyone Equally

We had no instruction manual for turning this historical gem into a luxury hotel. What we did have was a precise and shared vision. Sometimes the creation of a business plan happens at the most senior level. Commonly it then goes into a big folder that gathers dust on the top shelf. No one really knows what's in it because it's so big, too hard to understand, or remains unexplained, so everyone doesn't really know where they're heading.

At Ashdown Park, every member of the management team contributed to the annual business plan to achieve an engaging level of contribution and involvement from all. Each head of department wrote their own annual department action plan, which was then weaved into the ongoing master plan.

We knew we couldn't make a plan and expect everyone to follow it. To fully involve everyone with the vision for our culture and demonstrate our clear style of leadership, we went to great lengths to make sure it was meaningful for everyone.

We intentionally held a precise number of business and operational meetings because we didn't want to take any time away from looking after our guests. Each meeting was consistently inclusive and had clear intentions.

However, never would you be late for a meeting! They always started promptly on time, and walking in late was much worse than the embarrassment of being asked to leave the classroom at school . . . I painfully learned from the experience, more than once.

One of the greatest things I loved about our meetings—we were all encouraged to participate, and we all had equal voices. Whatever the meeting, we would always hear each other and leave changed in some way—either reassured, informed, or invigorated, and often, all three. Never did we leave scratching our heads wondering why we were there or confused by the message.

The Superpower of Number Eight

We expressed the sentiment of appreciation freely and frequently, amongst each other and with our guests. For the entire management team, there was nothing more rewarding than seeing everyone in the team progress, succeed, and flourish. This all came from the heart of a working environment that was richly embedded with gratitude. As a result, our team stayed with us longer; they didn't need to search for another more fulfilling role elsewhere. And as for our guests, they adored the feeling that our bright, appreciated team created.

Gratitude was our first language. This is when "*number 8*" became my personal little memory trigger and it's never left my mind through to today. For some unknown reason I simply counted the letters in the words *thank you*—8.

There are also 8 letters in the words *together, grateful* and *thankful*.

All the way through to the present day, whether I'm at home, in the office, with friends, or onstage speaking, I always have number 8 in my subconscious mind as my personal reminder.

Never Rest on Your Laurels

At some point around the anniversary of our first year, a number of us were summoned "*urgently*" to Graeme's office. We heard that a special parcel had arrived.

There on his desk in front of us was the esteemed award for Hotel of the Year from the Southeast England Tourist Board. We stood nervously around it giggling together in disbelief. Graeme then went off and proudly walked the prized trophy all around the hotel, into every department, to show every single member of the team that he could find and thanked them personally for their input. It was this shared pride that played a huge part in who we were becoming as a team—and as a business.

We didn't do what we did for trophies. We did it for the happiness and joy of our guests. Although, it was indeed the most marvelous and perfect way to show our whole team just how much their individual contribution was not only important, but also valued, recognized and appreciated.

Hotel of the Year wasn't the only award we received. We put enormous care and effort into the creation of our wine cellar, prompting the *Wine Spectator Magazine* to crown us with "One of the Best Wine Lists in the World." The Royal Automobile Club presented us with their coveted RAC Blue Ribbon, only given to hotels which reach the highest standards of excellence, which would later rise to the heights of Gold Ribbon for the finest standards in comfort, cuisine, and customer care and service.

Then within industry-record-breaking time, we received the AA's supreme accolade: Four Red Stars, presented to hotels selected as the best in the British Isles, as opposed to traditional hotel black stars representing, amongst other things, the level of hotel facilities. Red Stars are the AA's ultimate recognition for excellent levels of quality, outstanding levels of hospitality and service, with a dedicated team offering a personalized experience.

However, not once were we ever allowed to rest on our laurels.

Graeme reminded us of this each and every day from that point forward, that whilst we had Four Red Stars yesterday, today we started with zero, and they had to be earned all over again.

The Greatest Marathon of All

Taking on the momentum of endurance as a team *together* is one of the most satisfying and fulfilling feelings for everyone involved. Along with each of our imaginary musical instruments, we practiced long and hard, doing whatever it took to perform like the make-believe *orchestra* that we were, to perfect our *symphony*.

We composed many moments of wonderful imaginary music.

The hotel industry is relentlessly non-stop, and to establish the positive flow of a finely tuned workplace culture is no easy task. That's why the best hotels around the world make the spirit and heart of a connected team culture non-negotiable.

Imagine running a marathon, elated you made it to the end! Then, imagine the *finish line* immediately becomes the *starting line* and you have to head off all over again.

This is the daily endurance and resilient test of hotel life.

Successfully running a luxury hotel, the same as any other business, has no finish line. Tomorrow, it starts all over again.

Recipe 14 Recap:
SYMPHONY NO. 8

One of the most impactful secrets for creating team fluency is to make gratefulness your first language. Beyond that, great powers can be drawn from the mighty word *together*. This orchestral connected approach is what will create a highly connected business culture. Use this recipe to inspire you to create a team environment like the "orchestra" at Ashdown Park.

Ingredients:

★ Togetherness: lead the practice of working as an orchestra, rather than individual musicians.

★ The banning of "that's not my job" from your vocabulary.

★ Cross-training and shadowing across business areas: learn each other's instruments so you can play them whenever the song calls for it.

★ A fresh start to every day, never resting on your laurels.

Substitutions to Make this Recipe Your Own:

Whether you're running an organization, company, or a hotel, it is not a one-person show. Neither is the act of defining a vibrant team culture. You should involve absolutely everyone in bringing this to life. Your recipe will be customized by the vibrancy and insight of your team—your orchestra—as you create your culture.

Recipe 15:
BACKSTAGE, ONSTAGE

"

What happens "backstage" will end up "onstage." If we aren't friendly with each other . . .
smiling and saying, "good morning," then we'll have a similar attitude toward our guests.

Van France
Disney University Founder

Ashdown Park is a hotel, not a theater. We didn't perform on an actual stage, yet we thought of our work as a detailed performance designed entirely for the highest level of daily guest—audience—experience possible.

Companies and organizations may understandably not consider their work to be akin to putting on a "show," however it is a commonly practiced hotel metaphor, a way of working "*backstage, onstage*" that has a transferable place for any organization's culture.

At Ashdown Park, this is how we lived, thought, behaved, and prepared both our front and back of house—through the microscopic detail of our preparation and innovation backstage. That's why our team enjoyed their work as much, and why our guests would book with us over and over again. It was about how we made them feel, through our imaginary theater and ceremonial detail.

We considered our backstage to be any area that was invisible to our guests. The offices, wine cellar, equipment storerooms, kitchens, wash-up areas, the laundry, room service stillroom, walk-in fridges, boiler rooms, team rest areas, maintenance workshops, gardener's greenhouses, and the delivery entrance all combined. Backstage provided our heartbeat.

If the room service area was a mess, the guest experience would be the same. If we couldn't quickly navigate our large wine cellar, it would slow us down during service. Likewise, our guests would easily sense if our offices were disorganized or cluttered. Every detail mattered, otherwise it would break our harmonious flow and sabotage our promise.

If any aspect of our back of house areas were disjointed, it would spill over to our front of house guest experience—*onstage*. We treated both front and back with equal importance and pride. We purposefully went all out to create amazing memories and never got bored of doing it.

We were driven by the thrill of creating a continuous flow of memorable guest experiences and we thrived with a daily excitement in the way we would bring everything to life. We were impatient in our desire to inspire creativity with the smallest touches.

We worked and played hard backstage, tinkering with and preparing our experiences. Across the entire hotel team, it was the daily rituals of the human spirit in all its glory and the sense of ceremony between us that made the difference.

Never Too Busy for Connection

Our magic backstage experience began with a cheerful good morning to each other every day. Next would be the informal way we would jovially contest the polish of our shoes—a highly competitive daily ritual back of house, playfully arguing who had the best shine! Above all else, we all knew that no matter what challenges faced us each day, we were in the moment together, supported by each other through the habit of our daily rituals.

I enjoyed watching the way members of the team arrived for work to start their day. Our head chef, John McManus, was no exception. With the weight of a massive day ahead on his shoulders, he would always cheerfully walk into the kitchen every morning in his pristine chef's whites and go around every section with a bright "Good morning" and "I hope you have a great day" to all of his chefs. This was his little ritual, his way of creating togetherness and setting the positive tone for the day ahead. He did the same every day. Never was he too burdened, or too busy.

I obviously never realized at the time just how much I would miss moments like this in my latter corporate roles, where the day often started in silence with everyone with their heads down, reacting to emails, and answering all their meeting requests.

The Morning Meeting—Planning Wonderlicious Moments

Each and every day we created unexpected experiences and memories for our guests, none of which happened by chance but instead by being so closely in tune with each other. The success of our service culture came down to our attention to detail and the clear connection between each other. This all came together with one highly purposeful ritual that we performed standing up every morning at 9:30 a.m., 365 days of the year, with a representative from every department: our morning meeting.

It was a daily ritual we never missed. This wasn't just a meeting; it was our final backstage dress rehearsal. It was our way of gathering together and warming up our connection with each other before stepping into the present for what was literally about to happen. It was our daily moment to inform and encourage each other, ahead of the day that awaited us.

The early-shift duty manager would read out comments from the duty manager's diary from the previous day's highlights—good and not so good. We would frantically search Graeme's face for clues to his mood, and literally die if there had indeed been a complaint. We took the wrath, dealt with any inconsistencies promptly, and learned from the issue professionally as a team.

We studied and ran through the daily arrivals list with a magnifying glass, highlighting return guests, special occasions, and all specific requests.

Imagine Mr. & Mrs. Smith who were staying with us for the second time. By us all knowing this, any member of the entire team would be aware of the opportunity to say those magic words: "Welcome back." We would have taken note during their first stay that Mr. Smith likes the *Daily Telegraph* newspaper and Mrs. Smith prefers a firm foam pillow. So, both would be organized without them requesting. They have a dairy allergy, so at dinner we would proactively point out the suitable menu items *before* they had to ask us. It is also their wedding anniversary, so we would lavish them with simple wonderlicious touches. The early-duty manager would prepare a handwritten welcome card with the words, "Dear Mr. & Mrs. Smith, it is our pleasure to welcome you back to Ashdown Park on this very special occasion. We wish you a very happy and relaxing wedding anniversary. Welcome back and please make yourselves at home." These little touches were our way of making sure guests knew "We are paying attention. And we care." The thought and preparation from the front office team each day made it possible to do unexpected things like this

Missing the moment to say "Welcome back" to any returning guests would have been a disastrous missed opportunity. For all of us, our short morning meeting was a simple daily sequence that helped Ashdown Park exceed our guests' expectations.

When we had a bride and groom arriving for their wedding (or specific guests such as Mr. & Mrs. Smith), the Hall Porters would take their walkie-talkie up the driveway close to their anticipated arrival time and literally hide in the bushes! Once they caught sight of the guests, we would receive their call, "They're here! Driving down to the door now, thirty seconds away." These were genius (and incredibly fun) moments for us. It brought us such joy to see the reaction of sheer surprise and delight on our guests' faces as we magically appeared out of nowhere, to open their car door with a personal welcome as they pulled up at the front door.

These were all tiny touches that cost us nothing and yet meant the world to the people who came to stay with us.

During the morning meeting, our event coordinators would share and read through the day's event function sheets, highlighting the details of the conference and banqueting events for the day ahead. The restaurant manager would announce the guests who had lunch and dinner reservations, including special requests. Whether it was our department or not, we all had a window into the many touches of magic that would be taking place that day.

We left our morning gathering each and every day, ready together—to head out onstage.

Causing Differentiation with Ceremony

We knew that we only ever had one chance to make a memorable first impression.

Take our tea service as an illustration: We had an endless selection of teas, lovely bone china crockery, highly polished silver teapots, and wonderful home-baked chocolate-chip cookies we would serve to our guests as they ordered. We served it all with an air of attentive ceremony. It wasn't just a cup of tea; we were creating a feeling—a moment of nostalgia, a moment of pleasure—all brought to life with wonderlicious hospitality.

We plumped the cushions on the armchairs and sofas. We carefully placed the cups and saucers facing each place setting, with the cup handles to the right, and the handle of the teaspoons pointing diagonally below each cup handle. We would place a couple of extra logs on the fire then stand close to the front door ready to welcome our guests as they stepped inside.

Why did these extra efforts even matter?

Because we knew our guests had a choice. There were many other places in the local area that would serve them tea. It was the feeling and memory from our attentiveness that encouraged them to keep returning and also show us off to their friends. If we displayed any hint of being robotic, disorganized, or disinterested, it wouldn't have mattered in the slightest how good the tea was.

Backstage with our new team members, we demonstrated and rehearsed everything. How to elegantly place the silver tea strainer onto a teacup and then unassumingly, also ceremoniously pour the brewed tea. We practiced how to hold our little silver milk jugs and gracefully pour the milk into the cup. These were more than minuscule touches of ceremony, they were opportunities to define what simplistic, wonderful hospitality felt like, which for our guests, was everything.

The same skill and attentiveness were used when we presented and served a bottle of wine. I'm sure you have had your share of times in restaurants when the person taking the wine order either knew little about the wine list or embarrassingly tried to bluff their way through it, then proceeded to carelessly rip the important decorative foil off the bottle top and drip the wine across the tablecloth with no grace or care. Every moment like this was defined by involving the entire team with our approach to pleasure. We mastered everything like this by discussing and practicing it backstage together.

It was the same with how we would each answer the telephone. The second we picked up an external call from the main switchboard or any internal department, we were onstage. We knew that it wouldn't matter how nice our website looked, how expensive our marketing campaign was, or how well we had polished the windows if we were inattentive or careless with our telephone tone. We would be behind at the first hurdle; the opportunity inside the first impression would be gone, like a flash of lightning.

Embracing the Mundane

We didn't reserve the ceremony of our attentiveness for the fancy things. It was something we soulfully performed with everything.

We took great pride in the way a dinner table was attentively cleared between courses. The way any member of the restaurant team cleared the plates from a table was just as important as serving them; it was another skill that came with elegance and finesse. Any member of the restaurant team could magically clear a table of four in one go, but it was the way they did it. Not a big chaotic stacking of plates, but a graceful arrangement of the four main course plates, the four side plates, all of the cutlery, the butter dish.

I've witnessed my fair share of horrible table clearings. Whenever I go to a restaurant with family or friends, I admit it's something I can't help but always watch out of the corner of my eye around the dining room. I am fascinated by how commonly bad it is. Even if the culinary delights have been amazing at a restaurant, these simple service basics should match, so that each guest is left with an overwhelmingly positive impression.

When a table cloth was replaced during service, we did so with discreet etiquette. Instead of chaotically throwing a table cloth up into the air to unravel it and screwing up the old one with crumbs going everywhere, we approached the act with simplistic grace. Anyone could do it, like a blind-folded magician—gracefully unfolding the fresh table cloth across a table while gathering the dirty one at the same time.

Without this attention to detail and care over every touch, regardless of how polished we appeared, our guests would have soon forgotten about us.

It was the same as folding a triangular point at the end of toilet rolls in every single bathroom showed how much we cared. Washing the towels and drying them at the right temperature so that they were fluffy and not scratchy also accomplished the same. Our tonality and presence every time any of us said, "Good afternoon and welcome to Ashdown Park" was always warm and present—even if it was the hundredth time we said it that day. Undistracted sincerity toward each and every guest was critical.

Wonderlicious Subtle Ceremony

For many reasons, the restaurant at Ashdown Park was (and still is) beautiful. A traditional and wonderfully elegant dining room, which blends perfectly into the historical past of this glorious mansion house. For our guests, there was no hint of any disjointed formality, just a warm and inviting setting that came with exciting precision.

Creating a wonderlicious dining experience called for the multiple layers of ceremony that we put into everything, both backstage and onstage.

When our guests weren't taking in the uninterrupted views of the grounds and forest which stretched to the horizon, their eyes were drawn to the crisp, finely pressed white linen tablecloths and precisely folded napkins, the well-polished silverware, and the elegant bone china. We would smile warmly and knowingly when we knew that guests were thinking, "Oh my goodness!" in delight over the detail of the silver butter dishes that cradled equally cut slices of butter on a little bed of crushed ice. All of our subtle ceremony and details contributed to our guest experience, yet there was more to it.

The dining room was in good hands with a wonderful team. We partnered with a hospitality school in France, who loyally supported us with our recruitment. They helped us find many special personalities for our kitchen and restaurant team, all polished with the finest principles of hospitality. These hospitality graduates blended in effortlessly with our local team members. We earned an excellent reputation for our culinary style and standard—both the à la carte and daily table d'hôte menu providing an exciting selection with locally produced ingredients. The adjoining main kitchen was well structured and organized. All of this obviously contributed to our guest experience—yet there was *still* more to it.

This is what made the guests' experience and moments wonderlicious: It was how we enthusiastically brought everything together backstage ahead of each service—our endless preparation, consideration, rehearsals, training, tasting, testing, and tweaking. The ceremony of dinner service was always unique, and the level of preparation would probably make many heads spin with disbelief. This went all the way to how we polished our shoes as attentively as the silverware. Every inch of the restaurant carpet was vacuumed, the log fire was set and ready, the lights were dimmed to exactly the right level . . . All this, along with true passion for the job, is how you create wonder.

Take the polished shoes away, leave the lights on full beam, or miss doing the preservice team briefing and the experience would be entirely different.

No stone was ever left unturned. We created an amazing experience for our guests. Whilst it was fun and definitely hard work—it was never a chore. All we had clearly in our mind every day was evoking a feeling for our restaurant guests that we were expecting them, and it was our pleasure in doing so.

Full House Means Everyone Onstage

The final build-up to Saturday evening dinner service was always exhilarating. Each weekend we would commonly have a full house in the hotel, with anywhere up to two hundred guests staying with us. We would usually have a wedding reception in our main banqueting suite, various private dinner parties in various other event spaces, and roughly one hundred reservations in the restaurant. There would also be a steady flow of room service orders and the lounge service (along with the various bar areas). We were all systems go! All the hotel offices backstage were deserted because our entire orchestra was now onstage creating wonderlicious moments.

The restaurant team would be at their allocated stations around the restaurant, and the hotel management team in position all around the hotel public areas. We would be in the lounges, at the front door, in the main mansion house entrance hall—each of us strategically in position ready to unobtrusively share our warm welcome.

You might think that taking a dinner order from a guest was just a run of the mill routine process. Yet for us it was the multiple layers and secret touches of subtle ceremony which created a series of anticipatory moments that began long before a guest would receive their first course.

Any of the management team could take an order for dinner, which might sound easy enough but was far more intricate than just writing down an order and handing it to the chef. If I—or any member of the team—was chatting with some guests in the lounge and they asked me about the salmon entrée or how the lamb was prepared and couldn't answer, in a flash we would look amateur or like we didn't care. Likewise, no matter how busy we were, if we ever appeared hurried, flustered or disinterested, it wouldn't reflect well on who we were or what Ashdown Park was.

When a guest chose their main course, for example saying, "I'll have the beef please," not only would we write it down (the process), but we would then add the acknowledgment (ceremony) by saying something like, "This is an excellent choice!" It was all the little touches that created a special feeling and connection.

While serving, the restaurant team would never walk up to a guest's table holding the dinner plates and ask, "Who ordered the beef?" We didn't have to, because the person who took the order would have written a tiny guest description next to the item: beef (man red tie), salmon (lady blue dress). Subtle ceremony equaled wonderful hospitality.

When guests asked where the restaurant was, we never would just point them in the right direction and say, "It's down the hall and turn left at the end." We would walk them there, of course! Over and over again we would go back and forth from the lounges down the long hallway to the dining room. These were always our precious short moments (opportunities) for us to inquisitively search for additional clues on how we could enhance their experience further.

After dinner, we served a plate of homemade petit fours to accompany coffee, which obviously we took great pleasure in introducing, rather than just leaving the plate.

We took pride in the ceremony—the fullest expression of human-spirited excellence. And then, early the following morning, we would start all over again with breakfast.

Let Your Feet Be Happy . . .

Anyone who's ever worked in hospitality knows it's an environment that thrives on camaraderie.

Every aspect of Ashdown Park came to life through a united team spirit. We were given permission to be our best selves to create the best experience possible for each and every guest. It was about the little things . . . and the big things. Our reviews, recommendations, and awards ultimately showed that having a clear attention to ceremony would always provide us with a bounty of praise.

Had we worked separately, stayed stationary in our offices, or sat in constant meetings planning the future, producing reports, and thinking about the following day, we would have always missed the moments unfolding there and then.

Graeme would consistently remind us, "We can't look after our guests once they have checked out tomorrow."

The success of establishing a vibrant and exciting service culture comes with full credit to the often-unsung heroes—your feet.

Leave them stationery under your desk and *they* will be miserable. Allow them to move around and explore—they will gladly take you on the most wonderlicious adventures!

Only then will you notice how they become your *Happy Feet*. Encourage everyone to do the same and an entire culture (along with business growth and profitability) will radiate a special and invigorating rhythm that your customers can't help but get caught up in and fall in love with.

Recipe 15 Recap:
BACKSTAGE, ONSTAGE

Your team comes alive when you take the "backstage, onstage" theater-style approach to teamwork, logistics, and service. Choreograph moments of subtle ceremony that create distinctly connected moments for customers and guests and have them occur throughout every aspect of business operation.

Ingredients:

★ Happy feet: explore with them, move around on them, allow them to take you on the most wonderlicious adventures.

★ Subtle Ceremony: it is the difference between ordinary and wonderful.

★ Magic added to every detail of your business operation, no matter how small.

★ Daily morning meetings: begin each day together by sharing opportunities, warming up connections, and designing wonderlicious moments in the day ahead.

★ A theater approach to culture: embrace an environment of unity where every team member feels valued and included, whether they're backstage or onstage.

★ Keep your back of house—backstage—areas organized. Your customers will feel the difference.

Substitutions to Make this Recipe Your Own:

Turn every task, even the most mundane or seemingly unimportant, into the opportunity for enhancement. By infusing the attentive spirit of ceremony, you can elevate your guest experience from ordinary to wonderlicious, leaving a lasting impression that keeps guests coming back for more.

Behind the Scenes of the Ashdown Park Recipes:

At the time of writing these reflections, three decades have passed since I joined Ashdown Park. Never has a day gone by where I don't think about it and still feel like I'm there. The deep connection, and my eternal love for the property and the lessons I was fortunate to learn, still guide me today. I passionately share these lessons from stages around the world as a speaker, and any time I am faced with challenges in my day, I still often ask myself, "What would Graeme do or say?"

I had the huge pleasure of returning to Ashdown Park in 2018 for the twenty-fifth-anniversary celebrations. I flew in from Sydney, Australia and headed back down the long winding driveway, just as I did for my interview so many years earlier. It triggered exactly the same emotionally charged butterflies.

I was overwhelmed with happiness seeing the team as focused as we were on opening day twenty-five years earlier. Not only were their hospitality standards as good (if not better), they have also maintained a healthy business occupancy that has navigated through the stormy times of varying economic, political, and other highly challenging external influences. Graeme has been managing director of Elite Hotels since 1998 and remains based at Ashdown Park.

It was a thrilling reunion.

Along with a few tears of joy to accompany my Happy Feet, it felt like I had never been away.

SWEET FINALE

–

IMAGINATION

"

There is no life I know
To compare with pure imagination
Living there, you'll be free
If you truly wish to be

Willy Wonka

MISSION IMPOSSIBLE: A NEW ORBIT

*I*mpossibility provides a tantalizing crossroad.

This one single word carries enormous powers to deceive and manipulate, while simultaneously enticing and seducing.

It takes a split second to brush something off as impossible and with it, miss the potential of whatever it could have been. Human instinct has a clever way of dismissing things that appear too difficult and impossible. Taking sides with impossibility is the same as conforming with perceived reality.

Impossible isn't something that can't be done—it's only something that hasn't yet been done before.

Taking courage to confront impossibility is like standing at the edge of the dance floor, watching everyone in front of you get lost inside their moments of joy. With shy apprehension, your feet start to twitch and urge you forward. Before you know it and with uncontrollable impulse, you're on! Moving your feet and dancing to the beat, your freedom feels stronger than the music and the perception of others to your dance moves pale into insignificance. What if using your imagination felt like this—not a dance party, but like letting go, being free to dream no matter how others might scorn your ambition for doing something different.

To dare.

To play wildly and courageously with possibility.

This sweet finale comes with the purity of imagination. The last part of any menu is the moment where a chef aims to surprise, delight, and achieve that exceptional finishing note to an incredible meal. Chefs actually are often disappointed when their guests say no to dessert, because they know it's the perfect sweet touch to finish their culinary experience.

To add an extra twist to everything you've learned so far about wonder, I finish with a delicious example of what happens when each of the Wonderlicious Recipes up to now are all blended together, with the elements from each recipe combined to create the fullness of wonder.

The one thing that I have learned through my working life is that creating uncomplicated joy is just that—*un*complicated. Redefining impossibility is possible. Work can (and should) be the most exhilarating time of our lives. More than anything, wonder can create a thriving workplace and world-class business culture.

Managing and leading luxury hotels like we explored with Redworth Hall and Ashdown Park is one thing; transferring all the goodness of wonder and hospitality into an alien environment is another. I had to learn that the hard way when I left hotels and stepped into the corporate business world. With only the lessons of wonder in my heart, I had to master how to stay strong and deflect the non-belief of others and win over those who told me my methods of creating uncomplicated joy were ridiculous, absurd, and impossible. I learned to rely on the power of belief to encourage everyone to join me, and my happy feet, on the proverbial dance floor.

I find myself filled with music as I lead you perfectly into this sweet finale, tapping my toes to the beat and singing along with the lyrics of Lionel Richie as I envision all of us "Dancing on the Ceiling."

And why not?

Why shouldn't we aim to make our workplaces happy and joyful? After all, as Hugh Jackman sang, this is "The Greatest Show."

I left my beloved Ashdown Park Hotel and headed to Tower 42, the iconic landmark office skyscraper in the heart of the City of London, the once tallest building in the UK. Along with the magnificent collaboration of the owners and my on-site team, we dared to change everything. Our goal was to flip the commercial real estate industry on its head and through a culture of wonder become known as the best office building in the world.

In the words of David Bowie, "Let's Dance!"

Shall we?

Recipe 16:

IMPOSSIBILITY

"

The wonder of imagination is this:
it has the power to light its own fire.

John Landis Mason

Both emotions hit me at the same time. I was "*terri-cited*"—a nauseating mix, in sequence, of *terrified* and *excited*.

London is my hometown. I was born a stone's throw from Westminster Abbey, and no matter where I have lived and worked throughout my life, London is where my heart feels happiest. However, this day in 2002 felt different as I stepped out of London Bridge Underground station in the early morning rush hour. I reached the pavement and froze to the spot, overwhelmed as I saw the skyline in front of me. In a flash of panic, I asked myself, *What on earth are you doing?* Even hearing the familiar, usually endearing chimes of Big Ben echoing across the Thames offered no comfort.

I contemplated turning around to find the first train out of there or disappearing down a hole to hide. There in front of me towered the six-hundred-foot-tall building, Tower 42. It magnificently reached up into the sky and glistened in the early morning sunshine. At the time, it was the tallest office building in London's financial district, and it was to be my new place of work. I had been hired as general manager of this incredible property. Thankfully my feet took control of the situation and took me toward my first day. I navigated through the crowds of fellow workers in pinstripe suits, on their mobile phones, dashing in all directions to their offices.

As I got closer, the tower grew taller and bigger. Thankfully my heart seemed to reach a relatively normal pace and I switched from fear to an excited realization that this was it.

I wondered, in awe of the opportunity before me "Is this real? Is this moment actually happening?"

Once I stepped inside the entrance from Old Broad Street, away from the mass of red London buses and black cabs, into the breathtaking calm of the huge glass lobby, I came to my senses. This would be my working home for the next eight years—25 Old Broad Street.

The Blank Sheet of Paper

Several weeks earlier I had my final interview with the owners of the building—the Tower Limited Partnership, a joint ownership investment between Merrill Lynch Investment Managers (later becoming BlackRock) and Hermes Real Estate. I remember walking into the formal boardroom and meeting seven of the partners who were waiting to welcome me. It was both unnerving and exhilarating, I had never felt so far away from my comfort zone before in my life. I really wanted the GM role and I had one chance to prove myself. At the same time, I realized that I immediately liked the partners who sat around the gigantic rectangular board table.

They were seated to my left and right, so I had to carefully focus on where to direct my eyes without excluding anyone. I concentrated on navigating the crossfire of questions while they each considered if I was the one who could take care of their £226 million prized trophy asset, with targets to achieve a £20 million annual rental return. One might expect a stuffy, intimidating interview, but they surprised me. They were entirely prepared and present. It was an interview masterclass and an experience in itself.

One of the partners said, "It's common practice and would be considered normal in our industry for us to employ a general manager with an engineering or facilities management background." He looked at me and then to the other partners, and continued, "But we don't want to be normal."

Those words were music to my ears. I knew I would love working for this inspiring group of individuals. They all leaned forward and started joining in.

One partner explained, "We want to reimagine the tower and our five peripheral buildings into a multi-use city village, something that has a big heart. We want it to be a happy and exciting place where people love to come to work every day. We want to make it the best in London."

"Like a hotel without bedrooms," said another. "Like never been seen before."

I smiled eagerly in agreement and swallowed hard as I knew just how big London was. This was a formal meeting, but there was no uneasy interrogation or corporate jargon, just warmth and connection. They were genuinely interested to hear what I was saying and suggesting.

"We have to give you this," as they slid the official job description across the table. Then the moment happened that changed everything in an instant. To this day (some twenty years later), it remains another of my fondest and most career-defining moments. With perhaps the greatest recruitment strategy of all time, one of the senior partners, Christopher Lacey, then of Merrill Lynch Investment Managers, smiled as he slid another piece of paper across the table toward me.

He was a warm and likable character, as proven by what he said next: "But Peter, *this* is the most important piece of paper we would like you to concentrate on."

I turned it over. It was blank.

Christopher explained, "We don't fully understand the hospitality world you've come from, but we love it. Take this piece of paper and bring to life for us what you learned in hotels. More than anything, be yourself, and inspire the same in everyone around you."

I was lost for words but somehow managed a heartfelt, "Thank you."

"We won't interfere with your day-to-day leadership, but please know that we will always be here to support you."

I didn't realize at the time just how exceptionally far ahead they were in their determination to make a real statement in the property industry. Employing me, a hotelier, as their general manager was just one part.

I asked plenty of questions, but the most important one was finding out how many people made up my on-site team. "Seven," they replied. "You have a core team of seven."

They sensed my dismay that this 2.2-acre estate with six buildings and over three thousand resident occupiers was looked after by seven people.

"Oh! You mean the contractors! This is for you to bring to life, all of the service providers and contractors. You will find them all over the estate."

For anyone looking at the payroll of Tower 42, I was the only name that appeared on it. As is tradition in commercial property management, everyone else was either employed by the managing agent, appointed as a specialist associate, or contracted through one of the many service providers.

Never Lose Sight of What Makes You—You

I left my final interview feeling on top of the world, with the words of the owners going round and round my thoughts. "Like never seen before," they had said. I felt like Dorothy in *The Wizard of Oz*. I wondered if repeating her words, "There's no place like home, there's no place like home," would wake me up from my dream and send me back to reality.

Those four terrifying, exciting words, "Like never seen before," lived in my mind and guided my heart continuously throughout my time at Tower 42.

There is a special pride that comes from creating a place that brings happiness to people. For our team, our customers, and the owners, Tower 42 wasn't just a landmark building on the London skyline that leased office space. We were going all out to create a special place that would shine with heart. We wanted to become famous not just for being an efficient office environment with desks and chairs, but for having a vibrant atmosphere of joy.

I knew at this moment that I would never forget or lose sight of where I came from. I already had in my heart everything that I had learned from Mr. Müller's bakery and his frogs, from my pottery teacher at high school, from Malcolm Powell at Redworth Hall, and of course from Graeme Bateman at Ashdown Park. All of their lessons traveled with me in my heart as my box of magic tricks. I was excited and proud to now be able to share all of this far and wide with everyone else.

Backward, Forward, Left, or Right?

Tower 42 was more than a skyscraper of steel and glass. It had dominated the London skyline for thirty years and had multiple layers of historical significance. It was designed by Anglo-Swiss architect Richard Seifert and took ten years to build before being formally opened on 11 June 1981 by Queen Elizabeth II. Tower 42 was originally known as the NatWest Tower, having been built as the international headquarters of National Westminster Bank. Seen from above, the shape of the tower resembles the NatWest logo, with three chevrons in a hexagonal arrangement. With forty-seven levels above ground, forty-two cantilevered and lettable floors, the tower represented the heart of the estate with five other self-contained buildings and 473,000 square feet of high-quality office accommodation.

One thing remained more apparent than anything else: all of us together, the owners and my team, all felt incredibly honored to be the new custodian and didn't take this lightly. With concrete foundations going fifty meters deep into the London clay, we were about to mastermind a never-seen-before workplace culture and lifestyle equal to the size and stature of the impressive building itself—and to do so, with wonder.

We frequently found ourselves facing the crossroad of impossibility and the status quo. Retreating backward was never an option. At each opportunity, we strove to avoid all easy escape routes and instead, courageously pushed beyond whatever the rest of the industry was doing. We had our sights set on a new orbit that laid outside of the norm. We proudly looked past the *No Entry* sign and dove headfirst into impossibility.

Luxury hotels are one thing and office blocks are another. Each fulfills a different function, and they ordinarily *appear* to be planets apart. Try and ask the caretaker or receptionist to get you tickets to the theater, collect your guests from the airport, or schedule you in for a manicure at your desk and you are sure to be sectioned off to spend the next twelve months undergoing psychiatric treatment.

To successfully transform and operate Tower 42, a high-rise office building, as a quality hotel environment, we couldn't just *say* we were running the property uniquely as a hotel, we had to actually *do* it. Whilst marketing our trophy office building with the word *hotel* would have sounded nice and impressive on the surface, it had to be real. Every single minuscule part of it.

The best hotels around the world lead their market and industry because of their highly connected culture of wonder. Their success comes from the *feeling* they give their guests even more than impressive facilities. I kept that knowledge close to my heart as we started out on our quest to create something no one had seen before.

Stepping through the front door on my first day, I fastened my seatbelt, and, without any warning, the roller coaster departed immediately. I was all in for the ride.

Turning an Industry on Its Head

We lived inside a viciously competitive market, and all eyes were on us being at the heart of the world's leading financial center. We were the tallest and also the oldest property in a skyline filled with dozens of cranes which were busy building brand new shiny skyscrapers, with even fancier fittings and features. There would always be something new to compare ourselves with, so instead, we remained clear in our goals. Beyond our iconic status, we were going to do whatever it took to be the best.

The commercial real estate industry, for good reason, is contractual, transactional, and complex. Traditionally when companies take up space in an office building, they agree to formal terms of lease with a property agent representing the landlord. Once signed, they become a *tenant*, with general amenities and services provided via contracted services.

We wanted to go further than just high-quality office accommodations, air conditioning, innovative lighting, efficient plant rooms, intelligently crafted leasing terms, and attractive rental options. All of that alone wouldn't bring people through the door. What mattered most to the owners was a fully occupied estate. At the same time, we knew we couldn't force anyone to lease their office space with us. We had to make it irresistible in multiple and exciting ways. So, we set out to create wonder by applying hotel hospitality methods to our environment.

The only difference we saw was that we didn't have any bedrooms and our guests never checked out. They signed long leases and would be with us for anywhere from five to ten years, which was especially invigorating for us. The positive we took from this was that we would have the chance to form a deep understanding of what they actually wanted, needed, and expected. Then it was down to us to stay fresh and focused continuously on top of anticipating the exacting detail of everything—every single day.

Adding Simplicity to Head-Spinning Complexity

Our approach to life at Tower 42 was to radiate uncomplicated joy and efficiency. We ensured that no one would ever guess that behind our calm and welcoming presence lay the immense precision that went on behind the scenes.

The owners were beyond genius with their vision. It wasn't just me as general manager, or the on-site team, or our many external representatives that made Tower 42. It was a collective effort.

They appointed Greycoat Estates as the asset manager and trusted advisor, responsible for overseeing the financial and leasing strategy, liaising with the banks, and pioneering the master plan, which was led by Andy Craven. Based near the tower, Andy combined the charm and demeanor of Hugh Grant with the brilliance of Albert Einstein. We worked together in close partnership, with me leading everything from the ground, building relationships with existing and future occupiers, and guiding the on-site team.

BNP Paribas had the integral responsibility as our managing agent to employ the core management team and various service providers, while expertly managing all the owners' contractual obligations.

Our shared responsibility was like a gigantic bowl of complex spaghetti. Each strand represented something of significant importance, meaning we had to do whatever it took to keep everything untangled.

We were operating 365 days of the year 24 hours a day with over 3,000 resident occupiers and multiple lease arrangements. Every month we welcomed 12,000 visitors, delivered 50,000 items of post and 10,000 courier packages, security searched 3,000 visiting cars, served 8,000 cups of tea and coffee in the cafe, and screened 11,000 items of baggage through airport style security. On top of this, we had precise health and safety, legal, and environmental requirements to fulfill, leasing agents and press advisors to coordinate, and our close daily partnership with the City of London Police to manage. We had a master development plan, a communication strategy, and a financial commitment to the owners. There were multiple service providers, 20 passenger lifts making 300,000 journeys each month, and one could not forget all the windows that we had to keep clean.

As an extra challenge to all these near-limitless logistics, we couldn't—and wouldn't—*at any point* charge additional fees for providing excellent service and an innovative culture. This was on the house. Our occupiers already paid an annual service charge for all utilities and common area maintenance (charged per square foot), which included our salaries and services.

Just like a quality hotel, the wonder of our creative delight would be part of the experience, not a supplementary charge on the bill.

Amongst the countless details that went into each day, it would have been so easy to become totally lost amongst it all, swept away down the rapids of tasks and responsibilities. We focused our efforts on *simplexity*. It became our ongoing guiding light and our way of consistently applying and blending simplicity with complexity. Whatever faced us, no matter how challenging or confronting, we used *simplexity* to keep moving forward and growing with ease and momentum.

During moments of overwhelm, it is easy to forget what actually lights you up, matters most, or sparks uncomplicated joy. We used *simplexity* as a practice with our team and our customers. It helped us create the customer delight we believed in. We kept anything complex as simple as possible and used this style to take us toward possibility.

People became our superpower, and wonder was our unique ingredient.

The more we did it the more it became second nature. The more we did it the more the estate filled up. People from far and wide started talking about us, including the newspapers.

And this was just the beginning for what lay ahead . . .

Recipe 16 Recap:
IMPOSSIBILITY

Big transformative dreams take vision. Vision takes purpose and passion. And all of it combined takes a whole lot of wonderlicious ideas to make it all come true. It takes courage to push beyond the status quo and aim toward a new orbit with innovation and ideas. It takes even more courage—and simplexity—to inspire an entire industry. Above all else, the biggest changes come to life through the heart of people. What lessons will you apply to make your *Mission Possible?!*

Ingredients:

* Vision: share a blank sheet of paper with new employees along with permission for them to be adventurous and, most of all, to be themselves.
* Simplexity: put the focus on simplifying the otherwise complex to avoid getting caught up in the rapids of tasks and responsibilities.
* Terri-citement: blend the emotions of fear and excitement when tackling new challenges.
* Unending innovation: continuously play with innovation. The more daring, the better.
* Values: stay true to yourself and your values, drawing on them for inspiration and guidance.

Substitutions to Make this Recipe Your Own:

Whenever something seems beyond you (impossible), run toward it! Whether it is a new job, a complicated life problem, or a goal you want to achieve, this recipe helps you take pride and privilege in the opportunity to dare embracing impossibility, no matter how terrifying. By applying the principles of this wonderlicious recipe, you can transform even the most daunting challenges into opportunities for success and fulfillment.

Recipe 17:
IRRESISTIBILITY

"

You can dream, create, design and build the most wonderful place in the world . . .
But it requires people to make the dream a reality."

Walt Disney

What if treating people well was the common practice of modern workplace leadership?

What if daring to be different was a real way of life?

What if these two little words had the power to cause workplace transformation and the brightest of all team spirits?

What if were two words that we used a lot at Tower 42.

Together we consistently asked ourselves *what if* we tried this or said that. *What if* we changed this or played with that?

For any esteemed chef the world over, they purposefully allow time to stand still behind the scenes inside their kitchen and play with *what if.* To savor the construction of every dish, to decipher recipes and transform them, to play until they find that essential special ingredient and touch—that's what makes distinguished chefs so inspiring. We practiced the same method, taking the time to be still, giving time and space to think and practice. We found joy in experimenting with who we were and what we could achieve with *what if.*

Turning Impossibility into Irresistibility

To *make* something irresistibly special for our customers, we had to *do* something irresistibly special. Becoming the most desirable business address in London went far beyond the steel and glass of the property, or the lovely furniture, or even our energy efficiency and innovative leasing structure. Being irresistible could only truly come from the heart and passion of the day-to-day experience provided by the authenticity of our people—the entire Tower 42 team.

Sometimes life can throw out some mighty scary curveballs of absurd impossibility. The multi-contract set-up of Tower 42 was the biggest curveball I had faced up to this point in my career. It was a mind-spinning obstacle. Every representative of the on-site team was contracted or employed by an array of different companies and service providers. So, I relied on one of the biggest lessons I learned from my hotel days, which was to focus only on the possibility that this fascinating opportunity provided and build a single team culture that was united and together, no matter who technically signed their paychecks.

Tower 42 could only operate as one.

There were many more people than the *seven* that made up the actual on-site management team. We had over 250 wonderful characters—a mix of individual contractors and service providers—that we started to bring together as one cohesive team. Through my eyes, I didn't see the various companies they represented. I saw them as Tower 42 people, full of heart and potential.

If we had organized and run Tower 42 in the usual property industry style, with each of the service providers and contractors working separately and only within the scope of their own individual contact agreements, the team and customer environment would have been nothing more than that—contractual. It would have been a disjointed and reactive atmosphere. This way would have only created something "*seen before.*"

It was an unusually complicated prospect and something else that we masterminded with *simplexity.*

I wanted our team spirit to be fun and inclusive for everyone. Without a big instruction manual or book of rules, our approach was to practice a continuous flow of trust, care, and kindness amongst the entire Tower 42 team. This would hopefully aid us in our possibility of reaching *that* point—the point of doing something "*Like never seen before.*"

Like a jigsaw puzzle with 250 pieces in the box. If I left all the pieces unconnected in the box and held it at arm's length, our new culture of wonder would have never worked, or meant anything. Joining all the pieces together was like turning the lights on.

I threw the box away.

The Choice Between Joy and Suffocation

For anyone going to work each day, being part of a workplace culture can be nothing or it can be everything. It can suffocate your personality beneath the wheels of process, or it can inspire playful creativity. So many companies who create unbearable work environments exhaust their team with this fragile dance every day until they inevitably crash and burn.

It took everything I had in my heart and sight to inspire and lead a diversely interesting and deeply satisfying workplace in which everyone's potential and wisdom would be whole-heartedly celebrated.

At Tower 42, the team needed Lionel Richie's lyrics more than David Bowie's. We wanted to take our wonder culture higher, to "Dancing On The Ceiling" level, filled with uncomplicated joy.

For the thousands of people walking through the doors of Tower 42, I wanted them to not only marvel at this iconic vertical structure, but also feel the immediate difference in our team spirit—the purity of our humility and connection.

Not only this, but our intention also went further: we wanted everyone visiting or coming to their office each day to be fascinated by our imagination and brightness. We would do whatever it took to not allow any gray seriousness of the outside world to smother and lose sight of this.

I knew clearly from my time in hotels that people, whatever their role, thrived in the freedom to express themselves. They got a sense of belonging from being included as well as having their efforts noticed and contributions valued. By being consistently gracious and treating people—all people—with genuine care, only goodness would come back in return.

At Tower 42, there were no blindfolds to hide this away, only a resolute determination to bring exactly this to life. We celebrated every day, not with wild parties and champagne, but with recognition of all the incredible things our team was doing to better the lives and work of our customers.

We were creating a *never seen before* culture of wonder and this one focus of intention stayed clearer, brighter and ahead of anything else. *Every day* was a *human-spirited opportunity for wonder.*

At Ashdown Park, I had been part of a team that performed as an orchestra for the previous eight years. Ashdown was a luxury hotel. Tower 42 was an office skyscraper. I wanted to do it again and I wanted it to be as good (and famous) as the London Philharmonic Orchestra. When I shared this vision, I was delighted by the response. It was exactly as it had been during those profound grand opening meetings at Ashdown Park. The Tower 42 team were all in for creating a unique and joyful working harmony for our monumental estate.

Inventing Never Seen Before: Together

When I hear statements like "people are our greatest asset," I often cringe because they're often used by organizations as a marketing ploy and not a realistic culture statement.

I knew that it was the word *team* that would take us to our new orbit, with a strength of bond to inspire us beyond our never-ending finish line. Bringing all 250 personalities together as one team was our magic. Everyone gravitated to the prospect, because it was exciting and real. No longer were they powerless to help or forced to say those dreaded words, "That's not my job."

Onstage and backstage, we had 10 on our engineering team (plumbers, electricians, and a handyman), 23 security guards, a loading bay team, 7 front-of-house receptionists, an amazing concierge, a chauffeur, 4 window cleaners, 108 cleaners and waste disposal attendants, 11 post and print room operators, 2 lift engineers, a team of 17 in the health club, a hospitality team of 47 for our restaurant and bars, 7 for our private dining rooms, and 8 in the café.

Amongst them all we had eight fluent languages, a professional swimming coach, Michelin-starred chefs, one of the world's top master sommeliers, a team of physiotherapists, personal fitness trainers, and nutritionists. Overall, it was a broad and hugely fascinating collection of incredible personalities and expertise. The day-to-day operation could have so easily remained separated and also so easily gone awry. Bringing everyone together so tightly provided further magnetic strands to our point of difference of becoming a fascinating and aligned lifestyle brand.

Instead of limiting voices at the top, we welcomed all of our senior on-site contractor and service provider roles as part of our management team. For example, our cleaning contract manager became Head of Housekeeping. The core management team grew from seven to sixteen, adding more connected voices to our magical making of wonder at Tower 42.

If my leadership approach had been at arm's length and with the scrutiny of a magnifying glass, it would have been a pretty uninspiring existence for anyone on the team. Assessing everyone individually in the boardroom against the small print of their key performance indicators, reviewing performance within the terms and parameters of their formal service contracts, they would have only been focused on delivering this. I knew, from experience, that it wasn't the way to get the best out of anyone.

I was determined to create seamless collaboration across all areas of the daily operation, fostering a genuine willingness to support one another—a special connection that allowed us to bounce off each other effortlessly. For instance, for the security team to be in sync with the reception team, and for any member of the daytime housekeeping team to feel comfortable directing a guest to the restaurant, everyone would be willing to pick up a piece of litter or walk a first time visitor to the correct lift instead of pointing which way to go. All roles and departments had to feel connected, equal, and supported.

If anything, one of the easiest things to establish was the open and informal nature of our communication. This was made simple because everyone knew that our intention was authentic with no hidden agenda. At no point did we communicate in "contractor talk," only "Tower 42 talk," which moved us quickly to the point of subconsciously forgetting who, in fact, employed each other, because all we could see was the Tower 42 Team. This wasn't the norm for the industry, and we loved this difference.

Each of our various service providers were carefully selected and hand-picked. They were critical to our success, but in the face of each other, in front of our customers, and to the outside world, everyone was a proud and equal part of the Tower 42 Team, all part of the story and the experience of creating *"never seen before."*

Inspiring a Shared Belief without Instruction or Force

Both off-site and on-site, everyone involved with the running of Tower 42 was (in the nicest possible sense) like a bowl of nuts. The Peanuts (the believers) were easy and didn't need much convincing with our vision of doing something "like never seen before." They were very happy to let go of their simple shell and go all in. The Walnuts (the non-believers) were dubious and more challenging to crack! We obviously couldn't demand them to conform. Instead, I let them come out of their resisting shells by themselves. It was easier for me to show them that what we were doing—blending wonder with hospitality—came with genuine intention. One by one, we won the hearts of The Walnuts, and everyone joined in.

One thing that I consistently practiced from my time in hotels was imagining myself inside the shoes of everyone on the team, whatever their rank or position. Nothing mattered more to me than knowing everyone went home at the end of their day and shift, knowing they felt valued and appreciated. It's all I wanted. Nothing else was more important to me than making sure each person looked forward to coming back the next day to do it all over again.

Mastering Repetition with the 50/50 Approach

Apart from public holidays, we put on our show every single day, over and over, without pause. We didn't aim to rinse and repeat what we did the previous day. We were simply focused on making each one better than the last.

To keep everything fresh, we avoided formal rules and complications like the plague. One thing that remained our guiding force was our informal "50/50" approach. It became our habit for the management team to spend half of our day at our desks (to keep up with the fast flow of our office based tasks) and the other half spent out on the floor, interacting with customers, greeting guests, checking in with all departments and searching for clues to delight or things we could tweak. The thing I loved most about this, apart from its groundbreaking style—we didn't run it with a stopwatch, process, or spreadsheet. We just did it.

As role models, the management team and I went all out to show equal interest in every single role of the entire team. We did this by being out on the floor at least half of every day—visible and accessible inside the property—as highly invested in everyone as our own employees. Within seconds, we could be at the rubbish compactor in the basement talking to Sid (a fabulous, loyal character who cheerfully compacted the never-ending volume of rubbish coming down to his area from every floor), or we would be up on the roof checking-in with the window cleaners. We could be down in the security control room or behind the main reception assisting the team to welcome the never-ending flow of guests arriving. Every day, we were out and about assisting and connecting. We kept our interactions light and bright, not only asking everyone how their day was going, but more importantly, asking with our magic words: "Are you okay?"

Our open, blameless approach was the key to creating our vibrant, successful culture. We had each other's backs because we cared. Whilst we had a clearly articulated organization structure to define the complex responsibilities across the business, we relented from having a formal hierarchy chart. Never would there be any hint of *them and us*; it just didn't exist, nor would it be allowed.

Plain and simple, we were in it together and that made us feel invincible. Our connection was as powerful as the floodlights beaming inside a football stadium. If any of the individual cables or fuses were split or broken, the lights wouldn't work, and the football pitch would stay dark. We certainly weren't perfect and yes, sometimes our lights flickered, but thankfully only briefly. Never did they fail.

Within the cynical side of the industry, some undoubtedly questioned why this even mattered or they brushed it aside as unnecessary and time-consuming fluff. To us, nothing else mattered more. Our culture and our strength as a team were everything—our super powers.

You Can't Fake "Family"

We didn't casually say that we were a family, although this is how we felt and exactly how we behaved in supporting each other. Here lies the truth, the whole truth, and nothing but the truth, of that powerful little gem of a word in practice—*family*.

All of us connected together as one became a defining part of the Tower 42 story; it fueled the feeling that reached all of our customers and fired our engine with great tenacity.

If you ever use that word, or talk about your team culture as a *family*, it has to be truthful. You must show up for them like *family*. It is a word that must never be used falsely to sound impressive.

For anyone outside looking in, they saw a harmonious environment, with a huge team working generously together—polite and compassionate with each other. Being courteous was second nature to us, with "please" and "thank you" expressed freely and with clear sincerity. These common missing ingredients of modern business workplaces formed who we were. So many companies were missing the wonderful and effervescent connection created by the civilized and well-mannered interactions that were common in times gone by. But for Tower 42, these values became the heart of our presence.

Inventing a Language of Wonder—Together

Normal practice across the commercial real estate industry is for companies to sign a formal lease for their new office space and then contractually become *tenants*. We decided that wouldn't work for Tower 42. We asked ourselves, *What if we completely removed "tenant" from our vocabulary?* Since we despised this word, we playfully banned the use of *tenants*, replacing it with *customers* and *guests*.

We dared to make these changes together, tweaking our expression with what we stood for and adding extra layers of groundbreaking difference. In setting the stage, our mini dictionary of our unique expressions expanded . . .

> *Tenants and Visitors*—**Customers and Guests**
> *Contractors, staff, service providers*—**Tower 42 Team**
> *The Building Management Team*—**Tower 42 Management Team**
> *Weekly Team Meeting*—**The Gathering**
> *Cleaning contract*—**Housekeeping**
> *Reception Security Guards*—**Hosts**
> *New team onboarding*—**Welcome Party**
> *Survey*—**Your Views**
> *Newsletter*—**View from 42**

This simple play on words sent our culture of wonder into a vastly fresh direction and wholeheartedly changed the approach of the entire team. Our *customers* and *guests* enjoyed it too—they knew we were on their side and not handling them within the contractual constraints of the formal paperwork. Dropping *tenants* from our vocabulary cost nothing but created enormous additional value. Our customers weren't only signing up for a lease; we were providing an unrivaled place that they could call home.

Creating an Invisible Magic Code

We became similar in many ways to Secret Service Agents with our invisible ways, eye signals, and gestures between each other. In devising our cultural values, we avoided any reference to the word "rules."

Instead, we involved everyone across the team in bringing the vision of our magic code to life—to remind each other of what we proudly stood for as The Tower 42 Team. Real words to guide us. We wanted our customers and guests to feel like kings and queens walking into Tower 42 and we weren't prepared for anything less.

To the outside world our published team motto became "*We lead, others follow.*" It was a bold, daring statement and we all believed in it.

Internally, we had a more informal and memorable team catchphrase: "*Dare to be different.*" It was followed by our secret code:

1. *Take fun seriously*
2. *Be kind at every opportunity*
3. *Support and serve each other*
4. *Stay humble and unexpected*
5. *Move your feet*
6. *Communicate openly*

To the outside world and across our promotions and marketing materials "*So much more than just spectacular offices*" became our well-known statement.

People over Process: Critical Rituals

Before anyone stepped into their role, we shared with them who we were, what Tower 42 was, and why their contribution was so important. Each service agreement and contract had a specific headcount, and they could each ordinarily employ people as needed to maintain that contracted level of team numbers. However, imagine you are Mary, the new cleaner (contractor) arriving to start work at Tower 42. You would probably be overwhelmed and have no idea of how anything worked, apart from your vacuum cleaner. Instead of a disjointed and contractual company onboarding process, we shared our legendary "Welcome Party" and eagerly performed this as often as required—usually monthly, sometimes weekly. These were two precious hours that turbo-charged our culture with an encouraging celebration. It replaced the disconnected, arduous checklist of policy processes that was so common within our industry.

This was a simple moment of welcome connection, reassurance, and an invitation to anyone joining, along with a blank sheet of paper, to be themselves. I wanted the team to stay with us, to grow, develop and flourish, rather than us suffering from a revolving door of turnover.

One thing we practiced more than anything else was openly showing appreciation to each other. It became our natural flow, not only during the day but outside of business hours too. The core of our housekeeping team arrived late in the evening to clean each of our customers' floors, so we took turns visiting them during their night shift, not only to spot check standards, but to make sure they knew how much we appreciated them.

Apart from our own special in-house training and coaching, we took the management team of sixteen off-site for two days each year to go into the heart of our connection and to keep our "never seen before" vision thriving. This was a no-frills experience with no extravagant expense and was often themed around survival. One favorite occasion we headed deep into a remote forest with nothing, apart from basic food supplies and a survival expert. We had to build our own shelters to sleep in using only sticks and leaves, and we also learned how to make fire to cook.

It was a wonderful way to bond and plan for the future, but the real value came from spending time together, away from everything, to truly be ourselves and learn from and about each other. This was something else we did that was often scorned as time wasting fluff. "How was the holiday?" our neighbors would say on our return. We were quietly pleased that they didn't understand what we were doing and never would we have achieved anywhere close to the same outcome from being in a windowless training center boardroom for two days with spreadsheets and screens. Nor would it have created the same level of appreciation from everyone.

We purposefully located our management suite on level 24, so that we were all visible and centrally positioned together in the heart of the tower. One of *the* best ever things that we did at Tower 42 was acquiring our circular table for the meeting room of our management suite. Much of what we became was born around it. We all loved our table! It seated ten and, being a circle shape, there was no head chair; essentially, everyone felt equal.

Better still, the only thing electronic in our meeting room was the lights. We intentionally had no TV screen on the wall, and our special little meeting room was a sacred device-free zone, with just paper and pens.

Show Not Tell

Rather than continuously *telling* our customers and guests everything. We also *showed* them. People love to be shown things, like when we participated as young children with *Show & Tell* in the classroom at school. We were taught that the most important part was the show. If someone brought in their bunny rabbit, you didn't want them to describe their pretty bunny to you. You wanted them to show you—the bunny! So, the show part is more important than the telling part.

We had combined our large group of individual contractors into one magnificent and cohesive team—and wanted to show everyone the feeling of our collective heart, not just describe it.

Each year we arranged several little photoshoots with the team for our marketing materials and one time we captured a wonderful picture up on the roof of the entire on-site management team. All sixteen of us were in the picture smiling proudly at the camera. The thing I love and cherish more than anything with this particular picture is that anyone who saw it would have no idea that we were employed by twelve different companies.

Other times we gathered absolutely everyone for the annual Tower 42 team photo. Out went a message to everyone inviting them to meet us outside the following day in our courtyard at 9:30 a.m. sharp! As many of the team as possible stopped what they were doing and raced down for the ten-minute photo shoot. Apart from having to leave someone at the main reception and in the security control room, all the chefs, housekeepers, engineers, hospitality—everyone—enthusiastically joined in. Usually there were about one hundred of us in our family photo, all beaming with pride. Then as fast as they were there, just as fast they left to get back to what they were all doing.

To this day, I still see the pictures of property teams around the world with a handful of people from their core team only. To us, we were all or nothing and these *show* moments were amongst the ones that mattered the most.

We kept returning to the crossroads and continued to head forward; our embrace of impossibility found its own special rhythm. The downside? We found it challenging to sit or stand still but felt happy being aboard our rocket ship to a new orbit.

Our breadth of wonder gave the tower its own heart. With the team in a harmonious and happy flow, we next applied exactly the same attention to our customers and guests.

It felt like we could reach the moon . . .

IRRESISTIBILITY

The transformative and fog-lifting power of "what if?" can unlock the full potential of any organization's culture. Embracing this style of openness and imagination can spark a wildly radiant, irresistible team spirit and the limitless possibilities that come with it.

Ingredients:

★ Invisible magic code: invisible ways, eye signals, and gestures between team members that work to create an irresistible atmosphere and experience.

★ Showing, not (just) telling. You can't fake family. Customers (and team members) can see false attempts at connection from a mile away. Instead, live the values and culture you wish to inspire in your entire team.

★ People over process: Welcome parties instead of onboarding processes. An invitation to stay, grow, develop and flourish with the team as opposed to the culture and expense of revolving doors.

★ Daring to be different: break free from common convention and experiment outside your comfort zone.

★ Banning of the words, "That's not my job." If you're in, you're in it together.

Substitutions to Make this Recipe Your Own:

Use some or all of the ingredients above to create an irresistible culture and a team that acts as one. Add your own secret code of actions and values.

Recipe 18:
OUTRAGEOUS SUPER GLUE

"

There's a morning when presence comes over your soul. You sing like a rooster in your earth-colored shape. Your heart hears and, no longer frantic, begins to dance.

Rumi

"**A**re they up there again doing their flower arranging?"

We knew it's what people were teasing us about from our neighboring competitor buildings. We were also aware that they were watching us, maybe with big binoculars from their high-rise floors over to ours. They had given us the badge of *fluff*. With our culture of wonder that was continuing to rapidly bloom to life, we were aware of the comments flying around outside. "It's all fluff!"

Maybe it was jealousy, or that our embrace of possibility just seemed too absurd. If anything, these viewpoints of our goals and culture made us even more determined to persevere. We weren't scared or embarrassed by what we knew people were saying—quite the opposite. We were blissfully happy with our state of so-called outrageousness. The more it appeared scandalous to some, the brighter our lights shone, strengthening our quest to prove any naysayer wrong.

The commercial real estate industry had always operated in a relatively traditional way, with everyone tending to do what everyone else did or offered. That meant most dealings with tenants, leases, and contracts were much the same from property to property. We were breaking the rules and shaking things up a little bit with our wonderlicious approach.

Other properties would do pop-up events or one-off surprise cupcake days in an attempt to enhance their "tenant engagement." We took a much bigger stance. We wanted to produce maximum adhesion with our depth of service—fluff to some—and went all out to make every single part of the daily experience uncommon and unexpected.

Our hearts and minds were subconsciously gathered together at the base of Mount Everest, all of us eager in our mountaineering gear. Quite simply and proudly, no matter what anyone scorned—our tenants and visitors were our customers and guests, and our contractors were our treasured team. We had our assortment of special pens to bring color (wonder and hospitality) to our black & white (service). Paper glue wouldn't have been strong or sticky enough and only provided a temporary fix. We were manufacturing our own adhesive formula of difference—our Outrageous Super Glue, like the world had never seen.

Not even the biggest avalanche could have knocked us off course. We wanted to embrace the view from the top and together nothing could—or would—stop us getting there.

The Gathering

In fairness, I probably should have given the team white lab coats and safety goggles stepping into our weekly meeting. It was more like entering a laboratory, playing with Bunsen burners and brightly colored bubbling liquids, than a formal hectic team meeting.

This wasn't just another meeting. Well, it was, but not in the usual sense or style. We had already replaced two words—Team Meeting—with The Gathering and every Tuesday at 10 a.m. on the dot, it happened. The Gathering was our special moment of uninterrupted connection and alignment. It was a lot like our pit stop, pulling each of our cars off the race track to refuel and change our wheels.

The same as hotels holding their morning "team warm-up" and restaurants holding their inspiring "pre-meal" team briefing prior to service, we performed exactly the same hospitality ritual. It became the most anticipated experience and our most important sixty minutes of the week. This was our time to pause, our backstage moment to fine tune our orchestra—the outside world was closed, and it was something else that had an element of outrageousness about it. There was no agenda or minutes, and we wasted no time discussing anything that could be better communicated by email. It was light and bright, with no tension or complication, and neither was anyone apprehensive nor shy about speaking up. Everyone tended to arrive early and often had to bring a chair with them because it was always a full house. The door was open to everyone, and beyond the management team, others from the broader team were welcomed to join in too.

One thing we thankfully never suffered through our special culture was lackluster complacency—The Gathering provided the antidote.

It was a balanced "*what's next*" moment, with equal energy to get our teeth firmly into "*what's now*" while taking the time to carefully play with our why and how. When anything felt like an uphill challenge, as it often did, instead of a "head spinning headache meeting," it gave us strength and in unison added further layers to our trust. It took us from a large group of individuals into a cohesive and transformative team.

Around our beloved circular table each year, we all sat with a big pot of pens (and a big plate of mince pies) to hand sign our hundreds of Christmas cards. Around that table is where we designed and created joy. It was around that table where we invented and played with making our Outrageous Super Glue.

Taking fun seriously was top of our list of values, and this was our incubator. Those sixty minutes each and every week influenced everything, and I wholeheartedly believe if every single organization and business the world over held a version of their own weekly team meeting like this, workplaces would change forever. Just like ours did.

Redefining "World-Class" Together

The greatest lesson I learned from The Gathering was the importance of listening and acknowledging every single idea that came forward—especially the ones that were unconventional or preposterous, as those harbored the most exciting and transformative potential. We loved our flow of ideas and allowed each one, big or small, the space to breathe and often then just got on with doing it.

None of the small things were small. A seemingly insignificant tweak was everything— and we made *millions* of tweaks! Like when one of the team suggested, "Why don't we just get rid of the word survey?" We knew "survey" was a word that everyone loathed. And in a flash, our customer service survey became "Your Views." We introduced the idea and our response rate immediately increased.

I adored the open banter and sharing of ideas across the whole team. During The Gathering one week, I apprehensively relayed the owner's dream from my interview of making Tower 42 the best office building in London. I half expected a horrified response to the prospect, but instead, everyone sat forward, leaned in, and the table burst to life with ideas and enthusiasm.

"Small place London," one of the team said.

Someone else chirped up with, "What about being the best in the UK?"

"Small place the UK," said another.

Followed by, "How about Europe?"

"Let's do the world," from someone else.

There came an unusually long silent pause as those words sunk in with all of us around the table. The silence broke with a unanimous chorus of celebration.

In a matter of minutes, as a team, we had set ourselves the most audacious challenge. It seemed like an outrageous goal, which was perhaps why we loved the idea so much. With no fanfare, we left The Gathering smiling and in simple agreement: the world it was. We wanted to be the best office building in the world.

We knew that to be recognized as the best in the world, first we had to earn it, probably against hundreds of metrics. "World-class" wasn't a status that could be referenced if it was only our aspiration. We couldn't buy it, and lavish extravagance wouldn't achieve it. We had to fully live and breathe our team's motto, "Dare to be different." Our collective hearts of wonder kept moving us toward it and our Outrageous Super Glue would be the magic ingredient.

I reported to the partners at our following monthly board meeting and relayed the story back to them. They, too, sat forward. We had built a wonderlicious team culture that wasn't afraid to reach for the sky, and I could see they were thrilled by our goal.

Gathering Gold Beyond the Familiar Boundaries

We were ruthlessly honest with ourselves about the position in the market we were planning to create and the statement we were making. We were pioneering a different feeling and an experience that our customers wouldn't get from any other office location. We did this by staying open and honest with our vision, and thinking hard about who we were.

We kept a close eye on our neighboring office buildings (what they were doing and offering) but didn't become distracted or obsessed with them. We were chasing a different orbit, aiming far higher. We wanted only to lead—not follow—the industry. Every week different members of the management team would head off undercover and go through our competitors' buildings. We'd order coffee in their cafe, go through their security, and look at the presentation of their lobby. We had a huge list of things that we continuously watched—not for one-upmanship but for reassurance that we were on the right track.

For Tower 42 to establish an actual, realistic hotel reputation, I couldn't just tell everyone that we were operating as a hotel culture and expect them to know what it meant, so I took them to it. All across London, we had every famous luxury five-star hotel on our doorstep.

Once a month for an hour or so, I would gather as many of the management team as available to experience these famous hospitality landmarks. To simply walk through them, sense the environment, to notice and learn from the subtle touches and differences. Other times we called the hotel in advance to arrange a morning tea and tour with the hotel general manager. We were always warmly welcomed and loved upon. We returned the love and experience every time a hotel team came to us as an exchange visit. Every month we visited the likes of The Ritz, The Lanesborough, Claridges, Corinthia, and many others including my all-time personal favorite London hotel, The Dorchester. Even the fabulous three-hundred-year-old department store Fortnum & Masons was part of our tour.

Each time before we arrived, I asked the team to notice the arrival and sense what happened as we got to the front door. I encouraged them to fully slow down and feel the ambience as we stepped inside the lobby, to observe the reception team, and to watch their hand gestures and listen to their vocal tone. Amongst many other things, I especially wanted everyone to watch the way all of the hotel team moved their feet.

One special visit was to the wonderful Four Seasons, Canary Wharf, hosted with afternoon tea and a grand tour with the general manager, Michael Purtill. Having both worked together at Ashdown Park, it was an especially exciting reunion! Michael brought his senior team together to sit with us and answer our never-ending flow of questions about their magic ways.

Heading back afterwards for the short trip to Tower 42, the team members were beaming and eagerly interrupting each other with their favorite moments, with everyone agreeing that Four Seasons had the most amazingly clean restrooms they'd ever seen. "Did you see the way they folded the end of the toilet paper!" one of the team piped up. We had our own clearly defined cleaning standards, but it was easier and far more inspiring to show the team what "good" actually looked like. They were able to fall in love with brilliant standards themselves, rather than being instructed to conform or try to figure out "good" for themselves.

The team was always awestruck hearing the same message from each of these hotels, that they—the same as us—didn't charge anything extra for their breathtaking hospitality. They also learned firsthand that anyone the world over can say "good morning" at the front door—and that there are those that do it properly, with real meaning and sincerity.

Often, we can think that overcoming impossibility comes with a cost or is too hard and therefore not worth pursuing. This critically important monthly Tower 42 team ritual came with zero expense, apart from the times that we ordered a pot of tea. In return for the cost of the tea, we collected a treasure chest brimming with gold—fresh wisdom, excitement, and inspiration.

Effortless Simplicity—Not Razzle and Dazzle

The whole of Tower 42 had a big heart and everyone coming through our doors felt an attachment to it. Being greeted by name and attended to personally is what brought them to us. It's also what encouraged them to stay—which is also gold.

Our customers weren't just paying top rents for the prestige of the address, but also for the feeling they had each time they stepped through the front doors as a result of the caring, polished, attentive, responsive service we offered day to day. We influenced the success of their own business, and they expected us to provide continuous daily convenience, with really good moments of service throughout their working day. Their success came from our attentive presence, by anticipating their every need, and being acutely in tune with their wants and needs.

Our customers and guests were looking for effortless simplicity. They didn't expect or want "razzle and dazzle." They weren't looking for circus acts or any fanfare of extravagant things. Nor were they interested in us boasting about the latest gadgets, gizmos, widgets, or thingamabobs. They wanted a caring connection and merely expected everything to work efficiently with ease. They ultimately wanted us to not only anticipate their needs, but consistently and proactively attend to what mattered most to them:

- **Respond to their emails promptly**
- **Answer their phone calls**
- **Solve their problems quickly**

So, we built our entire culture around exactly that—effortless simplicity.

Every member of the Tower 42 team shared a sincere and bright "Good morning" with a little wave or a sincere smile to the several thousand arriving each and every morning. We would leave a happy birthday message on a customer's desk before the day began. Terry, our concierge (fondly named Terry The Ticket by our customers), would deliver someone's freshly laundered shirts up to their floor, rather than waiting for them to be collected downstairs later.

All of these simple touches became the trademark of our promise and the principal ingredients of our Outrageous Super Glue.

We started collecting a vast array of awards—not to gather trophies, but to show everyone the impact of their efforts. Taking to the stage with the team at London's Grosvenor House to receive the Customer Service Management Team of the Year award, across all industries and sectors, was a pivotal and defining moment. We were heading in the right direction. It inspired us to keep moving onwards and upwards.

Unexpected Magic Awaits Everywhere

Okay, so I admit it—I love to play with magic and detail, in equal proportions. At one of our management team's off-site training days, for fun we all decided to give each other black T-shirts to wear with a name—any name—written in gold fabric pen on the front. We did a surprise reveal at the start of the day and whoever made my T-shirt put *Mary Poppins* on the front of mine. Sadly, the name stuck! With embarrassment put to the side, the positivity that continued onward from this is that everyone knew of the detailed approach I was encouraging them to play with. A little bit of magic mixed with a little bit of perfection.

Just One Chance

It was one thing to establish Tower 42 as a prestigious destination. It was a whole other prospect to create multiple destinations within the destination! On top of this, make it all connected, seamless, and harmonious. Our highest priority was occupancy, and this was another unique way we maintained a full house.

Whenever we had vacant office space to let, our representative agents would bring interested groups of people through the estate. We could have just stayed in our office and quite easily left them to get on with it—our agents were excellent. However, our visitors would be considering other London locations and we had once chance to spin each moment with precise touches of magic, to make a standout impression.

Terry, our concierge, would be on the ground floor keeping watch for our leasing agent with the prospective customers to arrive. We always found out in advance if our agents would be walking to us or arriving by taxi. As they approached the entrance Terry would immediately send a flash of eye contact up to me up at reception mezzanine level—then would instantly step outside to share his "A very warm welcome to Tower 42." In sequence I flashed the same discreet head nod and eye contact to our front of house security hosts and the reception team.

We had many international organizations based with us. If a Japanese company was visiting us for the first time, we would raise the flag of Japan on the full-sized flagpole in front of Tower 42. (We proudly collected practically every country's flag and always hoisted up the right one). Before stepping through the door, our visitors would excitedly notice this in the seconds that Terry gave his welcome smile and words.

One of the housekeeping team would be polishing the main front revolving doors at the exact moment they stepped through them and shared the next welcome "good morning/afternoon" greeting. All of three seconds, but it was meticulously planned and executed as part of their arrival. This continued with the team popping up in specific places throughout each visit. These were just some of our wonderlicious moments that cost us nothing to do. They never appeared staged, but they showed we cared. They made a connection with our guests. It was always something that everyone loved performing— and also receiving.

Creating Awe—beyond Christmas

The week before Christmas we hosted our special family day, our signature annual event—The Children's Christmas Party. Our customers proudly brought their children into their place of work for a special moment of fun and every member of the management team took care of all the different elements. Several hundred children would arrive, filled with awe that they were coming into Mummy or Daddy's big office tower, and we went all out to cause extreme excitement. The team gathered to inflate the balloons and make the little party snack boxes, and our engineering team built Santa's Grotto. Our beauticians did face painting and we made a little disco to play Musical Statues and other fun games. We all sat together wrapping little presents and asked our customers for their children's names in advance so that Father Christmas would ceremoniously call on and present each child with a personalized gift when we reached that point.

Everyone played a part in the magic of transforming the management suite or an area of vacant office space, if we had any, into a special wonderland. We didn't bring in an expensive events company to do it, but made it all ourselves and only asked each other one question: "What else can we do to make it even more wonderful?"

Like the moment Father Christmas arrived. Easily he could have sat in a chair downstairs in the ground floor reception as the children arrived, that could've been fun. Or he could have just walked into the party ringing his bell . . . to us it wasn't wonderful enough. So, we took Santa to the roof, six hundred feet up, popped him inside the window cleaning cradle and lowered him slowly down the outside of the building to the exact level of the party. Just imagine, you're sitting in your office or in a meeting and Santa goes past your window waving to you!

In the seconds Santa suddenly appeared outside, the children went completely ballistic. They couldn't comprehend their eyes and started screaming in sheer disbelief. To us, this was another simple moment of wonderful connection. Yet it cost us nothing at all to do. Our customers loved that we did this for their children, who thought their parents worked in the coolest building in the world (we agreed)!

This wasn't just a Father Christmas moment—we applied exactly the same method the other 364 days of the year by adding continuous layers of customer loyalty and doing a little bit more than what anyone was expecting—with everything.

Daily Breakfast in Bed

Throughout my previous hotel career, we had provided room service, delivering in-room dining, especially breakfast, to guest bedrooms. I desperately wanted to do it again—a familiar hotel concept, delivering convenient and time saving experiences directly to our customers' offices. Not anything that would come with any hint of complexity or any additional costs to them—or to us.

Even though we didn't have a room service department or team, the investment to launch this groundbreaking philosophy was zero—apart from the insignificantly small cost of us nicely printing three thousand menu cards—one for each customer to have at their desks. That was the total expense for introducing hotel-style room service, with twenty experiences delivered to any desk, office or meeting room, on any floor.

On the menu, each service and experience simply had the direct dial telephone number and customers effortlessly paid directly for whatever the service was. We already had all of the services available that they could leave the office to get themselves. Creating "Room Service" was our way of taking it to them, especially if they were pressed for time. There were no added costs, surcharges or delivery costs. A physiotherapy treatment from the health club cost exactly the same delivered to their office as going to the health club for it.

Everything and anything from a cappuccino from the café to a manicure from our beautician or a sink that needed unblocking by our handyman was an effortless call on the menu. For your shirts to be laundered or tickets to the football or theater, the number went straight to Terry our concierge. Everything was then promptly delivered to your desk or office.

Additionally, we formed external service partnerships with a local language school, a boutique shoemaker, a speech coach, and a shiatsu masseuse. If you wanted a French lesson at your desk at 7 a.m. on Friday, a new pair of your favorite shoes, assistance with your upcoming presentation, or had a stiff neck, you just called room service and the service came to wherever you were based in the tower.

Does this all sound too absurd? Our customers would disagree! Manicures at people's desks and in their meeting rooms were the most popular room service experience. This said, it takes courage to do things like this, especially when it generates zero additional income. We were satisfied it went way deeper than this; it was valued and hugely appreciated.

Space Activation

Hotels are masterful at creatively utilizing every inch of unusable or dead space, or repurposing areas deemed unsuitable for anything especially interesting. With little things and big things, they transform and maximize their space—often unusable areas—into convenient and attractive concepts in imaginative ways.

Behind our main reception in the building core, we had this tall and empty windowless closet with buckets and mops. It was obvious, this would make a perfect beauty room and nail salon. With some modest investment from the owners, it became exactly that, a private destination where customers could come to get their nails done or visit for a quick massage during their day.

And here is part of the trick. Outrageous Super Glue can be big, extravagant things and it can also be little things that you uncover and breathe to life.

At the top of the tower was an empty narrow corridor that went around the central core, with floor to ceiling windows overlooking all of London to the horizon in every direction. The previous owner had used it as their viewing gallery with a private and direct high-speed lift from the ground floor. We knew this would make a stunning champagne bar and again with some precise designs and investment we did this to create Vertigo 42, the tallest bar in London. It went from dead space to a beautiful awe-inspiring destination that served five thousand glasses of champagne every month. We opened internally to our customers, also to the public, and soon established an average two-week waiting list for a reservation.

Hand in hand with this, we had to master playing the game *Dot to Dot*, connecting every moment and touch point together seamlessly. In the moments before our guests reached Vertigo, six hundred feet up at the top, if we didn't provide the best welcome down at the ground floor—not even the champagne could save us! This was yet another moment where the epitome of our one-team strength came to life.

Our health club, which was operated and leased by Bannatynes, was a classic example of impossibility made possible. Over three levels in one of the estate buildings, the two sub-basement levels had the original swimming pool from the bank on the bottom floor. But the middle level was entirely windowless and was probably better suited to lease as storage space. We could see past this and turned it into a cool New York style basement gym. We converted one corner into a mirrored aerobics studio and the other corner into a spin class room—we painted the walls black, added flecks of luminous paint and turned the lights off during each class, to give it the experience of spinning in outer space.

The Power of Partnership

Level 24 in the heart of Tower 42 was prime office space and we could have generated premium rents using it this way. Instead, and working in partnership with Restaurant Associates, the fine dining arm of the catering specialist Compass, we turned the area into a hospitality floor with a high-class eighty-cover dining room and a series of private rooms.

One of our greatest Super Glue strengths came through our power of partnership.

Never did we issue service contracts and agreements with external service experts, like Restaurant Associates, then turn our back. The success of Tower 42 came with our relentless pursuit of shared ownership. One Team was our way of life. Nothing more, nothing less.

The Tower 42 partners were experts in commercial real estate. Restaurant Associates were culinary and hospitality experts. The entire on-site team each had their own individual specialties. Combining the multiple layers of expertise into one shared ambition changed everything.

This was the case when Restaurant Associates pulled a rabbit out of the hat in bringing Gary Rhodes, one of the UK's best loved chefs, to help us pioneer the hospitality experience of the tower.

Ever since hotel school, Gary had been one of my greatest chef idols. I had all of his cookery books, and here he was, along with his restaurant and kitchen team, taking on the hospitality of level 24. Rhodes Twenty Four was born in 2003, with a menu featuring his simple British classics. Gary wasn't just a name above the door, or a celebrity chef never to be seen. He was based at the tower and loved being part of our connected culture of wonder.

Gary's team was based in our open-plan management suite, where we were all together as one, connected and in tune with each other. For our customers and guests, they now had further dining choices—an informal cafe at ground floor, fun Japanese noodles from Wagamama in the plaza, and stylish entertainment for their own guests with Vertigo 42 and Rhodes Twenty Four.

If there are any words that can send a bolt of terrified excitement through any restaurateur and chef, those words would be "food critic." The one and only Faye Mashler, along with Rick Stein, came in for lunch the second day after opening Rhodes Twenty Four. Our whole team went from being terri-cited to awestruck as Faye reported a generous four out of five stars.

Soon after, high-profile restaurant critic Marina O'Loughlin also visited us from the *London Evening Standard*. This is the one newspaper that everyone all across London buys on their way home, with hundreds of thousands of copies sold every day. The newspaper that went out that day with the headline "Gibbering in naked lust" had us all dancing on the ceiling!

> *"One dish has had me gibbering with naked lust ever since, giving recollection*
> *a rosy glow. I'd ordered the knee-trembling star of the show—a pudding of*
> *moist, squidgy but improbably light suet crust, densely packed with onions*
> *and slow-cooked mutton of truly noble flavor. It came with three little jugs of*

sauces: a silky, soothing onion soubise; a rather embrocation-y caper sauce; and a magnificently punchy mutton gravy. Note to self: do not order a suet pudding [dessert]—a heroically proportioned jam roly poly for two—after a suet pudding [main course]. This absurd greed left me in pain; almost worth it, though, for the heavenly home-made custard, which I spooned straight from the jug. Superior comfort food with a view—what's not to like?"

In 2004, SquareMeal awarded Rhodes Twenty Four with *Best New Restaurant* and history was made for an office building in 2005 when Gary and his team received their Michelin star, which they retained each following year. Another huge layer of difference that simply came from us daring to be different.

Big and small, magic is waiting to be uncovered everywhere. Creating a Michelin-starred restaurant from nothing is huge, but the principal is the same for anything and everything. Like raising a country flag, holding an exciting team gathering, turning a big broom cupboard into a beauty room, or introducing unusual words to an office space, such as room service, the key is to look for opportunities to create magic and then give it a go.

If at First You Don't Succeed . . .

There we were, at our table in the huge Denver, Colorado ballroom, a handful of the Tower 42 team dressed up in our tuxedos and ball gowns, in the place where *it* happened.

We were surrounded by over one thousand of the most influential representatives and leaders of the commercial real estate industry from around the world for the 2008 TOBY Awards, *The Office Building of the Year*. Heads of industry were in the room from China, Japan, New Zealand, Canada, South Africa, and many other countries. At this moment we were no longer competing against our neighboring London office buildings, but all of North America and the entire industry globally. We were the only representatives from the UK and sat in awe, taking it all in, as we had done for the previous four years.

This moment was our fifth attempt at the TOBY's—the four previous years we had been here as an international finalist, and each year when the words came out from the stage "*and the winner is . . .*" it wasn't us. At no point did we ever give up, but kept learning, refining, and fueling our determination.

In our pursuit of world-class, we had joined and made friends with BOMA several years earlier, The Building Owners and Managers Association, headquartered in Washington DC and representing the industry globally. Even BOMA's President and Chief Operating Officer Henry Chamberlain came to visit Tower 42 and became fascinated by our approach and efforts.

This year, we had once again survived the rigorous application and highly detailed

TOBY process, with all entries meticulously judged and whittled down by local association and region before getting the chance to compete at the international level.

Then came the huge build up to announce the winner; the picture of Tower 42 and
the other finalists flash up on the giant screens. No one could see us as we held our
breath and squeezed each other's hands under the table.

"And the winner is," followed by an excruciatingly long pause.

"Tower 42, London"

It felt like a hundred miles, walking across the gigantic ballroom to the massive
stage with the team. Facing the audience cheering us, we were all at once overcome
with every emotion. From the moment our team said *"Let's do the world"* that time in
The Gathering, to the experience of our wonder culture being scorned as *fluff*, to this
moment where we became the first building from Europe to win a TOBY, it was the
most bizarre sense of unexplainable joy.

Afterward, one of the judges stopped us to say, "I've never seen anything like it before."
Touching down at Heathrow Airport in London, the UK press had already released the
newspaper headline, "Tower 42 Beats America."

I proudly shared the same message with the entire team, one by one, presenting
everyone individually with our special big trophy "This is yours; you did this."

We had entered our new orbit and it felt outrageously wonderful.

PS About That "Fluff . . ."

If you ever hear those words, "It's all fluff!" said about your goals or vision, you know
what to do, don't you? Run harder toward it.

We did and our *fluff* led us to achieve industry record rents, consistently full occupancy,
and the accolades that come from winning the best office building in the world.

Tower 42 was an office skyscraper—and also, it wasn't. It was a full-of-wonder place
that everyone fell in love with. Not from its physical structure, from its heart. It was
outrageously adhesive and enhanced the lives of those who walked through its doors.

And it all came about with several good squirts of Outrageous Super Glue.

Recipe 18 Recap:
OUTRAGEOUS SUPER GLUE

The biggest business innovation doesn't always come from large or expensive things. Embracing the label of "*fluff*" as a badge of honor, Tower 42 went all out to become a beacon of unapologetic creativity, a relentless pioneer of wonderlicious excellence.

Ingredients:

★   A safe, inclusive environment that fosters transformative team alignment.

★   Gatherings, not meetings. Make weekly team gatherings a sanctuary for creativity, trust-building, and cohesion.

★   Audacious goals for recognition that you commit to earning through excellence.

★   Courage to shake up your industry, break through traditional "norms," and set a new bar for excellence.

★   Creative spaces. Explore any opportunity to transform mundane spaces and concepts into awe-inspiring destinations and experiences.

Substitutions to Make this Recipe Your Own:

Whether you turn a broom cupboard into a beauty room or an unused hallway into a champagne bar, there is the potential for magic opportunities in every corner. You only have to look for it.

PS Get a round table for your team meeting—it might just become your secret weapon, as it was for us!

Chef's Table Experience: Behind the Scenes of Tower 42

Sometimes even the most wondrous leaders lose their way and have to find their way back to the wonder of it all.

And so, it was for me. I moved with my family from my beloved Tower 42 to Sydney to work for one of Australia's large corporations. Even though it was hard saying farewell to London and leaving our home and friends, the chance was too irresistible to miss—a senior director role responsible for customer service nationally. I thought it was my Golden Ticket. I very quickly discovered it wasn't.

Late evenings at home my phone would keep pinging with a flow of forwarded emails asking, "Where are we on this?" and "Are you across this?" I would ask Suzy my wife if I was supposed to be replying to these emails now late at night? I soon realized that yes, I was. Each day, when I wasn't sitting through awkward meetings, I would work in a large silent office just trying to keep up with the torrent of complex emails. It felt like I had lost my voice. All of the magic in my heart ready to share from Tower 42 dissolved into the floor. My identity was slipping through my fingers, as was my consciousness.

After pioneering uncomplicated joy in London, I was feeling conflicted. I had my "onboarding" after four weeks and the more I desperately tried to push through, the more unhappy I became. I started to find it difficult to get on the bus to work.

After eight years at Ashdown Park followed coincidently by eight years at Tower 42, it was quite out of character to resign after nine weeks. But I knew it had to be done. I was personally and mentally at a point that I didn't like at all. In my resignation meeting, it was decided that I would leave immediately, concluding with their final words that cut my remaining strands of consciousness: "You have thirty-one days until your visa expires—good luck." I barely had the strength to walk to the elevator. It was mid-December and Australia shuts down for summer holidays throughout January. Nobody would be recruiting and within the following thirty-one days we would have to leave the country. The clock had started ticking. Zac was two years old and Jake six weeks and it was at this moment I truly felt a million miles from home.

I have always believed that everything in life happens for a reason. On reflection here and some thirteen years later, I can now look back and be pleased that it actually happened. If I could rewind time, I wouldn't want to erase it despite how horrible it felt at the time. I got to experience this other side and through it, I gained such a deeper appreciation through my connection with other people who are going through the same in their own work.

I frantically searched for roles online and by chance landed on an opportunity with the property management organization JLL (formerly Jones Lang LaSalle). Having sight of their logo brought instant familiarity, as they represented us at Tower 42 leasing our vacant space. I applied for a general manager role in Melbourne and heard back almost immediately.

"Can you come and meet us this week tomorrow, Tuesday?" came the message. I replied just as fast.

Followed by, "Mike George, who leads our Premium Asset Group is looking forward to meeting you!"

Seeing this warm and friendly face in front of me was nothing short of an overwhelming relief. Mike was fascinated by my Tower 42 story and after an invigorating and exciting conversation, he said with a smile, "Can you start next Monday?" They fast-tracked my references from London and that was it. Except, the actual role offered really did feel like my dream Golden Ticket as the national customer service lead for their premium portfolio of ten office skyscrapers, along with an open invitation to bring the Tower 42 wonder culture concept to life across all ten. I felt like I had arrived in Heaven.

Taking World-Class Further

It was as if I had landed on a treadmill at full speed of positivity. The answer was yes to everything I suggested, and I started to fly. My role grew to National Director, Head of Customer Experience across the entire property management business, with several hundred office buildings.

Here in this moment, I knew that Tower 42 wasn't a one-off wonder and the heart of its daring and wonderlicious simplicity had started to spread far and wide across Australia. I asked if we could enter the International Business Excellence Awards in Dubai and in 2015, we took to the stage, across all industries and sectors globally, to win Best Customer Experience in the World.

So, I think my message is simply this—whenever we are facing the worst or most confronting situations in life, there is always something brighter waiting around the corner. This book started with me telling you how we were born with wonder and lost it along the way. We can also lose it . . . again. But it doesn't need to, nor should it stay lost. Wonder is always available to us, with people who wholeheartedly embrace you for who you are, as Mike did with me and all of my many wonderful JLL colleagues.

So, if your skies are currently filled with more clouds than rainbows, just know that wonder is always available to you—sometimes you just need to find it elsewhere.

COFFEE & PETIT FOURS

—

SERENDIPITY

"

Sometimes life drops blessings
in your lap without you lifting a finger.
Serendipity, they call it.
Charlton Heston

WHAT GOES AROUND COMES AROUND

As a special close, I found myself contemplating the best way to tie a ribbon around everything with an appropriately heartfelt conclusion. I realized that I couldn't provide an ordinary or dull ending, instead some playful twists and turns with the fullness of wonderlicious. I wanted this to be more than a solitary closing message and a combination of all the recipes, as one last delicious thought. The answer became so clear and obvious, I could hardly gather my thoughts quickly enough.

One of the greatest realizations that has remained constant throughout my life is that whatever touches of imagination and kindness you share tend to always come back to you in one way or another—usually at a moment in time when you least expect it.

My parents always guided and encouraged me with this from a very early age, as have the exceptional leaders that I've worked with. Between them all, they instilled me with the spirit of, "What goes around, comes around." They each took great care in encouraging me to follow the simple belief that being thoughtful, having good manners, being grateful, and always remaining respectful will bring these same things back to me. The same as throwing a boomerang as far as you can—*if* you do it properly, it will come back to you.

They each impressed upon me a single word, that the more you do and give each day, *it* will always keep happening, often without you even realizing. *It* is often bewildering, sometimes mind boggling, and always heart-warming: *Serendipity*.

Some think of serendipity as something that happens when you're least expecting it or a moment of pure luck. I always like to consider it as "a fortunate accident," the effect of stumbling upon something truly wonderful, especially while looking for something entirely unrelated.

Serendipity

Throughout my recipes, I have poured my heart into examples and specific lessons of what teamwork and gratitude truly looks like—the essential ingredients of humility that create the difference between a connected and sparkling business culture and an average one.

At the time of writing, I am currently based in Sydney, Australia with my family and run my own speaking and advisory business. I was contacted in 2017 by "RUOK?"—Australia's wonderful national suicide prevention charity that promotes life-changing conversations.

I was invited to speak at their Leadership Symposium in Sydney and share a special message of "teamwork and gratitude." I eagerly jumped at the chance.

They asked me to send them the name of my presentation. "Be as creative as you like with the title," they suggested.

Teamwork and Gratitude? I found myself reflecting on what I had learned from Graeme at Ashdown Park Hotel over two decades earlier and it came to me in a flash. "Teamwork" had always been a *symphony*, and "gratitude" had always been symbolized in my mind by the number *8* (for the number of letters in the two words "thank you").

I have no idea why Beethoven then came into my mind.

And that was it. I named my presentation *Symphony 8*.

It felt exciting—they loved it and said yes!

Symphony 8

On a spring day in Sydney 2017, I proudly presented *Symphony 8* and relished sharing how I had performed as a member of an "orchestra" through my hotel career and relayed the day I was promoted by Graeme to become Ashdown Park's deputy general manager—with my new role as "the conductor." For the number 8 part, I shared the more recent tale of Ted, my local butcher, that you heard earlier. I described what I did to say "thank you" to Ted with pure heart, causing some gentle tears in the audience.

I wasn't prepared for what happened next.

Life's Wonderlicious Miracles

As I came off stage, Glenn Capelli—one of Australia's most celebrated professional speakers, who was hosting the special day and sitting in the front row—walked up to me. I will never forget the moment when he held us together in a firm handshake. With softly spoken words, he said, "There's someone I think you should meet. His name is Dobbs Franks. He's one of the most celebrated orchestra conductors the world has seen. He's in his mid 80s and lives in Melbourne. He's a good friend. I would love to introduce you."

Lost in disbelief, I tried to compose myself, realizing I could have easily burst into tears. I held myself together and managed an eager, "Yes, please!"

Smiling, Glenn went on to say, "He's from Arkansas and has performed in forty-nine of the fifty states of the US and just about everywhere else around the world, and for the Queen several times too."

I started trembling as he continued, "He's performed with Ray Charles, Leonard

Bernstein, Eartha Kitt, Leon Barzin, Jill Perryman and all the greats—he's a walking piece of history."

For over two decades this serendipitous moment of wonder had been simmering away and all came together—by pure accident. And that was it. Glenn sent me Dobbs's bio (all sixteen pages of it) and introduced us by email. Dobbs replied immediately:

From: dobbsfranks

Date: Wednesday, 17 May 2017

To: petermerrett

Subject: Don't forget to bring your seatbelt!

Peter,

How delicious to hear from you.

It would be terrific to spend some time with you here in Melbourne. I will happily collect you at the airport, which will give us more time to spend amusing the natives.

Looking forward to our rendezvous.

PS Don't forget to bring your seatbelt!

Yours,

Dobbs

Standing in Melbourne airport arrivals waiting for Dobbs, I see this jolly character walking slowly toward me. With his little walking stick guiding his step, he throws me into the biggest hug like we are long lost friends of years. Our playful banter started instantly, and it soon became difficult to keep up with the speed of our conversation.

As Dobbs weaved through the morning traffic, he playfully announced in his heavy Arkansas accent, "Imagine if you hadn't called your presentation Symphony 8. None of this moment would have ever come to life."

He smiled and added, "Or if Glenn Capelli hadn't been in the audience that day."

It was scary to think how easily this precise moment could have never happened. Stepping inside his home, I couldn't believe I was actually there, standing in his kitchen while he boiled the kettle to make us big mugs of tea. We drank a lot of tea that day while he talked me through his life as a conductor.

"Here it is!" as he excitedly pulled out the vinyl of *Beethoven Symphony 8*, placed it onto his record player, and gently moved the needle to the edge. I was head to toe with goose bumps as it crackled and burst to life.

Dobbs dissolved into the music and explained how Symphony 8 is a very happy, attractive, and upbeat piece in four contrasting movements, a symphony that he has conducted many times and always enjoyed sharing with an audience.

"I am sure Beethoven smiles each time you refer to it!" Dobbs giggled.

And Now . . .

As a special moment of wonder—rather than me explaining the wise lessons I learned from Dobbs, I asked if he could pop in here to share them with you personally . . .

The Coda:
CONDUCTING WONDER
A Surprise Encore
by International Orchestra Conductor and Pianist
Dobbs Franks

T hose of you who may know either or both of us will understand that the volume of words we exchanged during the famous day that Peter and I met would fill several volumes the size of this one. But there is one word in the language which has never applied to either of us during all our conversations since: "shy" or the phrase "at a loss for words."

The fact that Peter and I met is certainly, in my opinion, only possible because the Great Spirit in the Sky has a wonderful sense of humor and looked down and decided it would be interesting to see if two very unlikely to ever meet people were actually to meet and be forced, as strangers, to spend an entire day together.

That first day we met in Melbourne, we hardly drew breath from morning to early evening, discussing what a conductor is and what they actually do. He seemed fascinated with my ramblings, and I could hardly keep up with his inquisitive excitement, as his questions flowed faster than the rapids of a racing river.

We have, since our first meeting, talked at length about truth—and I don't mean our version of truth. But actual and unadorned truth. We have regurgitated many ideas, thoughts, solutions, plans, visions, concerns, revelations, proposed revolutions, and then moaned about the fact that we had to live so many years (he not nearly as many as I) before unanimously agreeing that happiness is really all that matters.

Conducting Wonder

Peter asked if I could have a go at condensing my sixty years as a conductor and add my flavors of wonder as a little summary of useful lessons. It is a joy to have this moment and I am pleased beyond words to be asked to close this beautiful book. Although there is no way the following does anything more than touch the edges—but here goes.

After a fair amount of debate (several hours), we both decided that it would be fitting to call this part The Coda. In music, a coda is the final part of a fairly long piece of music, which is added in order to finish it off in a pleasing way—a separate passage to reinforce the sense of conclusion and adds a final embellishment beyond a natural ending point.

ONE

Never Take a Solo Bow

Your team may force you to take a solo bow from time to time, but never initiate it. This is a very attractive habit to form. You will be loved and appreciated by both your team and your audience (which may be your customers, clients, or anyone you are assisting in life) if you display a clear air of modesty, and more importantly, publicly acknowledge the important contribution your colleagues or team has made to your success—assuming you have created such a moment.

As a conductor it is tradition to recognize and give individuals and/or sections of the orchestra separate bows at the end. I have to make sure that if, for instance, the principal French horn has an important solo during the concert that I provide him or her with a solo bow. Also, it is tradition for a conductor to give entire sections independent bows like woodwinds, brass, strings etc. It is very important at the close of a performance to properly acknowledge your colleagues—you will be admired and respected if you do the ending well, rather than drink the applause for yourself.

TWO

Be Entirely Present

Be yourself, be fully present, and exude absolute authority in the moment (because your audience, or whoever is in front of you, is clever and will see through you instantly if you are trying to be something you are not). Be prepared, be honest, and enjoy it—use your whole body and make sure that every part of your physical presence is passing on the same message and inspiration.

For instance, as a conductor, one has to be aware that when you are standing on the podium, the concertmaster's best view of you is your left kneecap, the principal trumpet is your right eyebrow and when you turn to the violins, your right elbow is what the cellists will see.

So, every part of your body has to send a specific message, and it takes a lot of work to physically control all of your body as you work and make sure that your audience, which could be your team, customers or clients, even your family and friends (orchestra for me) receives the right message and view at all times.

Remember that whatever it is that you are doing, the people in your audience won't all be focusing on the same part of you or even hearing the same intent as the person next to them. That's why it is necessary to make sure that you and your body—meaning all the parts collectively and individually—are giving the intended message to the person/s who are concentrating on that part of you and your body.

Don't overestimate the importance of your voice and words because they will be interpreted via the portion of your body they are concentrating on. So, being entirely present is an important element of your preparation for whatever you want to communicate to others throughout your life.

THREE

Keep Your Heart Wide Open

Recognize the humility of your whole team. Be the captain of their ship, embrace their individual personalities, and be there for them.

Your team will eagerly go the extra mile for you if you recognize that they do their job better than you could. As a conductor, when I stand on the box, I am very aware that there is not one chair or seat that I could sit in and pick up that instrument and play it as well as the person who is sitting there holding that instrument.

During any performance, nothing in the moment is about me. My responsibility is only to deliver the vision of the composer and cause pleasure for the audience. I hold a picture of the composer in my heart and the moment on stage is always about them.

PS

Do Better Next Time

Never give up making sure the next performance is better than the last one. If you are trying to repeat what you consider a success, you will fail, I promise. There is no true satisfaction in repeating last night's performance. Because it can always be better.

The moments, which will from time to time be sheer magic, must remain in your memory and heart with a clear promise that you never make an attempt to repeat them. Use the energy and inspiration at the next performance, but not to try to reproduce a specific moment or inspiration.

Always try to remember that you can do a better one and make sure you do.

No Finish Line

As you can see, Peter and I have no finish line that we can see or even want to head for. It is all on the way to perfection, which we know will keep moving further away as we keep getting closer to it.

This moment is very important to me, our friendship means the world to me, and I know I am richer for it as well as humbled by it.

I can't resist finishing here with some of my favorite words from the poet who has been a major influence in my life, Kahlil Gibran: "Work is love made visible. And if you cannot work with love but only with distaste, it is better that you should leave your work and sit at the gate of the temple and take alms of those who work with joy."

TURNING THE TABLES

I am highly honored that Dobbs wrote this for me, to share with you, and I hope that you find encouragement from his words of wisdom, which still guide and inspire my heart to this day. There is one more profound thing that he shared with me, that has nothing to do with his lessons—that for six decades, whilst selflessly conducting various orchestras all around the world, he had never witnessed the actual moment of joy from his audience, because as a conductor, he always had his back to his audience.

Sometime after my first meeting with Dobbs, I received a surprise phone call from Glenn Capelli—another moment that I will never forget. Glenn, known fondly by all his speaker mates as "Cap," was the convenor of the 2018 Professional Speakers Australia Convention. He asked if I would take to the main stage with Dobbs as a duo in the conference program and unpack the magic of his life.

Standing backstage with Dobbs seconds before we went on, we were giggling, as always, like two mischievous and full-of-wonder six-year-olds. We held a big hug as our introduction was being announced, he placed his walking stick to the side, looked me in the eye and declared, "I'm going to walk on without it."

Walking out onto the stage with Dobbs to the sound of applause from the Brisbane ballroom is a moment that will live on with me throughout all time. We had spent many weeks preparing our performance and all that I felt was the deepest sense of privileged awe.

Observing Dobbs next to me, in such a radiated state of happiness facing the audience that day, could have effortlessly sent me into continuous tears of pure joy. I had to concentrate on my composure as I prompted Dobbs with the glorious unpacking of his life to the adoration of everyone in the room. He finished by playfully conducting the whole room singing "Twinkle Twinkle Little Star," with his baton raised high in the air, dramatically throwing in long pauses between various words and lines. Everyone loved the moment.

In the closing seconds, we both said thank you to the audience and took a synchronized bow. That's when the whole ballroom stood up and gave an emotionally charged standing ovation. All the lights went up so Dobbs could see everyone on their feet applauding. Only I could see the purity of his complete disbelief. I instantly stepped sideways all the way over to the edge of the stage. This was his moment, not mine. With no one able to see, I was finally able to let my tears blissfully roll down my face.

We met back in the center of the stage and hugged in front of everyone.

"There's just one more thing," he said, and the ballroom fell into eager silence.

He turned to face me and said, "This is for you, I want you to have it." He handed me his conductor's baton. We both hugged again. The audience kept clapping.

* * *

And, just like the last note in the Coda . . . he too was gone.

Not long after writing this part of the book, Dobbs sadly passed away in 2023, just before his ninetieth birthday.

A short time beforehand, he played me a beautiful rendition of "Pure Imagination" on his beloved black Baldwin piano at home. We arranged for the moment to be filmed as a special surprise and a shared message of thanks for Glenn Capelli.

I feel nothing but blessed to have had such an incredible friendship for the last six years of his wonderful life. He was thrilled to write these words and I promised he would receive the first printed copy of *Wonderlicious* to celebrate. A moment missed by the smallest fraction of time.

DIGESTIFS

—

HOPE

"

A Toast to Your Wonder!

Allow it to play, the wonder within,
Sharing it around is never a sin.
It's so easy to miss, this moment right now,
Living here today; not the future, but how?

Connection our yearning, all can see,
Pause tomorrow for later, be free and with glee.
Inside of the present, life becomes glowing,
Not passing you by, without even knowing.

Just hold on tight and don't let it go,
The wonder inside you is ready to flow.
So let us embark on this quest profound,
Where imagination and joy in harmony resound.

Let leadership be a beacon, pure and bright,
With service embraced, for the magic of flight.
Through grace and awe, time becomes art,
The rhythm of curiosity, a dance from the heart.

May I encourage, along with great sound?
Go on, release your wonder and share it around!
Please don't be embarrassed, timid or stern,
Just open the floodgates and let it return.

Peter Merrett

The Swan Song:
OPENING THE FLOODGATES
TO A WONDERLICIOUS LIFE

U sually at the end of a performance, amongst the final applause from the
audience, the curtain goes down and everyone heads home. Thankfully, with
wonder—the curtain only stays up!

Thank you for joining me through a glimpse into my life, career, and love of wonder.
I admit, through my writing, it has sometimes been challenging for me and in places
bittersweet to look back and try to describe these moments and memories. Some stories
were much harder than others to share, some more beautiful, some felt like releasing
precious trade secrets into the wind.

All that was in my heart, though, was to show how any of us can live a wonderlicious
life—by passing on and sharing the joy of wonder with others. So, if any of the moments
in this book encourages you to live a life more wonder-filled, to bring color back to
anything gray, I have fulfilled my dream.

Is It Love?

At the core of all of this, I hope that you've enjoyed reading *Wonderlicious*. Maybe you
have fallen in love with the story of Ted the butcher, or you want to find your own nanny
in an orange apron on your next flight, or you are hoping to never come across that fish
and chip restaurant ever in your life! If the reflections from Dobbs have touched you,
if the stories about my two boys and all the other characters that I brought to life have
lit a light with you, this is all I wanted.

I surrendered to my senior corporate director role with JLL in Australia in 2018 and
worked an extra-long notice period so that I could finish exactly on the day of love,
Valentine's Day. I was massively grateful, but my soul was drawing me toward something
deeper. An uncontrollable magnet was pulling me—to help and encourage others to
rediscover their sense of wonder. It was that simple—and indeed, felt that hard.

Time to Play?

I sincerely hope for all of my recipes to resonate and bring joy, but in an underlying point
of reassurance to creating wonder in real life. Whether it's in a service environment or
an organization of any sector or industry, you don't have to run a luxury hotel, high-end

Michelin-starred restaurant, or be the world's best office skyscraper to provide wonder for people in business or for your loved ones at home.

Take my lessons learned in hospitality and experiment freely, they are all transferable into any situation or environment: play music at supper time at home, sleep at night with your phone left switched off in the kitchen, host fun team gatherings in the office where all ideas are celebrated, say "Good morning" with sincerity, and be at the front door to greet anyone arriving for an interview, then invite them with a blank sheet of paper to bring themselves to life.

Play with your words to express something differently, bake some cookies for an elderly neighbor or mow their lawn without them asking, fully listen to someone when they are speaking with you, hold open the door for a stranger, notice someone's kindness and share a meaningful thank you . . . even present your spare room at home so that your guests feel expected and welcome like they're at a nice hotel.

Just be fully and unapologetically present in every moment.

There are a million things that any of us can do in business and at home, in our work and with our own families, to create light and make things a little more interesting.

May You Live a Wonderlicious Life

As children, our once internal encyclopedia of wonder guided our every action and experience. As we transformed into teenagers and then adults, we turned our back to it and locked the gates with a big padlock and chain. We thought it didn't matter anymore. I never wanted this to be just another book, but the key to that padlock.

I have been more determined than anything for this to not only be a message of encouragement for my generation, but also for the future ones too. Everyone born to this world arrives brimming with a sense of wonder, and whatever happens from this point, I simply hope that my encouragement lives on, for all humankind, here with us now and for everyone yet to appear. I hope that anyone who picks up this book two hundred years from now gets as much out of it as you do today.

Just remember that no matter what you deem to be the boundary of your capability, comfort zone, or possibility, you can (and should) step outside of it! As a former school-boy who did well in pottery, not English, I wrote this for you.

This isn't the end . . . perhaps the beginning. A thankful heart to you and please know, the world is waiting for your wonder!

THE END

—

"

Goodbye? Oh no, please.
Can't we just go back to page one and do it all over again?
Winnie the Pooh

> "
>
> *You can, of course dear friends, start over—or,*
> *you can simply begin living your very own Wonderlicious life.*
>
> ***With happy wishes and thanks so much for being here!***
> ## Peter Merrett

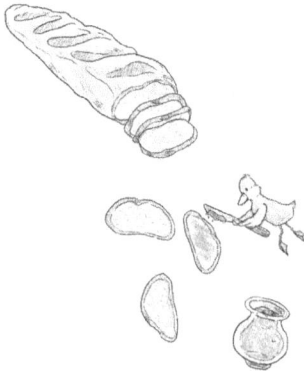

SPECIAL ACKNOWLEDGMENTS

*W*onderlicious has been simmering away in my heart almost constantly for several years. Even though every single part of writing this book has been one of the most daunting things I have ever attempted, it all came to life through the unwavering support of my former colleagues, friends and family, from every corner of my life. To everyone who continuously cheered me on from the sidelines and encouraged me to keep going with this—I am endlessly grateful!

Family Love

For my bride. My wonderful wife Suzy, I love you more today than when we first met. Thank you for navigating this wild roller-coaster ride of a life together and for always believing in me. During the countless months and hours I spent writing, you kept everything flowing at home with our teenage boys and never once did you complain. I am deeply grateful for my life with you, a daily adventure that is like having my fingers caught in the electric socket. I wouldn't change it for the world.

For my boys Zachary and Jake, who asked a million times if I was ever going to finish this book! If I could gather and combine all the words in the English language together, it still couldn't begin to describe how much I love you. What I feel for you is everything and I have no words to express my depth of pride for you both. I wrote this book for you.

The most sincere thanks to my father-in-law, George Burton, for meticulously reading the entire pre-edited manuscript from top to bottom and for the pages of suggestions and tweaks. Special thanks to my awesome brother-in-law Tim Wallace who, like me—a former chef—kindly helped me with Recipe 3 and then put his whole heart into the final post-edit proofread.

Special Thanks

True friendship is one of my favorite things in life. Some stand the test of time and never fizzle out no matter what. I have this with Terry Welsh, a special union that has so far spanned thirty-five years. Terry was the restaurant manager during my time at Redworth Hall. Later as deputy general manager of Ashdown Park, he encouraged me to join him once again. Terry then started the transformation at Tower 42 as general manager and recommended me to the owners as his successor. Throughout my time since moving to Australia, he has never left my side in support and consistently shared his ongoing belief in me. Dear Terry, my deepest spirit of appreciation to you, and for you.

Raising the Curtain

I have so many reasons to say thank you to Pam and Doug Lipp for the endless supply of encouragement and guidance. I will never forget sitting in the garden of your home in Sacramento, describing my ambition of writing this book. Thank you both for your continuous enthusiasm and joy, and Doug the heartiest thanks for saying yes to raising the curtain of *Wonderlicious* with your Foreword.

Thrilling Reunions

Throughout my writing, I am profoundly thankful for the many online and telephone reunions I have had with former teammates and colleagues, who each willingly shared many memories and reflections. Navigating life with you, alongside the complexities of work and the marvels of wonder, has been an extraordinary privilege. Thank you from the depths of my heart to each and every one of you.

Redworth Hall Hotel

I have the deepest appreciation for reuniting with my colleagues from thirty years ago: Marianne Lamb, Pam Mooney, and Lee Melville. Thank you for sharing your Redworth Hall memories and helping guide my thoughts to compose Recipe 2. It was a dream to write this one—to somehow express the sincerest gratitude to you, Malcolm Powell.

Ashdown Park Hotel

Happy Feet and Recipes 13, 14, and 15 took over two years and what felt like several hundred edits to finish. These reflections come with the greatest thanks to my former teammates for their huge input and reviews of my writing: Ian Pigeon, Jenny Sandells, Jon Webb, Colin Lee Davie, Nathan O'Reilly, Pauline Salvi, and Michael Purtill—all of these pages were written to express the biggest thank you to you, Graeme Bateman.

Tower 42

I had the weight of Tower 42 on my shoulders throughout writing the whole book. I knew I wanted to close with this but wanted to do it justice. Mission Impossible: A New Orbit and Recipes 16, 17, and 18 come with huge thanks to the shared reflections and reviews of my writing by Henry Chamberlain, John Webb, Adam Gray, Colin Lee Davie, Christopher Lacey, and Derek Williams.

Tower 42 still remains deep in my heart to this day. It was a colossal team effort and I remain in awe of everyone involved. It is simply impossible to name everyone . . . but special mentions to Andy Craven, Jeff Morton, Bob Dawson, Tim Elliott, Marcus Sperber, John Gentry, Steve Crossley, Kieron Nunney, Ludovic Bargibant, Laura De Wet Thorogood, Terry Burns, Lynda Fellstead, Joelma Rossi Paim, Robert Coupar, Kate Bourne, Debbie Cracknell, Eric Wilson, Phil Clark, and everyone who put their heart on the line in daring to be different!

Conducting Wonder

I lost count of the number of emails and late evening phone calls that I received from my dear friend Dobbs Franks throughout all of my writing. Dobbs was so eager and proud when I asked if he could compose The Coda to close *Wonderlicious*. I am beyond grateful for his constant free-flowing inspiration and immensely sad that he missed seeing this finished. *Dear Dobbs, we did it*!

A Shining Light

For the final part of my corporate career with JLL Australia, sincere thanks to Mike George for the eight fantastic years working with you and for your special way of shining a bright light of humility. Thank you for not only giving me the space and encouragement to play with wonder at great scale, but also for your support in us taking this to the stage of the International Business Excellence Awards in Dubai in 2015.

My Wonder Folk

Hearty thanks to the people who always support and inspire me through my ways of wonder—Catherine Lai, Neil Gopal, Connie O'Murray, Cindy Magouirk, Dana Getz, Pete Longworth, Sandrena Robinson, Michelle McNab, Stephen Cranage and Despina Notaras.

Thank you also to my dear friend John Pastorelli for helping me to gather and inspire my initial book ideas, and recording artist Matthew James Lyons for inspiring me to blend various musical references to my writing. And not to forget Nathan Griffiths in the Hunter Valley for the regular use of the kitchen bench at your vineyard staff-accommodation to escape and write. My heartfelt thanks to two of my best friends in life, Craig Hewett and Richard Macaltao, for their pre-print final review. Your ever-present friendship means the world to me.

Thank you to my amazing business coach Brad Tonini, my awesome web guru Gavin Rogut, and also my US Business Manager Jeffrey Rupp and his wife Linda for your ongoing kind support and regular input with my writing. Also, my speaker mates, who are never short of providing me with warm wisdom and guidance—Glenn Capelli, Michelle Bowden, Amanda Gore, Catherine Palin Brinkworth, Allan Parker, Kirryn Zerna, Maz Farrelly, Michael McQueen, Melinda Hird, Warwick Merry, Ian Stephens, Dale Beaumont, Winston Marsh, Jodi Richardson, Russell Pearson, Phil Preston, Neryl East and Danielle Dobson.

The Magic behind the Wonderlicious Scenes

In the first three or so years of writing, my manuscript was an incoherent mass (and mess) of words. Thank you to Kylie Bartlett for the initial guidance in giving structure to my ideas. Huge appreciation to Jaqui Lane, Founder of The Book Adviser, for the timely encouragement to persevere.

Then everything changed when I was introduced by chance to Crystal Adair-Benning, Founder of Word Magic—thank you Jessie Dee for bringing us together. Crystal became my writing coach, principal cheerleader, and literary fairy godmother. We met weekly for nine months and with much sparkling energy, everything started to gather purpose and clarity. Thank you, Crystal, for showing me the way, for embracing my message, and uncovering the fullness of my voice.

I owe a tremendous debt of gratitude to my incredible editor and publisher, Jenn Goulden, and masterful proofreader, Chris Arnold, of Entourage Media. Even though your edits made me go cross-eyed several hundred times, never once did it feel like a chore. I sincerely appreciate all of your enthusiasm, ideas, and the many Zoom calls! Your never-ending heart and depth of care have been instrumental in bringing this book to life. You went way above and beyond the anticipated edit, and from the bottom of my heart, thank you for believing in *Wonderlicious* and for helping me make it shine.

I am deeply grateful to Jasmine Hromjak at Entourage for her wonderFULL artistry, imagination and flair. Thank you for bringing my visual dreams for the book cover and interior pages to life with your stunning illustrations and beautiful art. It has been a pure delight and pleasure working together.

Lastly, in the midst of writing this, I lost my parents Eveyln and Chris Merrett, two humble and generous souls who encouraged me with the wonder of life. They were fascinated that I was writing this book and I wholeheartedly celebrate this moment in their memory.

NOTES

Presented below are the pivotal quotes that have helped to add a special touch of flavor to the Wonderlicious Menu and Recipes. I wish to express my sincere appreciation and admiration to the authors, whose words have been a guiding light of wisdom and inspiration. Every possible measure has been taken to ensure that the quotes in this book are attributed to their original sources.

Foreword: "Oh, What Wonder Awaits!"

xiii   **"Man does not suddenly become aware or infused with wonder . . .":** Sigurd Olsen, *Reflections from the North Country* (Alfred A. Knopf, 1976)

xvii   **"The trouble with people is they grow up, they forget what it's like to be twelve years old.":** Doug Lipp, paraphrase from Walt Disney

Aperitifs—A Toast to Wonder

2   **"All around you, in every moment . . .":** Lorin Roche, *The Radiance Sutras* (Sounds True, 2014)

Introduction: How It's Made

3   **"My mouth watered so much my taste buds put on shower caps":** Carole Fowkes, *Plateful of Murder* (Ink Lion Books, 2016)

Prologue: Let's Set the Table

6   **"I would rather have a mind opened by wonder, than a one closed by belief":** Gerry Spence, *How to Argue and Win Every Time: At Home, At Work, In Court, Everywhere, Every Day* (St Martin's Press, 1995)

Hors d'Oeuvres—Presence

12   **"We delight in the beauty of the butterfly . . .":** Maya Angelou (1928–2014)

Recipe 1: A Return to Wonder

15   **"You've always had the power my dear, you just had to learn it for yourself.":** *The Wizard of Oz* (1939, MGM)

Recipe 2: Leading Hand in Hand

24   **"As human beings, our job in life is to help . . ."**: Fred Rogers, *The World According to Mister Rogers* (Hyperion, 2003)

Recipe 3: Mise en Place

39   **"If you have a dream . . ."**: Marco Pierre White

44   **"Mise en place is the religion of all good line cooks . . ."**: Anthony Bourdain, *Kitchen Confidential: Adventures in the Culinary Underbelly* (Bloomsbury, 2000)

Appetizer—Heart

54   **"Seems to me it ain't the world that's so bad but what we're doing to it . . ."**: Louis Armstrong, spoken intro to "What a Wonderful World", 1970

Recipe 4: Giving Your Heart a Voice

57   **"Piglet noticed that even though he had a very small heart, it could hold a rather large amount of gratitude."**: A.A. Milne, *The House at Pooh Corner* (Public Domain, 1928)

Recipe 5: Fluency in Gratitude

65   **"Feeling gratitude and not expressing it is like wrapping a present and not giving it"**: William Arthur Ward (1921–1944)

Recipe 6: Becoming the King of Hearts

74   **"Three things in human life are important. The first is to be kind. The second is to be kind. And the third is to be kind."**: Leon Edel, *Henry James: The Master 1901–1916: Book Two: The Beast In The Jungle* (Avon Books, 1978), p 124

Sharing Plates—Curiosity

86   **"The whole world is a series of miracles, but we're so used to them we called them ordinary things."**: Hans Christian Andersen (1805–1875)

Recipe 7: Service Magic

89   **"I will reveal you who I am. I am your reflection"**: Santosh Kalwar, *Quote Me Everyday* (Lulu Press, 2010)

Recipe 8: Devils in the Details

102   **"It's not about how much you do, but how much love you put into what you do":** Mother Teresa (1910–1997)

Recipe 9: Making It Right

118   **"Well, here's another nice mess you've gotten me into":** Oliver Hardy, *The Laurel-Hardy Murder Case* (1930, MGM)

Side Dishes—Expression

132   **"Food, glorious food . . .":** Lionel Bart *Oliver!* (1960, musical)

Recipe 10: Magnetic Expression

135   **"What makes someone irresistible . . .":** Drishti Bablani, *Uns: Love, Let's Fall in Love with Love* (Drishti Bablani, 2016)

Recipe 11: Word Wizardry

146   **"No one cares how much you know, until they know how much you care":** Theodore Roosevelt (1858–1919)

Recipe 12: Gobbledygook Alternatives

157   **[Excerpt from memorandum sent to government employees 24 March 1944]:** Maury Maverick, Chairman, Smaller War Plants Corporation

Main Course—Rhythm

168   **"When hearts are high . . .":** from *Snow White and the Seven Dwarves* (1937, film)

Recipe 13: The Craftsmanship of Care

171   **"It's amazing what people will accomplish, when they know you believe in them":** Jon Gordon, *The Power of Positive Leadership* (Wiley, 2017)

Recipe 14: Symphony No. 8

181   **"No one can whistle a symphony. It takes a whole orchestra to play it.":** Halford Luccock, Scholastic Voice, Volume 18 (Scholastic Magazine, 1955), p. 89

Recipe 15: Backstage, Onstage

188   **"What happens "backstage" will end up "onstage . . ."**: Doug Lipp, *Disney U* (McGraw Hill Professional, 2013)

Sweet Finale—Imagination

200   **"There is no life I know to compare with pure imagination . . ."**: Leslie Bricusse and Anthony Newley, "Pure Imagination" from *Willy Wonka & the Chocolate Factory* (1971)

Recipe 16: Impossibility

203   **"The wonder of imagination is this: it has the power to light its own fire."**: John Landis Mason (1832–1902)

Recipe 17: Irresistibility

211   **"You can dream, create, design . . ."**: Dave Smith: Staff of the Walt Disney Archives, *The Quotable Walt Disney* (Disney Editions, 2001)

Recipe 18: Outrageous Super Glue

222   **"There's a morning when presence comes over your soul . . ."**: Rumi (1207–1273)

Coffee & Petit Fours—Serendipity

240   **"Sometimes life drops blessings in your lap . . ."**: Charleton Heston (1923–2008)

Digestifs—Hope

254   **"A Toast to Your Wonder!"**: poem by Peter Merrett

The End

257   **"Goodbye? Oh no, please . . ."**: from *The Many Adventures of Winnie the Pooh* (1977, Walt Disney)

258   **"You can, of course dear friends, start over . . ."**: Peter Merrett

274   **"If you allow the creativity and love of wonder inside you—anything is possible!"**: Zachary Merrett (2009)

INDEX

"

IF you allow
the Creativity
and love of
wonder inside
you- anything
is possible !!
☺

Zac Merrett

(Aged 9)

ABOUT THE AUTHOR

Peter Merrett has always considered chefs to be wizards. When he began training as one thirty-five years ago, he was captivated by the way simple ingredients could create magic, pleasure, and emotion. He took this concept for using many small details to create a large impact, and he expanded on it. As he moved into hospitality leadership, his exciting approach led his teams to win the prestigious UK Hotel of the Year award twice.

Transitioning into commercial real estate, Peter became General Manager of Tower 42 in London, where his team pioneered a groundbreaking office-hotel concept that won the Best Office Building in the World award from BOMA International. Later, as a leader within JLL Australia's property division, he inspired a hospitality-driven service culture that earned the organization global acclaim for Best Customer Experience.

Today in Australia, as a Hall of Fame professional speaker, mystery shopper, trusted advisor to the world's biggest brands, and Founder of The House of Wonderful, Peter has worked across eleven countries and numerous industries. He's shared stages with his mentor, Doug Lipp, former Head of Training at Disney University. He is also a Fellow of BOMA International, a judge for the Customer Institute of Australia, and has served on the Board of Directors for Professional Speakers Australia.

Now, Peter coaches leaders worldwide on how to trade employee handbooks and KPIs for teams that feel genuinely valued, appreciated, and excited to show up and treat your business as their own. Whether he's tying red ribbons around asparagus, hosting potato-peeling competitions with top executives, or wearing a superhero cape over his three-piece suit, his wonderlicious approach brings heart and joy back into the workplace, leading to extraordinary results.

Peter lives in Sydney, Australia, with his wife, two sons, a friendly house hippo, and a battalion of rubber duckies.

ON THE WONDERLIST

Join Peter Merrett (*petermerrett.com*) as he coaches leading
organizations and mystery shops the world for
all things *Wonderlicious...*